Fearless Living and Loving

Christian Hope for the Sick and Their Caregivers

John A. Love

WESTBOW
PRESS
A DIVISION OF THOMAS NELSON
& ZONDERVAN

WestBow Press books may be ordered through booksellers or by contacting:

WestBow Press
A Division of Thomas Nelson & Zondervan
1663 Liberty Drive
Bloomington, IN 47403
www.westbowpress.com
1 (866) 928-1240

Scripture taken from the Holy Bible, NEW INTERNATIONAL VERSION®.
Copyright © 1973, 1978, 1984 by Biblica, Inc. All rights reserved worldwide.
Used by permission. NEW INTERNATIONAL VERSION® and NIV® are
registered trademarks of Biblica, Inc. Use of either trademark for the offering
of goods or services requires the prior written consent of Biblica US, Inc.

Because of the dynamic nature of the Internet, any web addresses or links contained in
this book may have changed since publication and may no longer be valid. The views
expressed in this work are solely those of the author and do not necessarily reflect the
views of the publisher, and the publisher hereby disclaims any responsibility for them.

Any people depicted in stock imagery provided by Thinkstock are models,
and such images are being used for illustrative purposes only.
Certain stock imagery © Thinkstock.

ISBN: 978-1-4908-4678-1 (sc)
ISBN: 978-1-4908-4679-8 (hc)
ISBN: 978-1-4908-4680-4 (e)

Library of Congress Control Number: 2014913649

Printed in the United States of America.

WestBow Press rev. date: 01/07/2015

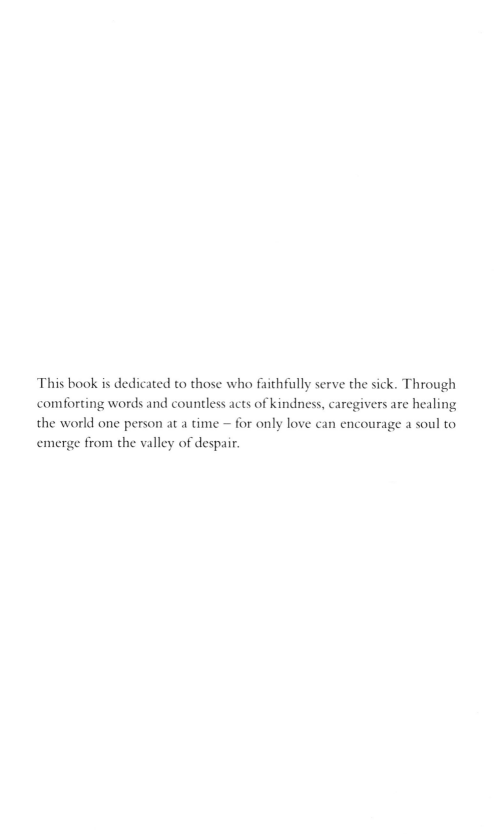

This book is dedicated to those who faithfully serve the sick. Through comforting words and countless acts of kindness, caregivers are healing the world one person at a time – for only love can encourage a soul to emerge from the valley of despair.

CONTENTS

PART ONE

ESSENTIAL REFLECTION

PRELUDE TO REFLECTION

Part One is a series of spiritual reflections which explores a wide range of topics. Each reflection is an independent, stand-alone composition. This holds true for the included poems and prayers as well. Accordingly, it may seem as though there's little connection between one piece and the next. Indeed, you can read these reflections in the sequence presented, or in any order you wish. And it may prove helpful to read some of the pieces more than once. Still, if you find that you're struggling with a particular topic – if it isn't capturing your interest or touching your heart – simply move on and perhaps revisit it later.

Part One's material provides the needed spiritual foundation for the meditations offered in Part Two. Therefore, readers are encouraged to finish Part One before starting Part Two. Bear in mind that most reflections have deeper levels of assimilation. Thus, the more time and effort you spend on each piece, the more you will benefit. And while Part One's reflections are, individually, whole and complete, they build upon one another. Together, they form an experience which transcends the separate parts. Together, they create a singular journey of self-discovery.

Reflection is an opportunity to open our minds and hearts to God. It's the gentle prodding needed to lift the veil of human illusion and discover divine reality. Reflection helps us focus on the meaningful as we sort through life's distractions. It's the quiet, solitary time which allows us to connect with God. And as we look inward and identify our true essence, reflection promotes a greater sense of safety and well-being. It leads to an acceptance of God's will and gives the gift of peace. Finally, reflection helps us perceive the world in a more enlightened way; and it reminds us that we are never truly alone when facing life's trials. Reflect and be grateful, for God has a magnificent plan for you. Reflect and be mindful, for God's presence is with you. Reflect and be joyful, for you are deeply loved!

1. The Cosmic Room

Imagine falling asleep at home, only to awaken in a strange, mystical place. Of course, curiosity compels you to explore your new surroundings, a large room containing thousands of dials. These dials are like the ones found on radios that have control knobs to change stations and to adjust the volume. And like radio dials, they're labeled. But here, the similarities end. Pausing to look closer, you see a label that reads *Sun's Temperature*. The next dial is tagged *Earth's Temperature*. Another one reads *Gravity*. Yet another is labeled *Atmospheric Conditions*. Moving along, you find a control knob titled *Light Speed*. Notable others include *Stars, Planets,* and *Black Holes*. And next to those are ones labeled *Time, Energy,* and *Space*. There's even a dial named *Big Bangs*. Before long, you realize there are controls designed to regulate each solar system and every galaxy in the cosmos.

Then, questions arise. Who engineered this celestial control room? How was it built? And who is operating it? The scientific community agrees that our universe is indeed "finely tuned." Yet, many scientists deny the existence of God. And this point of view inevitably sparks other questions. Could an ever-expanding and interconnected universe be born without a Creator? Is it likely that our world – more precise than a Swiss watch and more harmonious than a grand piano – is random and rudderless? Has all of this happened with neither a Maker of dials nor a heavenly Calibrator? Has life not flourished under a Shepherd's watchful eye?

Countless galactic mysteries remain unsolved. Still, there have been illuminating discoveries as well. For example, we've learned that our highly structured universe functions within a flexible fabric of time and space. And current evidence suggests that the same universal laws govern both the unthinkably small and the unimaginably large. In addition, we know that separate gravitational, nuclear, and electromagnetic forces are synergistically interwoven among energy, matter, and antimatter. Leading physicists believe that the slightest variance in today's elegant, cosmic dance could spell instant doom. It's thought that the tiniest change within the intricate balance of our universe might extinguish all life as we know it.

History has shown that people commonly draw different conclusions from identical evidence. So perhaps an open mind is our surest portal to truth and reality. Yes, faith is part of believing and trusting in God. But honest scientists will admit that they, too, rely on faith. As it happens, scientific conclusions are not entirely based on the results of laboratory tests. Many theories gain wide acceptance when, in fact, they cannot be tested at all.

And so it is that each person arrives at one of three theological destinations: There is a God; there is not a God; or there's uncertainty as to God's existence. People who believe in a Higher Power will often choose to nurture a personal relationship with their God. And those who feel connected with a Supreme Presence typically view themselves as spiritual beings traveling a spiritual path. Ultimately, people who see life as a spiritual journey perceive the world differently from those holding secular views. And from this observation, a final question arises. Do spiritual perspectives reflect universal truth more accurately than secular ones?

★★★

Within our universe, the infinitesimal is unified with the infinite; and the physical is joined with the metaphysical.

★★★

Carl Jung said, "Believing requires faith, while knowing does not. I *know* God exists."

★★★

Spiritual growth is aided by an open mind and a yearning heart.

2. Physics, Metaphysics, and Creation

Scientists claim that our universe is made entirely of matter, energy, and space. Curiously, matter has a counterpart which scientists have named "antimatter." And acclaimed physicist Steven Hawking suggests that matter and antimatter may have coexisted in equal amounts shortly after the Big Bang. If this were true, then matter and antimatter essentially cancelled one another. So in a mathematical sense, the net sum of our early universe was zero. That's one of the reasons why Hawking dismisses God's existence. If the universe initially contained nothing – that is, its mathematical identity totaled zero – then a Creator wasn't needed; for in fact, nothing was created.

Still, natural laws and structure are integral to the physical universe and to human lives. Our world, for example, has at least three dimensions: height, length, and width. And some consider time to be a fourth dimension. However, the theoretical physicists who endorse String Theory believe that the universe has additional dimensions – perhaps as many as eleven, though the exact number is under debate. Simply stated, there are parts of creation that we can neither sense nor experience at this point.

Scientific consensus promotes the Big Bang as the event which created our universe and the beginning of time. Time is not only directional, it's variable as well. Influenced by forces such as gravity, time can slow down or, in extreme cases, stop altogether. Yet the human experience is immersed in time. Our lives appear to unfold in a chronological order that features a past, a present, and a future. Applying the laws of physics, Hawking concludes there was no "time" prior to the Big Bang, and this belief serves as his second reason to deny God's existence: There was never a time in which a Creator could be present before the birth of the universe. Additionally, he suggests that the Big Bang was a natural phenomenon, not a supernatural one. In other words, Hawking claims that science doesn't need God to account for the world's presence. But is it possible that Hawking, despite his brilliant mind, has overlooked something? Are there universal realities that, to this point, have eluded scientific detection? Is it really *nothing* to listen to the music of Beethoven? Can mathematics explain what we find by looking into the eyes of a child? And is there a scientific formula which captures the essence of love?

Physics includes the study of the very small, quantum mechanics, and the very large, cosmology. At the subatomic level, matter is thought to be comprised of tiny vibrating strands of energy. And there's shocking evidence indicating that these infinitesimal energy strands are shared among different dimensions within our universe. Clearly, there are things happening which go completely undetected by human eyes. What's more, scientists have proven that all objects, regardless of their size or density, are mostly just empty space. As a result, there's one thing known for sure: Much of what we see is an illusion.

In humankind's quest to discover the secrets of our universe, new theories are presented all the time. Radical ideas occasionally gain mainstream acceptance, only to fade like the night sky as dawn approaches. Even the theories of revered physicist Albert Einstein have not escaped intense scrutiny. His belief that our universe is infinite in size is undergoing a present-day challenge. Currently, prominent theorists speculate that our universe may actually be finite; that it has a defined shape and a limited size. Moreover, it has been suggested that our universe might be just one of an infinite number of universes. And if this is so, are Big Bangs ordinary, ongoing events? For now, scientists think it's impossible for energy, including a human body, to travel from one universe to another. But this speculation raises more questions. Is it likely that other universes, if they exist, are the same as ours? Big Bangs aside, are there other means by which new realms are born? Could both natural *and* supernatural forces be at work?

Turning to planet earth, most scientists conclude that it took eons of time for just the right mix of climate and atmosphere to form the supporting backdrop for life as we know it. Academicians suggest that life began in a primordial "soup" of single-celled microbes. Then, an evolutionary process unfolded. Millions of years later — and after countless genetic mutations and adaptations — we have the diverse array of flora and fauna seen today. Searching the deepest seas and the most remote forests, scientists continue to discover new species. Some are flourishing, while others are not. But is evolution alone responsible for the world's plants and animals? Or has intelligent design played a role in forming and shaping our planet? Was our world created in six days as described in Genesis? Could a single day be something far greater than twenty-four hours? And finally, is it possible that creation is a divine process which includes evolutionary and adaptive changes?

People of faith believe that a Higher Power is responsible for life as it appears today. Moreover, a significant number of scientists have concluded that natural selection and other evolutionary theories solve some, but not all, of the mysteries surrounding carbon-based life. For instance, genetic mutations are typically spawned by a slow, random process. If this is true, have the supporting climate and atmosphere been in place long enough for incremental mutations to sufficiently explain today's immense diversity of life? What's more, mutations occur within existing species. And if that's the case, can mutations and other natural events account for all of the *new* species living on our planet?

There's at least one point of agreement among scientists: Ours is a universe of energy. Fueling the human body, energy sustains our heartbeat, our pulse, our breathing, and the electrical impulses found in our brain. And thoughts, too, are energy. Although it never disappears, energy does change form. And while energy is eternal, it is forever imprisoned by physical laws. But are there formless realms as well, worlds where energy cannot be found? Physicists and mathematicians have neither proved nor disproved the existence of metaphysical domains. Yet, it's certainly possible there are realms in which energy, matter, and time are absent. Perhaps even space is missing in such supernatural worlds.

So, does energy define humanity? Is life wholly explained by tiny, vibrating strands of energy? Or is spirit part of life's equation? Historically, philosophers and theologians have strayed from science when defining human life. Those who believe in God often draw distinctions between spirit and energy. The soul, or spirit, is viewed as an eternal life force. And unlike energy, spirit is not trapped in time or governed by natural laws. Philosophers and theologians explore both the physical and metaphysical aspects of life, meaning they study form *and* formlessness. Does spirit dwell in all realms, those with form and those where form is not? Is spirit able to roam among parallel universes and their many dimensions? Does spirit define human self-realization? Is it the essence of individual and collective consciousness? And in domains absent of space and time, could spirit be both everywhere *and* nowhere in perpetuity?

Globally, hundreds of millions of people believe in a Higher Power. Each day, there are many who call out to God, Krishna, Buddha, Allah, and Christ. But again, science can neither prove nor disprove a divine presence. And that's why human beings wrestle with faith. Ultimately, each person decides whether faith leads to folly or to truth. Is belief in God a crutch, or is it a gateway to illumination? For centuries, similar questions have prompted reflection among people determined to seek and find reality. Intellectual curiosity is a compelling motivator. For some, only science and logic can reliably lead to truth. Yet others choose to follow their hearts. They travel a different road while searching for wisdom and insight. And truth waits patiently, unaffected by the popularity of the path which discovers it – because absolute truth is eternal, unyielding, and unchangeable.

★★★

The Greek prefix *meta* means "above." Therefore, the metaphysical is above or beyond the physical.

★★★

If God is present in timeless realms, then it makes perfect sense for a Supreme Creator to have existed "before" the Big Bang phenomenon.

★★★

Like the colors of a glorious sunset, life is always changing. Evolution and adaptation, it would seem, are part of life's beauty and wonder.

★★★

Has God not created the natural and the supernatural; the organic and the spiritual; the temporal and the eternal?

★★★

Organic life is a structural manifestation of divinity. Yet, divinity is unstructured and, therefore, cannot be wholly expressed within the boundaries of organic life.

3. Earth School

It's the first day of school in a classroom filled with first graders. Desks are arranged in rows which face an enormous chalkboard. Girls sit quietly and attentively. Boys squirm in their seats – nervous energy makes it harder for them to focus on the tasks at hand. All eyes are wide with wonder and excitement. Each of these young minds is like an ocean sponge ready to absorb the numbers, letters, facts, and dates that come their way. Each child has the potential to unlock the mysteries of our universe. It's a new beginning.

★★★

You are a lifelong learner, and God has blessed you with an unimaginably long life.

★★★

Earth School's classes are now in session. Though life's curriculum is mandatory, you can choose *when* to learn its lessons. Still, you receive the lessons that you need, not the ones that you want.

★★★

You must first learn to read and to understand *see Jane run* before completing a dissertation on quantum physics.

★★★

Why is history always repeating itself? Perhaps it's because people can be stubborn and arrogant, which makes them very slow learners.

★★★

First, think of hardship as if it were a teachable moment. And next, reflect on these questions: What's the most difficult part of your life right now? Why?

★★★

Has God created the organic universe so that we may have a classroom? And could spirit realms serve as classrooms too?

4. Astronauts

Only twelve human beings have landed and walked on the moon. Another twelve have orbited the moon without landing. Their missions literally gave these men a unique perspective of our planet. Some of their insights are captured in the following quotations.

"For what I was feeling at that moment in time, science and technology had no answer. I felt the world had too much purpose, too much logic, and was just too beautiful to happen by accident. I mean this in a spiritual sense. There has to be a Creator of the universe who stands above the religions we've created to govern our lives." Gene Cernan, Apollo 10 & 17

"The earth reminded me of a giant Christmas tree ornament hanging in the blackness of space. As we got farther and farther away, the earth got smaller and smaller. Finally, it shrank to the size of a marble, the most beautiful marble you can imagine. I felt the power of God as I'd never felt it before." James Irwin, Apollo 15

"We learned a lot about the moon. But what we really learned a lot about was the earth. From the moon, you can extend your thumb and hide the earth. Everything you've ever known – your loved ones, your work, and all earthly problems. They can disappear behind your thumb." Jim Lovell, Apollo 8 & 13

"After our return, we visited countries around the world. I heard the same thing over and over. From large, enthusiastic crowds, people shouted, 'We did it! We did it!' At first, I thought this was strange. Then, I understood they were right – *we* did it. It was ethereal." Mike Collins, Apollo 11

"The biggest joy was on the way home. Passing by my cockpit window were the earth, the moon, the sun, and the whole 360 panorama of the heavens. It was a powerful experience. I felt an overwhelming sense of oneness and connectedness. Then I realized, 'That's me! That's all of it! It's one thing!' And it was accompanied by an ecstasy, a sense of, 'Oh my God! Wow! Yes!' It was an epiphany." Edgar Mitchell, Apollo 14

5. Made in God's Image

Remember that God *is* love;

And made in God's image, your essence is love.

Made in God's image, you are a spiritual being.

Made in God's image, you are creative by nature.

Made in God's image, you are free to choose.

Made in God's image, you are a light of the world.

Made in God's image, your soul is eternal.

Made in God's image, there is a spark of perfection within your heart!

6. Our Complex and Connected World

Each day, our morning sun rises in the east. But in order to fully understand a sunrise, you must be aware that its theater is comprised of the entire cosmos. This same principle holds true for the things that happen to us each day. That is, life doesn't unfold within a vacuum. People are interconnected and so, too, are events. As a result, there are no isolated, individual experiences.

Some events are pleasurable, while others are not. But details aside, the whole universe serves as a backdrop for each day's experiences. So before dismissing the rising sun as an ordinary, uncomplicated phenomenon, should you not first learn how it coexists with the countless stars and planets of the Milky Way? And before judging people and the things that happen to them, should you not first understand why God has created an indivisible world?

★★★

Jesus was teaching about interconnectedness when he told the parable of the sheep and the goats. Christ's message was straightforward: Whatever you do for one of my brothers or sisters, you do, in truth, for me. It reminds us that people are inextricably joined together. And just as importantly, the things we say and do – each word and every deed – are shared experiences.

For instance, someone who becomes sick might turn to doctors or family members for help. Thus, his experience is shared, in part, with others. And if a person walks alone in the woods, will his journey not include interactions with birds and animals, plants and trees? Even if someone were to lock himself inside a dark, empty room, would this event go undetected by a collective consciousness? And can anything occur outside the awareness of God? Where is the earthly experience that is not shared with our Heavenly Father?

★★★

Scientists have proven that humans, animals, and even insects which band together develop group intelligence. In all cases, their collective intelligence is superior to the individual intelligence of its members. With ants, for example, the problem solving ability of the colony is far greater than the problem solving ability of any individual ant. And with primates, breakthroughs in problem solving have inexplicably travelled from a single, isolated family to primate groups around the world.

★★★

A growing number of theoretical physicists believe that the universe itself is a living, thinking, and highly complex life form.

★★★

The universe is immeasurably vast and sophisticated. And scientists say that a living universe would have a memory beyond description; it would have computational capacities beyond comprehension; and it would have limitless regenerative and creative power. People of faith may see such attributes as Godlike.

★★★

The world is seldom as simple as it appears to be. Yet through innocent eyes and an open mind, the smallest thing may be recognized as a miracle.

★★★

By design, the infinitesimal can become the infinite.

7. Divine Promises

A covenant is a holy agreement founded on love. It is a sacred promise which embraces God's will. To his children, God has promised an immortal soul, an individual identity, the freedom to choose, and the ability to experience life. What does it mean to *experience* life? Think of it this way. Can you revel in calm seas if you've never faced turbulent waters? Can you rejoice in the sun's warmth if you've never been numbed by the cold? Can you celebrate the light of dawn if you've never feared the night? And can you wholly know love if your heart has not been broken?

8. An Upside-Down Perspective

Physicist and cosmologist Charles Hellaby teaches at the University of Cape Town in South Africa. Because he has studied both the smallest and the largest components of the universe, Hellaby has gained a well-rounded perspective on the workings of our world. And as one might expect, his research has attracted a great deal of attention within the scientific community.

Hellaby is convinced that those who study life by starting from the simple (the small) and then working upward to the complex (the large) are likely to be misled. Instead, he urges scientists to explore the universe beginning with the complex and working downward to the simple. This "upside down" approach has led to startling insights.

According to Hellaby, physics and mathematics explain much of the world, but not all of it. Physics, for example, deciphers how a violin produces sound. Yet an orchestra cannot function without a conductor. In other words, structure and cohesiveness must be in place prior to making beautifully complex music. Helaby posits that, in a similar way, mathematical and physical constructs had to exist *before* the birth of the universe. Otherwise the universe would have been chaotic and dysfunctional from the very beginning. And without a structured, cohesive universe, life as we know it can neither exist nor evolve. Hellaby suggests there's but one question remaining: Who created the mathematical and physical laws which were in place before the birth of our universe?

★★★

There are gaps within our human understanding of how the universe works. We are missing bits of knowledge, and grand mysteries remain unsolved. So you might ask: Where can we find this missing knowledge? And how will we solve these grand mysteries? In truth, only love can build a bridge that takes us to the unknown. And only love can provide answers to far-reaching questions. For what else is there? What else will lead us to the face of God?

★★★

We can debate it or deny it. We can kick and scream and hold our breath. But the fact remains: Human beings are *spiritual beings* made in the image of a Supreme Creator.

9. An Evolving Circle of Love

Spiritual growth is simple, but not easy.

Begin each morning with a prayer asking for God's help and guidance.

Understand that every thought, every word, and every deed is either an expression of love or a crying out for love.

As your day unfolds, remain focused on expressing love in all that you think and say and do.

As you learn to express love more consistently, your faith grows.

As your faith grows, you experience a higher level of awareness and self-understanding.

As your awareness and self-understanding expand, you become more open-minded and less judgmental.

As you become more open-minded and less judgmental, you are more willing to forgive.

As you offer forgiveness more consistently, you experience greater joy and inner peace.

As you experience greater joy and inner peace, you feel God's presence more profoundly.

As you feel God's presence more profoundly, you express love more consistently.

As you learn to express love more consistently, your faith grows.

And so it goes – an evolving, everlasting circle of love.

10. Prayer and Christianity

God wants to hear from you. He wants you to share your thoughts and feelings; your fears and worries; your troubles and your triumphs. God wants you to have a close, personal relationship with him. And we haven't always understood this. For instance, most people living in the times of the Old Testament believed God was distant and unapproachable. But Jesus helped people view God from a new, more illuminated perspective. In his ministry, Jesus taught that God *does* want a relationship with his children. And one way to nurture a personal connection with God is through prayer. That's why Jesus often prayed in front of his disciples. He wanted to show them how they could feel God's presence more profoundly. Prayer is powerful. You can pray for anyone, anywhere in the world, at anytime. You can pray for individuals or groups of people. When offered for the benefit of others, they are prayers of intercession.

And there are many other kinds of prayers, including ones of praise, thanksgiving, confession, and petition. A prayer of petition normally asks for a specific result, such as reconciliation. It might sound like this: "Gracious God, help me to reconnect with my daughter. She's struggling right now, and I love her so much. I want to support her and be an important part of her life again. Amen." A prayer of praise honors and glorifies God as we worship him. It could be something like: "Heavenly Father, you are a glorious God; a God of infinite love and grace. You are all-knowing and ever-present; the supreme Creator of all that is good. May I forever bathe in your Light. Amen."

In a prayer of confession, we acknowledge our mistakes and ask God for forgiveness. It might sound like this: "O Gracious God, I've done things that have hurt the people who love me. I deeply regret my choices and mistakes, and I humbly ask for your forgiveness. Please guide me as I make amends and try to ease the pain I've caused. Amen." And finally, a prayer of thanksgiving expresses gratitude for the blessings we receive from God. It could be something like: "Divine Father, thank you for your unconditional love and forgiveness. I'm grateful for the abundance of gifts you provide, for the beauty I see in nature, for the support I receive from family and friends, and for the peace I find through prayer. Amen."

Prayer has no limits. You can ask for strength, guidance, wisdom, insight, comfort, courage, perseverance, patience, protection, vigilance, or self-discipline. You can ask for help in building strong character. You can pray for help as you try to be more kind, compassionate, loving, and forgiving. You can ask for help in building better relationships with family members, friends, or coworkers. You can ask for help with your job or guidance on finances. And your words can be spoken out loud, or they can be silent. Either way, God knows what is on your mind and in your heart. Whether you feel good or not, whether you're dressed up or in pajamas, whether you're driving a car or taking a shower, you can always talk to God. Those who are wise have learned that good habits lead to healthy routines. Are you willing to start and end each day with a prayer? Can you choose to make this one of your good habits? And as each day unfolds, are you willing to share your thoughts and feelings – to keep up your conversation with God? Can you choose to make this part of a healthy routine? Remember, there's never a time or place where a silent prayer will not be appropriate and helpful.

Scripture suggests there's no need to "babble on." There's no reason to think that God favors longer prayers. Effective prayers can be simple, direct, and concise. And ideally, they should be genuine, pure, and heartfelt. For example: "Gracious God, help me to feel your presence and be an instrument of your will. Use me as a conduit of your Light, love, and peace. Amen." or "Heavenly Father, may your will be done on earth as it is in heaven. Allow me to see your truth and to understand your plan for me during this difficult time. Amen."

It's confusing when our prayers seem to go unheard. But could it be that prayers are sometimes answered in a different way from what we desire, or at a time other than what we expect? For instance, a man may ask God to heal his body; and perhaps his body will be healed, but not immediately. Then again, a prayer for physical healing could be answered with opportunities for emotional or spiritual healing. Or maybe God will help heal a broken relationship instead of a broken body.

God always responds to the prayers which come from our heart, the prayers which express love; for such prayers are aligned with his will. Indeed, prayers of the heart are destined to receive God's blessing. Ego-driven prayers, however, have little to do with love; and such prayers may go unanswered. Or, to think of it another way, God's answer might be, "No." And there's one more scenario which can lead to confusion. Sometimes, we simply don't recognize that God *has* answered our prayers.

Jesus said, "Your Father knows what you need before you ask him." So perhaps you wonder: *If God already knows my needs, then why should I bother to pray?* There are at least two reasons. First, by reaching out to God, you're making a conscious decision to seek his help, thereby honoring the covenant of free will. And second, with each prayer you offer, your relationship with God grows stronger. Jesus promised that when we seek, we shall find. When we knock, the door shall be opened. And as we grow in love and faith, we shall see the glory of God.

★★★

It's troubling when your desires appear to conflict with God's plan. Yet, your most fervent desire is to enter the kingdom of heaven – a yearning that's forever in harmony with God's will.

★★★

Prayer and meditation promote physiological changes. Your heart rate slows down and your blood pressure stabilizes. Muscles relax and tension begins to ease. And your brain releases endorphins that promote a sense of safety and well-being.

★★★

There is no substitute for a relationship with God. Fortunately, we can build a meaningful relationship with God from anywhere – in our home, in a hospital, or even in a prison.

★★★

After communing with God, Moses was radiant. Indeed, his face shone so brightly that he had to wear a veil. Such is the brilliance of God's Light!

11. Science, Ownership, and Truth

Could scientific methods one day prove that indivisibility and infinity are identical? Will scientists discover that, in fact, there is but one Source for all that is seen and unseen, for all that is animate and inanimate, and for all that is unthinkably small and unimaginably large? Perhaps physicists shall one day prove that love is the foundation of our universe and that spirit is the essence of our world. And thereafter, atheism will attract less interest than the Flat Earth Society.

★★★

Scientists pretend to be nothing more than detached, objective onlookers; when actually, they are busy poking and prodding the world. There's nothing wrong with hands-on research. Yet, scientists have already proven that the mere act of observation – not to mention poking and prodding – produces behavioral changes at the subatomic level. And if this is so, are their results always trustworthy?

★★★

Everything has a name, and there's a practical value to labeling things. For without names, language would be imprecise. Dialogue would be more confusing and communication would be plagued by frequent misunderstandings. Names, at first, appear to be innocent. Yet once something is named, a sense of ownership quickly follows. And ownership includes an element of control, which implies a level of understanding. Unfortunately, names can lead to a *false* sense of ownership, a *misleading* element of control, and a *misguided* level of understanding. The mind seeks only to explain, not to understand.

★★★

You cannot change faulty thoughts with more faulty thinking. The best way to solve a problem is to rise above the problem, then examine it and find a true solution. And the best way to rise above a problem is through prayer, reflection, and meditation.

★★★

Self-discovered truth is often more meaningful than lessons taught by a teacher.

★★★

Sometimes, more can be learned by listening and observing than by talking and doing.

★★★

Truth is like gravity. It works whether you believe it or not.

12. Spiritual Journeys

People often try to delegate their personal search for divine truth. They end up believing the lessons of someone who has a religious title. Or they trust a person who claims to have special gifts. Or maybe they follow a leader who offers nothing more than a dynamic personality. It's understandable why these things happen. Spiritual pathways are, after all, filled with potholes, hairpin turns, and dead ends. What's more, it can be surprisingly difficult to distinguish truth from falsehood. So it's easier to let others blaze the trail.

Yet, while delegation is an easy choice, it may not be a wise one. Remember that life is much more than just a final destination. Life includes the tough road trips which move us along the way. Indeed, bumps and bruises are essential to learning. And the people who allow someone else to steer their spiritual journey will surely miss an exhilarating ride.

★★★

Is there only one pastor, one rabbi, one mullah, or one priest whose lessons can be trusted? Is God found only within the walls of a church, a synagogue, a mosque, or a temple?

★★★

Is it really possible to give *your* spiritual journey to someone else? Can another person determine what rings true in *your* heart? And finally, can someone else grow in love and faith on *your* behalf?

13. The Lord's Prayer

Our Father who art in heaven,

Hallowed be Thy name.

Thy kingdom come, Thy will be done,

On earth as it is in heaven.

Give us this day our daily bread,

And forgive us our trespasses,

As we forgive those who trespass against us.

And lead us not into temptation,

But deliver us from evil.

For Thine is the kingdom,

And the power,

And the glory, forever. Amen

14. Making Plans

Think of the many times you've made plans, only to see them fall apart. It's natural to be disappointed when a dream is crushed. You may feel frustrated and angry as well. But if Plan A fails, then people of faith will pause, regroup, and ask God to help them devise a Plan B. And here's where things get interesting. Back-up plans often bear sweeter fruit than the original ones. For example, the job you didn't land may open the door for an even better career opportunity. The apartment you couldn't rent might prompt you to find a place closer to your favorite park. And your broken relationship may pave the way for a new, more enduring one.

★★★

While you make a plan for growing older, God makes a plan for you to grow wiser. And while you make a plan for saving money, God makes a plan for saving your soul.

★★★

God's plan for you is far grander than any plan you make for yourself.

15. God with Us

The virgin will be with child and shall give birth to a son; and he will be called Immanuel, meaning God with us. (Matthew 1:23)

★★★

When the angel, Gabriel, told Mary that she would give birth to the son of God, Mary asked: "How will this be, since I am a virgin?" And the angel answered, "The Holy Spirit will come upon you and the power of the Most High will bless you . . . For nothing is impossible with God." Mary replied, "I am the Lord's servant. May it be to me as you have said." (Luke 1:34–38)

Fulfilling the prophecies, Mary gave birth to a son and she named him Jesus. He was the Christ, the anointed one. While on earth, Jesus healed the sick and his ministry offered hope to the oppressed. He reached out to the poor and the disadvantaged. Jesus taught lessons of love and forgiveness while chastising the hypocrites who ruled the synagogues. Christ the healer, Christ the teacher, Christ the comforter, Christ the redeemer: Jesus is the shepherd whose voice you know. For unto us a child was born, and his life transformed the world.

★★★

Lord Alfred Tennyson wrote, "God is nearer than breathing, closer than hands and feet."

★★★

Think of the Holy Spirit as God's guiding voice, his divine Sanctifier.

16. A Path to Inner Peace

Can inner peace be won like the grand prize in a sweepstakes? Is equanimity received like a birthday gift from your favorite aunt? The human desire for inner harmony is so compelling that even a counterfeit, drug-induced peace can be addictive. Yet, lasting peace must be earned. It's the result of hard work, and there are no shortcuts. Inner peace blossoms as you grow closer to God. At first, you might experience only fleeting moments of calmness. But as your spiritual work unfolds, those moments of tranquility will occur more frequently. Not only do periods of peace offer encouragement, they affirm that you're on the right path.

Still, frustration is inevitable, especially when progress seems painfully slow. You may even feel despondent. At such times, prayer is helpful. Ask God for guidance, patience, and perseverance. Disciplined spiritual work will gradually elevate your consciousness. And in time, a profound and lasting peace will be within your grasp. Jesus reminded his disciples, "If you remain in me and my words remain in you, ask whatever you wish, and it will be given you." Jesus was referring to his words about love. For in truth, it is love that smashes all barriers between you and inner peace.

17. Angels

Humankind has enjoyed an ongoing fascination with angels. We admire their beauty and grace, their strength and compassion. And of course, we envy the wings which swiftly carry angels from one place to the next. We imagine what it would be like to have the wings of an angel.

The Judeo-Christian tradition teaches that angels serve as God's messengers and as human protectors. Angels also help with healing and they promote God's will. Some angels serve as attendants or guardians. Nativity scenes reinforce this perspective, as angels watch over the Holy Child. In fact, Scripture contains so many references to angels that, during biblical times, people must have been bumping into them once or twice a week. And herein rests the mystery: Where have all the angels gone? Today, sightings are rarely mentioned. Indeed, many people have never seen an angel.

Yet, we lose touch with God just as often as the men and women who lived long ago. And because of this, our Merciful Father continues to have his angels watch over for us. Our Loving Creator blesses us with guidance as well. God might send his message through a thought, an inspiration, a dream, a voice, a vision, or a special encounter. Or perhaps an angel will appear. Angels gather around us in greater numbers as we face difficult challenges. They come to us when we are overwhelmed, sad, or frightened. So as we feel God's presence, could we also be feeling the love of his heavenly angels?

Most people say, "I will believe it when I see it." But according to Native American wisdom, those who are truly wise say, "I will see it when I believe it." This insight sheds light on the earlier question: Where have all the angels gone? In truth, they haven't gone anywhere. Angels are among us still, just as they were during biblical times. But, you have to *believe* it. You must reach out to them, extend your hand, and *expect* to feel an angel's gentle touch.

★★★

Angels serve as protectors: When facing arrest, Jesus told his followers not to defend him. He said, "Do you think I cannot call on my Father and he will at once send me more than twelve legions of angels?" Note that twelve legions total more than 60,000 angels. *Holy Bible*

★★★

Angels guide us to divine reality: No one can fail who seeks to reach the truth. Angels light the way so that all darkness vanishes and you are standing in a light so bright and clear that you can understand all things you see. *A Course in Miracles*

★★★

Angels serve as holy messengers: And God sent the angel Gabriel to a virgin named Mary. The angel went to her and said, "Greetings, you who are highly favored! The Lord is with you." *Holy Bible*

★★★

Angels instill calmness: You do not walk alone, for God's angels hover near and all about. Love surrounds you, and of this you can be sure: You will never be left comfortless. *A Course in Miracles*

★★★

According to an ancient Greek legend, God will kiss the unborn soul of a baby. Then, an angel escorts the innocent soul earthward to be joined with a tiny body. Along the way, the guiding angel begins to sing. So somewhere, deep in every soul, there's a memory of that divine kiss. And somewhere, deep within each heart, there's an echo of that heavenly song.

★★★

Like the wind, an angel's presence isn't something you see, it is something you feel.

18. A Caregiver's Reflection

A stranger's smile is disarming. Love is the source of friendliness.

The phone call from a friend is uplifting. Love is the source of holy relationships.

An uncle's words are encouraging. Love is the source of helpfulness.

A mother's embrace is affirming. Love is the source of blissful peace.

A father's labor pays for food, clothing, and shelter. Love is the source of honest providing.

A wife's tender kiss consoles her husband. Love is the source of sacred covenants.

A chaplain's prayer promotes spiritual healing. Love is the source of inspired ministry.

A social worker nurtures physical and mental well-being. Love is the source of advocacy.

A psychologist's intervention leads to healthier choices. Love is the source of wise counseling.

A nurse's watchful eye and gentle touch are reassuring. Love is the source of compassionate care.

The sponge bath from a nurse's aide is soothing. Love is the source of heartfelt serving.

A physician's visit brings pain relief. Love is the source of comfort.

A surgeon's blade removes a tumor. Love is the source of hope.

A stranger, a friend, a family member, and a parent; a spouse, a chaplain, and a social worker; a counselor, a nurse, an aide, and a doctor; each one bears a healing gift. Each one is an irreplaceable link in the chain of caregiving.

Helping, encouraging, uplifting, and reassuring; nurturing, consoling, and providing; caring, comforting, protecting, and serving; ministering, counseling, and affirming; each blessing flows from an endless wellspring of love. And God is the Source of love.

★★★

Caregivers join people on their journeys and walk with them for a short while.

★★★

It's impossible to know how someone else feels because it is their pain, not yours.

19. Goodbyes

It can be awkward, or even painful, to say farewell to someone you love. And the word *goodbye* sounds so formal and cold. There's an implied sense of permanence or finality. But in Germany, people say *auf wiedersehen* as they part ways with friends and loved ones. It translates "until we meet again." Spanish cultures use *hasta la vista,* meaning "until I see you." And Hawaiians say *aloha* when greeting someone and *aloha* once more when preparing to leave. As it happens, these global variations for saying goodbye are not only warmer and kinder; they're closer to reality as well.

★★★

Can those you dearly love actually go away forever? Or will you surely see them again?

20. Looking for Love

You never know where or when your life will be touched by love. It may happen in a mansion, or in the most humble of homes. Someone of great wealth might offer you heartfelt love, or perhaps an impoverished person will bear this gift. An outpouring of love may come from a person of lofty status or from a social outcast; from someone highly educated or from someone with little schooling; from the healthy or the infirmed; from the mighty or the meek. Yet warmth, kindness, and helpfulness are welcomed blessings, regardless of their source. And isn't it curious how love is often found in a place where you least expect it, but at a time when you most need it?

★★★

Love can be expressed by a gentle touch; through an act of kindness; by giving or receiving a gift; through affirming words; and by attentive listening.

★★★

Is love ever wasted?

21. One Day at a Time

One day at a time, with its failures and fears
With its hurts and mistakes, and its sorrows and tears
With its portion of pain and its burden of care
One day at a time, I must meet and must bear

One day at a time, but the day is so long
My heart's not too brave and my soul's not yet strong
Oh glorious God, be You near all the way
Give me patience and courage and strength for this day

God's answer comes swiftly, so clear and so sweet
"Yes, I will guide you through hardships you meet
I shall never forget you, and though you may stray
I shall never forsake you or leave you this day"

Not yesterday's load are we called on to share
Nor tomorrow's sadness and strife should we care
Why look forward with worry, or back with dismay
Our needs, as our triumphs, are gifts for today

One day at a time, to be faithful and strong
To be calm under trial and be kind under wrong
Then, life's troubles shall pass and my worries will cease
They will weaken and flee as the night ushers peace

One day at a time, and this is God's day
He shapes precious moments as though they were clay
God's grace is sufficient, I walk not alone
For the love I find daily comes from His own

Adapted from the poem by Annie Johnson Flint (1866-1932)

22. Rest and Renewal

Find a quiet place to seek rest and renewal. Find a sacred place for times of introspection and healing. Find a holy place to seek forgiveness and guidance. And find a majestic place for times of worship and praise. Of course, you needn't travel anywhere.

★★★

Just as water is the natural environment for a fish, the grace of God is your natural environment. And like a fish in water, you are so immersed in God's grace that you have no awareness of it.

★★★

Like moths to a flame, humans are drawn to worship, praise, ceremonies, rituals, and sacraments. These holy experiences fill a need which cannot be satisfied with substitute activities.

★★★

Is your relationship with God more important than your beliefs about God?

★★★

Laughter, like grace, is a healing gift from God.

★★★

May God bless you and keep you.

May God's face shine upon you and give you peace.

May God's angels gather to guide, protect, and comfort you.

And may you feel the Light and love of Jesus Christ. Amen

23. **Contemplations of a Cardinal**

Born in Columbia, South Carolina on April 2, 1928, Joseph Cardinal Bernardin was the son of Italian immigrants Joseph and Maria Bernardin. At age 24, the young Roman Catholic was ordained as a priest. In 1972, Bernardin became Archbishop of Cincinnati; and ten years later, he was appointed the seventh Archbishop of Chicago. Pope Paul II elevated Bernardin to the Sacred College of Cardinals in 1983. Bernardin had gained respect as a compassionate priest, an insightful theologian, a capable administrator, and a trustworthy ambassador of the Church.

Then, his world was shattered by allegations of a horrible crime. Stephen Cook, a former seminarian, charged that Bernardin had sexually abused him. With a stained reputation and a shaken confidence, Bernardin questioned God. The Cardinal would later write: "When I was wrongly accused of sexual abuse, I asked: *Why, God, did you let this happen?* Still, I knew that my accuser needed prayers as much as I did. Those days were painful, but also filled with grace. I felt an outpouring of love and support. Above all, it was a time of spiritual growth." Cook eventually recanted and Bernardin was exonerated. Shortly thereafter, the two men met face-to-face. The Cardinal said this reconciliation and healing "filled me with new life."

But there was a second crisis waiting in the wings. In 1995, the Cardinal was diagnosed with pancreatic cancer. These are his words: "My father died of cancer when I was six years old. So when I was diagnosed with a tumor, I already knew that cancer changes lives – not only the life of the person carrying it, but the lives of loved ones as well. When I learned that I had an aggressive cancer, I kept asking myself: *Is this real? Is it true?* There were many tears and periods of sadness. When we are sick, everything changes."

Bernardin underwent extensive surgery, followed by post-operative radiation treatments. It was a grueling period in his life. But the cancer was in remission and Bernardin remained hopeful. During this time, he became a crusader and spiritual leader for the sick. He visited children's hospitals and community nursing homes. Then, fifteen months later, the cancer returned. Declining further curative options, Bernardin held a press conference. He told reporters: "In all sincerity, I am at peace. I consider this as God's special gift to me."

Bernardin chronicled his life's triumphs and trials in his heartfelt book *The Gift of Peace*. The Cardinal died on November 14, 1990 at age 68, just days after he completed his compelling autobiography which includes this message: "Growing up, I spent years looking through my mother's photo albums. I carefully studied my parents' homeland in northern Italy. As time passed, I came to know the mountains, the trees, the houses, and the people. The first time I actually travelled to that part of Italy, it felt as if I had been there before. As soon as I entered the village, I thought, *My God, I know this place. I'm home.* Somehow, I think this is the way it will be in the afterlife. As I enter heaven, I'll have the feeling that I am home."

★★★

The following contemplations are representative of the Cardinal's Christian beliefs.

The good and the bad are always present in our human condition. If we "let go" and place ourselves totally in the hands of the Lord, the good will prevail.

"Letting go" means releasing from our grasp those things that inhibit us from developing an intimate relationship with Jesus. It's a lifelong process, and it isn't easy.

Each day, open wide the doors of your heart to Jesus and his expectations of you.

Learn to distinguish between life's essentials and life's peripherals. Essentials guide you to love others, while peripherals steer you to focus on yourself. Spiritual growth blossoms as you devote more and more time on the essentials.

Suffering may cause a sense of loneliness, even abandonment. Yet suffering, as proven by Christ, can also be redemptive and life-giving.

Whenever we are with people who suffer, it becomes evident that there is little we can do to help them other than be present with them; to walk with them as the Lord walks with us.

If we are to love more as Jesus loved, we must first come to terms with suffering. We must accept the purposefulness of suffering before we can become effective instruments in our mission to help others.

It's tough to watch loved ones struggle with pain. But we must believe that by being strong and supportive, we make an enormous difference.

As we minister to those who are hurting, we encounter the living God.

Jesus opened his arms wide as he embraced little children. And as he opened his arms wide on the cross, Christ embraced the whole world.

The things people remember most are small acts of kindness and thoughtfulness.

It is during times of sickness that we need people the most.

By embracing pain, by looking into it and beyond it, I have come to see God's presence in even the worst situations.

Without prayer, you cannot be connected or remain connected with the Lord. You cannot experience lasting peace.

When you are sick, put yourself *completely* in the hands of the Lord. He will never abandon you. This is what gives us hope.

Jesus never promised to take away our burdens, but he did promise to help us carry them.

Death is my dear friend, the one who will lead me home to God.

24. Life's Opportunities

Are you willing to perceive hardship, pain, and disappointment as opportunities to . . .

Grow in faith?

Rely on God?

Examine life's meaning?

Redefine your identity?

Discover grace?

Make empowering choices?

Count blessings?

Overcome adversity?

Accept change?

Persevere?

Build character?

Foster hope?

Withhold judgment?

Launch a new beginning?

Trust God?

★★★

During a crisis, reaching out to God is a natural response. We have an intuitive desire to connect with God when facing hardship.

★★★

To produce a pearl, the oyster must first have an irritant.

25. Faith Means Reaching Out

It's a well-known children's song and the story is simple. The itsy-bitsy spider climbed up the water spout. Down came the rain and washed the spider out. Out came the sun and dried up all the rain. And the itsy-bitsy spider climbed up the spout again. And so on, and so on.

But wait. Could there be an existential conundrum hidden within this silly lyric? Is the itsy-bitsy spider a stubborn dolt, doomed to perpetually repeat the same mistake without ever learning or growing from his life experiences? Or is the itsy-bitsy spider a model of persistence, faith, and perseverance as he faces adversity?

★★★

An intellectual fisherman sat on the riverbank. The fish weren't biting, so he amused himself by watching a young, playful squirrel. The squirrel cavorted among several nearby trees, and it boldly explored branches that stretched well beyond the water's edge. Suddenly, the squirrel lost its grip and fell awkwardly into the river. It was apparent that, without aid, the squirrel would quickly drown. Deep in thought, the fisherman wondered: *Is it the squirrel's destiny to drown? If so, I wouldn't want to interfere with divine will.* But then he thought: *Maybe the squirrel's destiny is to be rescued by a fisherman who just happens to be close by. I could help this poor creature. Perhaps this is what God wants.* Paralyzed with indecision, the fisherman watched in horror as the young squirrel was swallowed by the murky water.

★★★

There's nothing wrong with contemplation. And it's okay to reflect on God's will. Yet in the end, faith isn't merely an intellectual exercise. Faith is to be *lived*. And living one's faith includes helping people when given the opportunity. It means being kind and compassionate. It includes loving those who are difficult to love. And it means forgiving those who have hurt you. When you are willing to love unconditionally, God works through you to make our world a better place. So don't just stand there. Reach out to the next person – or to the next squirrel – in need of your help. Jump in and *live* your faith!

★★★

Jesus said, "Go and make disciples of all nations." As you live your faith, you are teaching Christ's commandment to love God. And as you live your faith, you love your neighbor as yourself. Is the Great Commission, then, not advanced by those devoted to *living* their faith?

★★★

Riddle: Five frogs are sitting on a log. Three decide to jump off. How many frogs are left on the log?

Answer: Five. Although three frogs had decided to jump off, none of them actually did it.

★★★

Act like the person you wish to become.

26. Cancer Has Limits

Although this reflection focuses on cancer, its lesson applies to most diseases and disabilities.

Cancer has limits . . .

    It cannot cripple love.

    It cannot shatter hope.

    It cannot erode faith.

    It cannot smother peace.

    It cannot destroy confidence.

    It cannot kill a friendship.

    It cannot erase memories.

    It cannot silence courage.

    It cannot invade the soul.

    It cannot dampen the spirit.

It cannot extinguish eternal life.

It cannot diminish the power of resurrection.

★★★

Cancer *does* change lives. In addition, the body's betrayal often triggers a mix of strong feelings such as anger, fear, frustration, anxiety, and sadness. Yet, those who face cancer's challenges can make positive choices, including how they choose to perceive their illness.

Adapted from an unknown author

27. Human Nature

You're naturally drawn to like-minded people, those having interests and values similar to your own. It's the same human nature which also prompts you to spend more time with those holding similar theological views. And as you spend more time with people, some of them are bound to become new friends. A few may even earn your admiration, respect, and trust. And of course, these are the people you turn to for advice.

Yet when seeking guidance, especially spiritual guidance, it pays to be passionately discriminating. Or to say it another way, it's important to follow your heart. Do the words of your counselors ring true? Are their lessons teaching kindness and unity? Be cautious of a narrow-minded message laced with fear-based judgments. Usually, this type of advice is offered by someone promoting a self-serving agenda.

Remember, this one life is *your* spiritual journey, and the peace of God awaits you. Therefore, go boldly into the world. Knock on doors. Seek and find. And rejoice as your search unfolds. You'll have plenty of help along the way, but no one else can walk the path for you.

28. In God We Trust

As our faith grows, perhaps there shall be a time when we surrender to God. Perhaps there shall be a day when we honestly ask for God's will to be done, not ours. And as our faith grows, perhaps there shall be a time when we ask the Holy Spirit to guide us. For in truth, these choices prepare us to be devoted servants of the Lord.

With our Father's help, we can extend kindness to those we meet; we can be more accepting of different cultures and religions; and we can offer forgiveness to others and ourselves. With God's help, we can choose to be in the world, not of the world. In other words, we will begin to distance ourselves from the relentless drama of the human experience. And we will resist the temptation to make fear-based judgments.

Life is ever-changing. We celebrate great triumphs, but we endure bitter disappointments as well. In our darkest hours, we can turn to a Merciful Father. And by listening to our heart, we will know that divine plans are perfect, even as they remain a mystery.

God is omnipotent and omniscient; a Supreme Creator beyond description and comprehension. His love has no end, and his grace has no boundaries. By placing our trust in God, we can experience a profound and lasting peace. We can maintain an underlying sense that all is well. And as we grow to trust him more and more, we will see the glory of God.

★★★

Jesus approached his disciples as they were huddled on a boat. The men were shocked and amazed, for Jesus was walking on the water. Empowered by a deep trust, Peter left the boat and walked on the water towards his teacher. Peter believed with his whole heart that nothing could stop him from reaching Jesus. And in fact, Peter's walk of faith was going well until doubt and fear crept into his mind. A moment later, he began to sink.

★★★

Like every journey, faith has a starting point.

29. A Pop Quiz

Your responses to the following eight questions just might change your life. Please select one answer per question.

1. When facing an uncertain future, you would:
   A. Stockpile food and water.
   B. Apply for a Concealed Carry permit.
   C. Form strategic alliances with like-minded neighbors. Or,
   D. Make prayer and meditation part of your daily routine.

2. When trying to avoid catching the flu, you would:
   A. Wear scuba gear.
   B. Cancel your doctor's appointment.
   C. Stay locked in your bedroom until the coast is clear. Or,
   D. Make prayer and meditation part of your daily routine.

3. When struggling with financial problems, you would:
   A. Borrow from your child's piggy bank.
   B. Call a rich uncle.
   C. Purchase a Power Ball ticket. Or,
   D. Make prayer and meditation part of your daily routine.

4. When trying to improve the relationship with your spouse, you would:
   A. Consult with the nearest bartender.
   B. Forget your wedding anniversary.
   C. Bring home a McDonald's happy meal. Or,
   D. Make prayer and meditation part of your daily routine.

5. When seeking a reprieve from stress and the daily grind, you would:
   A. Listen to heavy metal music.
   B. Bang your head against a favorite wall.
   C. Book a cruise. Or,
   D. Make prayer and meditation part of your daily routine.

6. When looking for help and inspiration to work through life's problems, you would:
   A. Read old columns of Dear Abby.
   B. Ask a gang leader.
   C. Crack open a fortune cookie. Or,
   D. Make prayer and meditation part of your daily routine.

7. When trying to discover life's meaning and purpose, you would:
   A. Climb to the attic and look inside that antique trunk.
   B. Play a game of Monopoly.
   C. Take a deep breath and hold it for as long as possible. Or,
   D. Make prayer and meditation part of your daily routine.

8. When seeking to experience lasting happiness and inner peace, you would:
   A. Buy a new sports car.
   B. Sign up for ballroom dancing lessons.
   C. Join a study group on the Book of Revelation. Or,
   D. Make prayer and meditation part of your daily routine.

Are you beginning to see a trend? Spiritual exercise boosts your emotional well-being, and research has proven that emotional stability strengthens the body's immune system. In other words, prayer and meditation actually promote better health and lessen your risk of becoming sick. So as you pray, you really *are* fending off those flu viruses!

30. Pain and Suffering

There are different kinds of pain; and if it were possible, we would avoid each one of them. Yet, a closer look at human pain reveals some surprising benefits. For instance, physical pain is an alarm, a warning which tells us there's a problem with our body. If not for pain, many ailments would go undetected and, therefore, untreated. And without treatment, a problem may become more serious, perhaps even life-threatening. So while you may not be grateful for the pain, you can be grateful for knowing that something is wrong. And though certain conditions are chronic or incurable, most health problems respond favorably to medical treatments, especially if they're received right away. In this sense, pain is a helpful friend.

Physical, emotional, and spiritual pain are endured by nearly everyone. These woes are common to the human condition. Suffering, however, is a perception. It has very little to do with pain, and much to do with the thoughts and feelings associated with pain. Ultimately, then, suffering is a choice; it's something the mind can actually dismiss as unreal. In other words, while pain is a mandatory lesson of the world's curriculum, suffering is an elective.

For Christians, pain holds the potential to strengthen faith and bring believers closer to God. Moreover, pain can motivate people to examine their attachment to the material world, and such introspections often lead to spiritual growth. Psychiatrist Victor Frankl was a Nazi concentration camp survivor and an early pioneer of existential psychotherapy. During his imprisonment, Frankl observed that men and women were willing to bear extreme pain as long as they could see meaning in it. And he noticed that people who attached meaning to their pain were more likely to survive.

It's important to understand that God is not the source of human pain or suffering. In truth, poor decision making – and the resulting consequences – are among the leading causes of pain. But here again, discomfort is an ally because it prompts us to make wiser choices. Pain urges us to stop making the same mistakes over and over. And there's at least one more benefit: If not for pain, could we fully appreciate pleasure?

★★★

It's impossible to know how someone else is feeling. Nor can you experience another's pain. Yes, you can offer empathy, compassion, and support to those who are hurting. You may even have angst and sadness over another person's pain. Still, it won't be anything like what the other person is experiencing.

★★★

Attempts to resist or "fight" pain will actually intensify it. Acute pain can trigger fear which, if left unchecked, may escalate into full-blown terror and panic. Yet for those who are able to accept pain and "surrender" to it, their pain seems to be much more tolerable. In fact, people have used a combination of surrender and meditation to undergo invasive surgery without the benefit of anesthesia. Meditation cues the brain to release the body's natural chemicals that mitigate pain and promote a feeling of well-being. And a prayer which asks God for courage, calmness, and comfort may also provide effective pain relief.

★★★

If trapped, wild animals will battle to regain their freedom. And strengthened by a rush of adrenaline, an animal will either fight or flee for its life. But after receiving a mortal injury, all running and fighting stops. Endorphins help block the pain. Muscles relax and breathing slows down. And there's no perception of suffering or feeling of self-pity. The animal isn't necessarily accepting its impending death. Rather, it is surrendering to the circumstances of the present moment. It is simply accepting what cannot be changed. And by doing so, the animal dies more peacefully.

31. An Eye for an Eye

It has been taught: An eye for an eye, and a tooth for a tooth. But what does it mean? Jesus suggested that if one cheek is struck, turn the other. He also said that if you are sued for your coat, offer your shirt too. And if you are forced to walk one mile, walk another one as well. The point is: No one can truly harm you. Even if your body has been broken and you've lost your possessions, your soul is untouched. Your spirit, the immortal part of you, remains unscathed regardless of what happens in the world. Therefore, Christians are urged to offer forgiveness in lieu of revenge. We are asked to offer grace in lieu of retribution. And we are to be mindful that it's God's task to balance the scales of justice.

★★★

Christ's ministry transformed the world. Yet, his revolutionary message can be summarized in just a few words: Love God, love yourself, and love others as you love yourself.

32. The Serenity Prayer

God, grant me serenity to accept the things I cannot change;

Courage to change the things I can;

And wisdom to know the difference. Amen

33. Structure

Most people function more effectively when structure is integrated into their lives. Indeed, those who follow a daily routine are, by definition, living within established boundaries. These habits are deeply rooted, driven by a primordial backdrop of circadian rhythms and cycles such as daylight and darkness, high and low tides, lunar phases, and changing seasons. Structure helps us maintain stability, constancy, order, and a sense of control in a seemingly chaotic world. Yet, too much structure stifles innovation; a real problem for humans who, by nature, are creative.

That's why balance is so important. Eastern religions have long recognized the advantages of maintaining a balanced life. Ideally, everyone should strive to keep a healthy balance between work and play; career and family; scheduled time and free time; the secular and the sacred; and to keep a balance between disciplined behavior and spontaneity. But the Judeo-Christian tradition recognizes our need for balance as well. In fact, the Fourth Commandment sets aside one day in seven to worship and to rest. Unstructured time – even a single day – promotes healing. So God has directed that all people and domesticated animals are to receive this blessing.

34. The Sacred Heart

In the Catholic Church, the physical heart of Jesus is a source of devotion. Known as the Sacred Heart, artistic images of Christ's heart depict both the pain of his crucifixion and the transformative powers of his love. Jesus demonstrated that a loving, faith-filled heart is the wellspring of miracles. Yet, at least one additional mystery is tied to the Sacred Heart's divine nature.

There are those who believe that, much like a human body, each soul has a heart as well. And it, too, is called the Sacred Heart. It has been taught that the Sacred Heart is the center of your soul, the very essence of who you are. Your Sacred Heart holds the precious treasures of your life; all of your fondest memories; every loving thought, word, and deed.

Your Sacred Heart is immortal and invulnerable. It's an impenetrable vault where no thief comes near and no moth destroys. It shelters keys that unlock the secrets of the universe. And its bounty cannot be plundered.

Within your Sacred Heart dwell divine perfection and endless love. Its holy chambers guard your innocence, your wonder and awe of creation. It protects all that is good and beautiful. It's the home of peace and joy.

Your Sacred Heart is the genesis of heavenly music and praise. It speaks the language of inspired truth. It sees the face of God. And inside your Sacred Heart, all whom you've known and loved are with you for eternity.

★★★

Your Sacred Heart is unfamiliar with barriers. Neither the highest mountain nor the deepest valley can block its path. Able to cross oceans of time, the Sacred Heart is a gateway to spirit realms, a portal to infinity.

★★★

The Sacred Heart remembers your wholeness when you feel broken and your beauty when you feel ugly. It remembers your innocence when you feel guilty and your purpose when you feel confused.

Adapted from the teachings of Glenda Green

35. Those Troublesome Monkeys

When Great Britain ruled India, the British built a golf course in Calcutta. But the men playing the new course faced unexpected challenges. This exotic land was home to thousands of playful monkeys who didn't know that the lush grass and the intriguing golf balls were off limits. First, the British built a fence to solve the monkey problem; but the curious creatures easily climbed over it. Next, the British tried capturing the monkeys; but this plan failed as well. Finally, the men gave up and adopted a new rule: Play the ball where the monkey drops it!

Sometimes a ball landed in the fairway, but a monkey would pick it up and drop it in a sand trap. Other times a ball landed in the rough, but a monkey would pick it up and drop it into a water hazard. Still, there were occasions when a mischievous monkey would pick up an out-of-bounds ball and drop it onto the green.

Life is much the same; we can only strike the ball from where it lies. Everyone must face hardship, yet there are always choices to make. Not only can we bless the monkey and the ball, we can bless wherever the monkey drops it. In other words, we can choose to make the best out of every situation, learn from it, and play on.

★★★

While waiting for a storm to pass, why not dance in the rain?

★★★

A long time ago, men vented their anger by beating the ground with sticks. Today, it's called golf.

Adapted from an unknown author

36. Unity

Individual consciousness is uniquely linked to a person's life experiences. Yet, there's also a collective, unified consciousness shared by all of humanity. Much like individual consciousness, collective consciousness is ever-growing and ever-changing. Yes, the world is comprised of unique identities and personalities. But on the level of collective consciousness, we are just one big family of brothers and sisters. Jesus pointed this out by saying: "Whatever you do for one of the least of these brothers of mine, you do for me."

★★★

When we categorize people – when we view them as young or old, rich or poor, black or white, student or teacher – there's a risk of establishing arbitrary, unnatural boundaries for what we expect to give and to receive. Yet, if everyone we meet is simply seen as a child of God, equal in every way that matters, then we are prepared to exchange miracles!

★★★

Summarizing the world's troubles, Mother Teresa said, "We've just forgotten that we belong to each other."

37. Contemplations of a Crusader

William "Billy" Graham, Jr. was born in Charlotte, North Carolina on November 7, 1918. He grew up on his family's dairy farm and worshipped at a nearby Reformed Presbyterian Church. After high school, Graham earned a diploma in biblical studies from Trinity Bible College. He later received a bachelor's degree in anthropology from Wheaton College. Soon after he began to preach, Graham earned a reputation for having an honest voice and a convincing delivery. Eventually, he was ordained as a Southern Baptist minister.

In 1949, Graham gained national fame as his sermons were broadcast on radio. Then, NBC offered Graham a lucrative contract and his own weekly television show, but he turned it down. By this time, Graham was focused on his "Crusades." Like the Revivals on which they were modeled, a Crusade might last several days. The venues, however, were much larger and would often draw ten thousand people or more.

During his career, Graham led over four hundred Crusades and travelled to more than one hundred countries. It's estimated that Graham has personally converted over 3,000,000 people to Christianity, making him one of the world's foremost evangelical preachers. In addition, Graham was a spiritual advisor to U. S. Presidents Harry Truman, Dwight Eisenhower, Richard Nixon, Ronald Reagan, George H. W. Bush, and George W. Bush.

Throughout his long career, Graham has remained an outspoken critic of communism. At the same time, he's also been a fierce advocate for Civil Rights. Graham has authored more than thirty books, including several bestsellers. And for the past sixty years, he's ranked among the most admired people in the world.

★★★

The following contemplations are representative of Graham's Christian beliefs.

The most eloquent prayers are the prayers offered through hands that heal and bless.

A keen sense of humor helps us overlook the unbecoming, understand the unconventional, tolerate the unpleasant, overcome the unexpected, and outlast the unbearable.

My one purpose in life is to help people find a personal relationship with God, which I believe comes through knowing Jesus Christ.

God has given us two hands, one to receive with and the other to give with.

Being a Christian is more than just an instantaneous conversion. It is a daily process whereby you grow to be more and more like Christ.

The Christian life is not a constant high. I have my moments of deep discouragement. I have to go to God with tears in my eyes, and say: *O God, forgive me. Help me.*

The word of God hidden in one's heart is a stubborn voice to suppress.

God's love was proven on the cross. When Jesus bled and died, God was saying to the world: "I love you!"

When wealth is lost, nothing is lost; when character is lost, all is lost.

Comfort and prosperity have never enriched the world as much as adversity has.

God doesn't take away something from your life without replacing it with something better.

The will of God shall not take you where the grace of God cannot sustain you.

The happiness your soul aches for is the happiness undisturbed by success or failure; it's the happiness which is deeply rooted and gives you inner peace and contentment, no matter what the outer problems may be.

If God eliminated evil by programming people to do only good acts, we would lose the ability to make choices. We would be nothing more than robots.

God wants your fellowship and has done everything possible to make it a reality. He has forgiven your sins and has blessed you with the priceless privileges of prayer and worship.

I feel sorry for those who have never known the thrill of taking a stand and fearlessly sticking to it. Moral courage offers immense rewards. Like a shot of adrenaline, moral courage floods the spirit with vitality.

38. Halcyon Seas

On this day I'm sheltered from the battering storms of life
I've found a quiet harbor safe from malice, pain, and strife

Tomorrow I will surely sail on tranquil, blue-green seas
And drifting past the face of God, I shall revel in his peace

39. A Message of Hope

Jesus understood that he was to be crucified, and he knew it would be a painful death. Indeed, there was a moment when he asked, *Father, are you sure?* Yet, Jesus accepted his destiny knowing it was God's will, and that his sacrifice would help heal a broken world. Maybe Jesus, understanding that his earthly journey was nearing an end, took a moment to reflect on his life and ministry. And if such reminiscence happened, perhaps Christ shared the following thoughts.

"Heavenly Father, I've taught your lessons just as you've asked, using parables to touch the hearts and minds of my brothers and sisters of all backgrounds and faith. Many have watched me pray to you. And through you, Holy Father, I've fed gatherings of thousands with just a few loaves of bread and a handful of fish. Through you, Gracious Father, I've cast out demons and healed the sick. Those who were blind can now see, and I raised my friend Lazarus from the dead. And Father, all of this has been done for your glory and to show my brothers and sisters that you have sent me."

"Still, many will not know me as your Son. Many will never believe what I've done through you. Some find it difficult to accept what they do not understand. Others were expecting a warrior king, not a Prince of Peace. They were looking for a Savior who would conquer their enemies, not forgive them. Yet, I shall *vanquish* death, this world's greatest fear. I will show my brothers and sisters that life *is* everlasting.

I will prove that the body's demise is but a new beginning. And Father, for those who believe, the truth shall set them free."

"I've taught my brothers and sisters not to worry about when they will eat or what they will wear. I've shown them that life is more than food and the body is more than clothes. I've assured them that when seeking heaven, their earthly needs are provided as well. I've offered my brothers and sisters a new way in which to perceive the world. I've taught them how to pray and to grow in faith. But above all, I've shown them how to love. Holy Father, mine is a ministry of love, not fear; and of forgiveness, not revenge. And Father I ask that, through you, my legacy shall be one of life, not death; of joy, not suffering; and of resurrection, not crucifixion. My spilled blood will end all need for sacrifice. And I pray that my teachings will remain a beacon of hope."

★★★

Grace is where faith and mercy are one with God; where the horizontal and vertical components of the cross are joined in perfect harmony. Even where joy has vanished, there is love.

★★★

Christ's resurrection is more real than anything which can be seen or touched.

40. Divine Love

Divine love transcends even the highest, purest form of human love. And remember that God not only loves; God *is* love. Ancient Greeks used the word "agape" to describe God's love. Agape, then, is the very foundation of life, the wellspring of creation. It is the ultimate, everlasting, and unfailing love which God bestows upon his children. Sometimes, the meaning of agape is expanded to include the special love people have for their heavenly Creator. Still, agape is just a word used to express the ineffable; a word used to explain the unfathomable. And words are entirely inadequate to capture the essence of God.

41. Epiphanies

After waking from a restful night's sleep, we typically feel an elevated awareness – a heightened sense of reality – when compared to the world of dreams. This is similar to the way people feel after an epiphany. They may think: *Oh yes, things are much clearer now. How could I have been so foolish? **This** is what's real!* And so it goes until their next awakening, and the new reality which follows.

Some epiphanies are as subtle as a tropical breeze, while others strike like a bolt of lightning. Either way, sudden bursts of inspiration can lead to new insights and discoveries that transform our world. Human frontiers are ever-expanding. Our horizons stretch further and further.

Breakthroughs in science, mathematics, and medicine are occurring around the globe. And the fields of music, art, and design are moving forward as well; for life is seldom static. Yet, each new discovery is spiritual in nature – and each epiphany is a holy event – because someone's heart has been touched by God.

★★★

Immediately, something like scales fell from Saul's eyes, and he could see again. (Acts 9:18)

42. Canine Companions

There's a special bond – a covenant, really – between people and dogs. A long time ago, wolf-like canines lingered just beyond the glow of human campfires, hoping to scavenge scraps of food. The most trusting of these animals eventually became our friends. At some point, people and dogs recognized the mutual benefit of joining forces. And welcoming these furry companions into our lives changed the course of human history.

A symbiotic union is thriving in our modern world. Dogs receive food, shelter, medicine, benevolent leadership, and a sense of purpose. On the flip side, we benefit from their service, loyalty, companionship, and a host of significant intangibles. Working dogs help us hunt, herd, and retrieve. They assist in search and rescue missions and are able partners in law enforcement. And as devoted family members, dogs provide protection as well as instinctive and creative interaction unmatched in the animal kingdom.

Today, trained service dogs guide the blind and assist the paralyzed. They detect cancer and forecast seizures. They can be their master's eyes, ears, and hands. And licensed therapy dogs offer people more than just a calm presence. It's been documented that a therapy dog can help lower heart rates, ease breathing, relax muscle tension, and reduce stress. People suffering from cognitive disorders like dementia often respond favorably to therapy dogs. It's believed that a friendly dog can stimulate long-term memory and trigger fond thoughts of past experiences.

Unfailingly loyal, dogs never question their master's worthiness. Nor do they compare their life situations with those of other dogs. Because they love unconditionally, dogs promote healing and a general sense of well-being. And if that's not enough, research has shown that dog owners live up to ten years longer than people who lack a relationship with man's best friend. Though many animals have been domesticated and have served our interests, dogs maintain a completely unique and unbreakable bond with their human partners.

★★★

Dogs are very aware of human feelings. They look into our eyes, study our body language, and pay close attention to the tone of our voice. If a dog senses sadness, he just might place his head onto that person's lap as a way to offer comfort. No other animal is so sensitive to our moods and so attentive to our needs.

★★★

Things we can learn from dogs: Dogs never hold a grudge. Dogs enjoy exercise. Dogs show love in small ways. Dogs are not afraid of silence. Dogs always remember to greet us. Dogs let go of guilt. Dogs are content to be themselves. Dogs are great listeners. Dogs remember to have fun. Dogs live in the present moment. Dogs are trusting. Dogs never take things personally.

★★★

Loving relationships shared by people and their pets are testaments to the inherent connectedness of God's creatures.

★★★

Heaven's rooms are a bit like hotels. Some allow pets, while others don't.

43. Life's Meaning and Purpose

This reflection requires a contemplative response to six timeless questions; queries that, for thousands of years, have prompted passionate debate among philosophers and theologians. There is no limit to the possible responses, so your views may be vastly different from the ones suggested for reflection. Either way, you will have plenty of food for thought.

Question: What is life's purpose?

Reflection: From the eyes of a spiritual seeker, life's purpose may include pursuits such as growing closer to God; achieving spiritual healing and wholeness; glorifying God; discovering divine truth; building strong character; reassessing worldly desires; promoting the greater good; growing in love and faith; seeking higher consciousness and self-realization; and finding spiritual salvation. Based on your Christian beliefs and values, how do you define life's purpose?

Question: How is spiritual growth achieved?

Reflection: Spiritual growth is broadly defined as drawing closer to God. With this in mind, Christians may reach new spiritual heights by opening their hearts to Christ's Light and love; by offering unconditional love and forgiveness to others and to oneself; by providing selfless service; and by expressing kindness and compassion through words and deeds. Identify the things in your life which have helped you to grow spiritually. What changes can you make to promote additional spiritual growth?

Question: How is a personal relationship with God developed?

Reflection: Spiritual teachers have suggested that a close, personal relationship with God is nurtured through study, prayer, meditation, reflection, and worship; and by living in the present moment; by drinking fully from the cup of life; and by looking inward, not outward; and through childlike innocence; an open mind; humbleness; and joy and laughter; and through holy relationships; through discipline and vigilance; through freedom and spontaneity; through love and forgiveness; and through sacred silence. Psalm 46 exhorts, "Be still, and know that I am God." For Christians, what might this Scripture mean? What can you do to improve your personal relationship with God?

Question: What is life's meaning?

Reflection: Could life's meaning be defined by each person's unique search to discover divine truth; by each person's singular journey to find God and to know him? Is life's meaning defined through someone's quest to experience lasting inner peace; by someone's personal pursuit to live joyously? Identify whatever it might be that gives your life meaning. What do you attach value to? What brings you a sense of joy? As you examine your Christian beliefs, what is worth living for? What is worth dying for?

Question: What is faith?

Reflection: Having many dimensions, faith has been viewed as surrendering to God; trusting God and asking that his will be done; accepting personal worthiness of God's love and grace; feeling God's presence; listening to divine guidance; recognizing and appreciating life's blessings; letting go of guilt; overcoming fear; dismissing thoughts of worry and lack; relinquishing *all* judgment to God; and knowing that God is ever-present. How do you describe faith? Take a moment to remember something from the past that has happened to you, or to someone else, which caused you to lose your trust in God. Moving to the present time, has your faith been restored? Why or why not?

Question: Is there a purpose to life's suffering?

Reflection: Pain – whether it's physical, emotional, or spiritual – is an ever-present element of the human condition. Moreover, pain can come through no fault of our own. For example, the death of a loved one will trigger pain. And as our health declines, we may feel pain of a different kind. Are these not opportunities to reach out to God, to love him more deeply? Additionally, we feel pain each time we make a poor choice. Suffering, in these cases, may provide a chance to *choose once again*. In other words, pain can motivate us to make better decisions, including how we choose to perceive our suffering. As we make more positive choices, our lives are enriched and we grow spiritually as well.

Scripture teaches that, ultimately, suffering leads to hope. Most importantly, it's not a futile hope, but one that is well-founded on God's love. Saint Paul wrote, "Suffering produces perseverance; perseverance, character; and character, hope. And hope does not disappoint us, because

God has poured out his love into our hearts by the Holy Spirit, whom he has given us." Think back to an earlier time when you endured hardship or suffering. Now, identify the personal strengths you had at that time – whatever it was that helped you cope with adversity. Are those strengths still part of you today? How can they help you work through your present challenges? Do you have any newly acquired strengths or added confidence? In closing, please reflect on the following questions: Are your current strengths a source of hope? Will your present challenges bring you closer to God? Why or why not?

44. Calendars, Clocks, and Photographs

There are moments in our lives when calendars, clocks, and photographs seem to separate us from the people we love. Calendars can mark the days when loved ones are elsewhere. Clocks can track the time when someone you love is absent. And photographs may spark memories of people who have died and are still deeply missed.

Because of this, God has made sure that heaven has no calendars. So there are no days in which loved ones can be elsewhere. And God has made certain that heaven has no clocks. So there is no time in which someone you love can be absent. And finally, God has promised that, in heaven, photographs and sorrows shall no longer haunt you. For where is grief when all whom you've known and loved are forever within your Sacred Heart?

45. Hope and Faith

Wherever there are people, you find problems. Yet, it's also true that where there are people, you find hope. In every corner of the world, human hearts are filled with hope. According to the dictionary, hope is to want something to happen and to believe that it will happen. Hope is a brother of trust; and wherever you find meaning to life, you find hope. Indeed, hell has been defined as a separation from God and the loss of hope.

Like life itself, hope is never static. Hope evolves and changes but doesn't go away. We, therefore, live and die with a sense of hope. If diagnosed with a serious disease, for instance, we hope for a cure. If a cure isn't available, we hope for a new treatment to be discovered. If a new treatment fails to materialize, we hope to live longer than the doctors expect. If we cannot live as long as we wish, we hope to be comfortable and pain free. At the very least, we hope to *not* be a burden to our loved ones. And finally, our hope is to have a peaceful death.

Love is the wellspring of hope. But what *is* hope? As we observe our world and experience life, it's clear that, like the air we breathe, expressions of hope are all around us.

Hope is a cloudless blue sky.

Hope is a gentle touch.

Hope is saying, "Please forgive me."

Hope is rain falling on a freshly plowed garden.

Hope is the pine tree clinging to a rocky ledge.

Hope is the first spring daffodil to penetrate the snow.

Hope is a wobbly foal at its mother's side.

Hope is the sunrise which conquers darkness.

Hope is a baby cradled in loving arms.

Hope is a silent, starry night.

Hope is blowing out candles on a birthday cake.

Hope is an ocean wave breaking on the shore.

Hope is a soaring eagle.

Hope is the solitary wildflower in front of vacant building.

Hope is looking deep into the eyes of a child.

Hope is asking, "Will you marry me?"

Hope is a heartfelt hug.

Hope is a comforting breeze.

Hope is the fragrance of a rosebud.

Hope is the warm smile offered to a stranger.

Hope is an endless horizon of amber grain.

Hope is the rainbow after a storm.

Hope is a resurrection.

Hope is heaven on earth.

Hope and faith are joined as one. Hope and faith cannot be separated any more than warmth can be separated from the sun. And when combined, the greatness of hope and faith exceeds the sum of each part. Faith is as multifaceted as the finest diamond. And faith, like a precious gem, is found in all colors, shapes, and sizes. Faith isn't limited to a specific religion or to a particular race or culture. Nor is it tied to age, gender, wealth, or status. In truth, it's easier to understand faith by watching someone *live* it. Faith's recipe starts with a heavenly blend of perseverance and persistence. Then add a cup of trust, a dash of commitment, and a sprinkle of unfailing optimism. Mix vigorously and bake until done. The result is divine.

Love is the wellspring of faith. But what *is* faith? As we observe our world and experience life, it's clear that, like the light of day, expressions of faith are all around us.

Faith is letting go of the past.

Faith is facing the future without worry or fear.

Faith is feeling God's peace in this very moment.

Faith is saying, "I forgive you."

Faith is working through pain, sadness, or disappointment.

Faith is following your heart.

Faith is accepting your worthiness of love.

Faith is having an open mind.

Faith is remaining humble.

Faith is answering, "Yes, I will marry you."

Faith is welcoming God's grace.

Faith is doing the right thing.

Faith is building a relationship with God.

Faith is making healthy choices.

Faith is praising God.

Faith is to trust the invisible and the intangible.

Faith is growing closer to God during troubled times.

Faith is keeping promises.

Faith is asking for God's help.

Faith is expressing love.

Faith is praying for others.

Faith is closing your eyes and opening your heart.

Faith is to know that, with God, all things are possible.

46. Coping and Care Giving

Different people cope with adversity in different ways. And as someone struggles with a life-threatening illness or a life-changing event, there are no rules requiring a calm acceptance of the future. Nor are there laws requiring a pleasant, cheerful demeanor. People say hurtful things, especially as they deal with physical pain and mental anguish. Sometimes, they withdraw from the world. So try not to take things personally. Try to understand that, when someone is hurting, he may act differently; he may not be the perfect patient.

★★★

Terminal illness turns the world upside down. It changes everything. It changes the way each day begins and ends. It changes what is important, and what is not. Suddenly, there is so much information to process – so many choices to make and so many feelings to sort through.

★★★

Caregivers are often focused on healing physical wounds. Yet, the invisible wounds caused by emotional and spiritual pain need mending as well.

★★★

For the sick, your kind words, your warm smile, your gentle touch, and your thoughtful presence are precious gifts.

★★★

Sometimes, a compassionate caregiver will be called an "earth angel" by appreciative patients.

47. A Prayer for Help, Protection, Guidance, and Comfort

Heavenly Father, help me this day to be an instrument of your will. Help me to be a conduit of your Light, love, and peace.

Protect me this day from all harm, and protect me from evil and malice in all forms.

Guide me through any obstacles that might prevent me from expressing the love that I am.

Allow me to feel your presence and experience your peace.

And for those who are hurting emotionally or spiritually – and for those who are sick or dying – I send them my awareness, my love, and my willingness to be with them in spirit. Amen

★★★

Daily prayer, reflection, and meditation prepare you to receive God's gifts and blessings.

★★★

Daily expressions of gratitude will nurture a positive attitude and promote a greater sense of peace. Saint Paul explained it this way: "Whatever is true, whatever is noble; whatever is right, whatever is pure; whatever is lovely, whatever is admirable, excellent, or praiseworthy; think about such things and the God of peace is with you."

48. Gifts of Grace

Each human being makes countless real-life choices, blazes a one-of-a-kind trail, and carves out a personal legacy that can never be duplicated. And so it is with the final steps of every earthly journey, the last few steps which take one's soul from here to the hereafter. Each transition is unique. Every passage is one-of-a-kind.

Yet, just as life has shared experiences, there are common elements found in death as well. As we draw closer to our final breath, God may offer an opportunity to gaze at heaven's beauty, a gentle reminder that there's nothing to fear. Sometimes, God allows the vision of a loved one to appear, a familiar presence which brings comfort. Other times, a white light may shine forth, a healing luminance which instills a sense of peace and well-being.

Or then again, perhaps God may send us an angel; for an angel's touch is so gentle and tender. Angels are both loving caregivers and vigilant protectors. Therefore, why would we be surprised to learn that God uses angels to escort souls across the bridge from this world to eternity? Would a God of grace not make provisions for a calm, safe crossing? And would a God of love not make plans for a joyous homecoming celebration?

★★★

Bedside visions are real. They are gifts of grace which cannot be explained by opiates, low blood oxygen, or brain deterioration.

★★★

People gather around loved ones who are either coming into this world or leaving it. Could it be that way in the spirit realms as well?

★★★

During your transition to the afterlife, you will never lose your awareness or sense of self. Indeed, you will feel more alive than ever before.

49. Enlightenment

As one's consciousness elevates, there's greater certainty of God and greater clarity of God and self. There's also a better understanding of how the natural and the supernatural domains of creation are interwoven. Eventually, the metaphysical is recognized as more "real" than the physical. At this point, anxiety gives way to a lasting inner peace.

Enlightened human beings have been touched by God. They perceive themselves, others, and the world with unfailing clarity. Because they are wholly in tune with divine reality, they live and die fearlessly. Master teachers have similar gifts, plus the ability to help people move forward in their spiritual journeys, to help them grow in love and faith.

At any given time, there are only a handful of enlightened teachers in the entire world. They might be found anywhere. Some are devoted to a particular faith tradition or spiritual philosophy, while others are not. But always, they teach lessons of love and kindness. The fortunate few who are merely in the *presence* of a Spirit-guided teacher will experience a heightened consciousness. And by practicing the lessons of a master teacher, followers can achieve incredible breakthroughs in awareness and self-realization.

Yet, of all the teachers from all the ages – of all the prophets, gurus, saints, and mystics throughout human history – God sent just one master teacher who was destined to be a Savior as well. And the world was forever changed by his lessons of love and forgiveness, by his ministry of sacrifice and resurrection.

★★★

There's a paradox within heightened consciousness. As humankind collectively achieves higher levels of awareness and self-understanding, God seems to be, at times, more distant than ever. Our developing minds produce a relentless stream of obstructive thoughts, and God's very existence is doubted. Yet, once humanity emerges from this valley of disillusionment – after we vanquish our sense of separation and quiet our busy minds – we will grow exponentially closer to our Source. Ultimately, we shall connect with God in a way which was never before possible.

★★★

Everyone is confused. It's just a question of how much.

50. Natural Beauty and Worldly Offerings: A Guided Imagery

Your journey begins on a path which leads through a tranquil forest. Picture the forest floor blanketed by lush ferns. Their rich green color blends perfectly with the emerald trees shading your path. On the distant horizon, majestic rock formations penetrate the clouds, and you're in awe of nature's beauty. As you walk along the path, there's no sense of time or urgency. You feel a sacred connection with God. Now, your ear detects the comforting sounds of a nearby stream. Going a bit farther, you see crystal clear water cascading over polished rocks. To your right, an inquisitive fish explores the boundaries of a secluded pool. As you resume walking, birds glide from tree to tree, and their whistled melodies offer an unexpected serenade. Playful animals are all around: daring squirrels, timid rabbits, darting chipmunks.

Now, the path leads to an opening, to a distinct change in landscape. Magically, you stand at the edge of a vast meadow – a vista graced by an abundance of wildflowers. Vibrant reds, yellows, oranges, and purples stretch as far as you can see. You reach down, pick a blossom, and lift it to your nose. A glorious fragrance greets you – then lingers in the air. You examine the fragile petals one at a time. Each is intricate, yet simple; each petal is an elegant expression, a gift from God. But there are more gifts to discover. Finding a single drop of nectar, you taste it and marvel at the sweetness.

The path ahead is so inviting, you take off your shoes. While walking barefoot, cool grass soothes your feet. You smile as soft moss tickles the tender skin between your toes. The blue sky is dotted with cotton-like clouds. You feel the warmth of a golden sun, and a gentle breeze touches your face. To your left, a deer stands watch over her fawn. Like all young life, this fawn is so innocent, so frail — so dependent on its mother's vigilance. Yet, its future holds such promise. Now, your gaze is fixed on a butterfly. Its fluttering wings are relentless, tireless. As this curious creature disappears from sight, you sense a genuine kinship; because it, too, follows a whimsical path leading to an unrevealed destination; it, too, must confront uncertainty.

Walking farther, you view something ahead — something that seems strangely out of place. Yet, your attraction to it cannot be denied. Drawing closer, you see a structure of some kind. And getting closer still, you're surprised to learn that it's made of marble and adorned with gold and precious gems. At last, you recognize what you've come upon. It is an altar. More importantly, you know this sublime altar is a special gift and that its discovery is not an accident. You've found a holy place and you sense God's closeness.

Feeling humbled, you choose to kneel in front of the altar. And listening to your heart, you know exactly what to do. On this altar, you place your pain and suffering. You place your grief and anger on the altar. You lift up to God any guilt or shame. On this altar, you place your fears, your worries, and your anxieties. You place your regrets, mistakes, and disappointments on the altar. You lift up to God any unfulfilled dreams, broken promises, unrealized legacies, or failed relationships. And God loves you so much that he gladly accepts your offering of earthly burdens. He is pleased to relieve you of your fears and worries, your regrets and mistakes. He is eager to help you heal emotionally and spiritually. God wants you to commune with him and grow closer to him. God wants you to feel whole.

As you rise from your knees, you feel so much lighter — so renewed and joyous. You feel a profound inner peace; a calmness far greater than you've ever felt before. You pause to bathe in the Light of your Creator.

And now that you know where to find this altar, this sacred place, you can revisit it as often as you wish. You can revisit it anytime you start to feel once again weighed down by earthly burdens. Be assured that God is merciful, and understand that you shall never be left alone or comfortless.

51. A Caregiver's Prayer

Gracious God, I am here to be kind and helpful.

I am here to represent the One who has sent me.

I do not have to worry about what to say or what to do, because you will inspire me.

I am content to be wherever you wish, knowing that you travel with me.

And I know that I will be healed as you teach me how to heal others. Amen

Adapted from *A Course in Miracles*

52. God and Love

The physical universe is a manifestation of God's love. Therefore, love is the master of structure and form. Through love, all things are accomplished. Through love, you will quiet the winds and calm the sea. Through love, your command will move the mountain from here to there. If you cannot do these simple things, then grow in love today and try again tomorrow. For when you truly believe in love, all things are possible. And when you truly believe that you *are* love, you will be a master of worldly things.

★★★

Love is the power which drives human progress, including advances in technology. The universe isn't frozen in time. By design, breakthroughs in consciousness happen everywhere in the world. They may occur at any moment, just as they always have. When Moses walked in the desert, there were no doctors performing open heart surgery. And when Saint Paul preached to the Gentiles, there were no astronauts landing on the moon. Such advances offer proof of an ever-present, ever-expanding love which thrives on our planet.

53. Love, Forgiveness, and Healing

LOVE . . .

People are obsessed with it. We think about it, write about it, and read about it. We talk about it, we look for it, and yes, we even sing about it: *Love makes the world go 'round. Love is a many-splendored thing. All you need is love.* Interestingly, our world seems to have different kinds of love. There's an intimate love shared between life partners, a warm love that's freely given to family members, a genuine love that's offered to close friends, and a nurturing, heartfelt love that a mother extends to her newborn child. But what kind of love does God have?

The New Testament teaches that God *is* love. But what does that mean? Are there words that describe divine love? Perhaps the following ones are appropriate: unconditional, incomprehensible, enlightening, transforming, uplifting, unfathomable, debilitating, all-consuming, and overwhelming. Some of the words chosen to define God's love might have been expected, while others not at all. So let's take a closer look at divine love. People with firsthand experience of God's unfiltered love – those who have felt its *full* force and impact – share similar stories.

For example, a man named Saul was traveling on the road to Damascus. Without warning, he was struck by God's overwhelming love. Saul, a man who had persecuted Christians, was instantly, completely, and permanently transformed. In a very real sense, he was debilitated. That is to say, he was unable to function in the world for a long while. Saul needed time to recover from an epiphany which affected him physically, emotionally, and spiritually. Saul became Paul, an enlightened apostle, an instrument of God's will, a man born again. He was changed beyond recognition and bore no resemblance to the man he used to be. Though Paul encountered extreme hardship later in life, his faith never wavered. His inspiring ministry was God-directed and passion-driven. For Paul, divine love was all-consuming.

Closer to home, meet Howard Storm, a former art professor at Northern Kentucky University and a self-proclaimed atheist. Storm openly ridiculed those who embraced religion or believed in God. Then, a near-death experience changed his life. While in the hospital with a life-threatening illness, Storm was guided to what he later described as a "timeless realm of complete darkness." From there, a horrific journey unfolded. Storm endured intense suffering, torment, guilt, despair, and shame. But his experience didn't end there. Ultimately, he received the gifts of divine forgiveness and salvation.

Storm said he felt an unfathomable love that was offered unconditionally. He explained that the full force of God's love is beyond human comprehension. Upon feeling the unrestrained impact of divine love, Storm was overwhelmed. He couldn't bear to face this world again. Storm was debilitated to the point that his emotional and spiritual recovery took many months longer than the time needed for his body to heal. He was instantly, completely, and permanently transformed. Storm never returned to his job as a college art teacher. Instead, he entered seminary and went on to serve as a church pastor. Today, Storm remains a faithful servant of the Lord.

There's a dimension of love which people experience when the road is smooth and life's challenges are easily managed. But there's also a deeper, richer side of love which we discover only by enduring hardship and by remaining steadfast in troubled times. This was the lesson learned by Job, a lesson that each of God's children will face. As we grow in love and faith, the road becomes smooth once again and life's challenges are more easily managed. As we grow in love and faith, we experience a more meaningful relationship with God, and all of life's blessings are laid at our feet.

Scripture contains many references to love, both divine and human. Psalm 100 describes God's love in one short proclamation: "The Lord is good and his love endures forever." And in his first letter to the Corinthians, Paul describes human love in its highest form: "Love is patient, love is kind. It does not envy or boast. It is not proud or rude. Love is not self-seeking or easily angered, and it keeps no records of wrongs. Love always protects, always trusts, always hopes, and always perseveres. Love rejoices with the truth. Love never fails." For human beings, these are lofty standards indeed. And Paul's reminder that love keeps no record of wrongs is a perfect introduction to . . .

FORGIVENESS

Are you aware that forgiveness is part of love? In truth, love and forgiveness are inseparable. Think about it. Do you really love someone if you cannot forgive them? Do you really love yourself if you cannot accept the forgiveness given to you by others? But to explore these questions and to understand forgiveness, we must go back to the very beginning – to the original sin. Adam and Eve chose to eat the forbidden fruit. Desperate and fearful, Eve blamed the serpent, while Adam blamed Eve. But their attempts to project blame and escape accountability were ineffective, and their choices led to catastrophic consequences. No longer in Paradise, Adam and Eve felt unloved, and they believed that God would never forgive them.

Some Christians believe this was a literal event, while others view it as a metaphorical one. Either way, the resulting pain is very real. And from that moment forward, humankind has been tormented by guilt and shame. It's both a collective and individual burden still carried today. Even when guilt and shame are not forefront in our mind, they remain active in our subconscious thoughts and fears. So every now and then, a faint inner voice tries to convince us that we are unworthy of God's love and undeserving of God's forgiveness. Occasionally, a soft voice whispers that we deserve to be punished, we deserve to suffer, and that God will never forgive us.

Perhaps Satan is the force behind this inner voice which tries to deceive us. But many psychotherapists point to the human ego as the menacing culprit lurking in the shadows of the mind. Still, the next time you hear a devilish inner voice of guilt and shame, stop for a moment. Pause and remember: If God *is* love, then God *is* forgiveness. And if God's love is unconditional, then God's forgiveness is unconditional as well. So in truth, there is nothing we can think or say or do that is beyond God's forgiveness. In reality, divine love has no boundaries.

People routinely underestimate God. We wrongly project human weaknesses and limitations onto God. Though created in a divine image, human beings are just that – human. We make mistakes, we're not infallible. In short, we are not God. Nor is God human. Our Creator doesn't have human frailties. That's why there are no limits to divine love. Our unwillingness to forgive doesn't influence God.

Jesus taught lessons of love and forgiveness. His ministry was inclusive, reaching out to those who were largely ignored or shunned. He touched the hearts and lives of criminals and prostitutes, the sick and the poor. He walked among the outcasts of society. Ultimately, Jesus forgave Judas who betrayed him, Peter who denied him, Pontius Pilot who condemned him, and the Roman soldiers who crucified him. Jesus *was* forgiveness. He also taught that God wishes us to live joyously. Jesus said to his disciples, "Obey my commands. I have told you this so that my joy may be in you, and that your joy may be complete. My command is: Love each other as I have loved you."

There are some things in this world that we know for sure. We know that we cannot live joyously while clinging to guilt and shame. We cannot live joyously in a state of self-loathing. And we cannot live joyously while thinking we're unworthy of God's forgiveness. Make no mistake, expressing love is spiritual work. Offering forgiveness is spiritual work. Accepting forgiveness is spiritual work. And spiritual work sets the stage for lasting joy and happiness.

Forgiveness is a process, a journey of many steps. The first one is to identify the people who have hurt you in some way: physically, emotionally, spiritually, or perhaps financially. Make a list of their names. Maybe God will be on your list; and if he is, that's okay. Yet, remember that love holds no grievances. Therefore, the next step is to offer genuine forgiveness to each name you've listed. Truly "let go" of past wrongs. After this, try to identify the people *you* have hurt. Embark on a thorough life review and make a list of those who were burdened by something you said or did. Then, take ownership of your behavior. Don't project blame onto someone or something else. Admit that people were hurt because of *your* mistakes and *your* choices. Ask God to forgive you. And after this, pray for guidance as you apologize to each person on your list, as you ask to be forgiven, and as you make amends.

Bear in mind that apologies and amends are offered only when you're certain they will not cause further harm. You might wonder, "How can I ask for forgiveness? How should I apologize and make amends? I've lost touch with many of the people on my list, and some of them are no longer alive." One solution is to write a series of letters. Letters can be written to both the living and the dead. You can even write a letter to God. And if you're unable to write, consider dictating the letters to someone you trust. Understand that you can mail the letters or destroy them. Either is okay, because repentance which serves the greater good is not unheard or wasted.

At last, you've reached the final step in your forgiveness journey. Knowing that God has already forgiven you, accept the empowering gift of self-forgiveness. Choose to love yourself, to let go of all guilt, and to embrace your worthiness of God's love. Though it may seem like a daunting task, reflect on these questions: If God really thinks you're unworthy of love, then why did he send you a Savior? And how could any loving father believe that his precious child is undeserving of forgiveness? It isn't by chance that this forgiveness pathway is similar to the ones found in twelve-step recovery programs. And that brings us to . . .

HEALING

Why do people abuse alcohol and take illegal drugs? For the most part, it's to escape their pain. Why are they in pain? Often, it's because – unconsciously – they feel broken and incomplete. Addicts feel unworthy and unloved. In essence, they are unhealed. Eventually, they come to despise both their addictions and themselves. Why are twelve-step programs such a beacon of hope for people struggling with addictive behaviors? Why have these programs proven to be so successful? First, addicts must accept that healing requires help from a Higher Power. In addition, they attend meetings where everyone receives respect and love; where everyone is given nonjudgmental acceptance and support. If there's a relapse, they are still treated with dignity. They are still respected and supported.

Addicts are also taught that, in order to stay clean and sober, they must seek forgiveness and make amends. Gradually, they learn to love and to forgive themselves. Gradually, a healthy self-image emerges and their confidence is restored. No longer a burden on anyone, they are changed beyond recognition. They are completely transformed and their pride is justified.

Pain is interwoven among all three levels of human life: the body, the mind, and the spirit. So it's natural for healing to occur on each of these levels as well. Physicians have long recognized that problems within the mind can cause physical ailments, like migraines and chronic pain. Prescribed medicines can, thankfully, manage physical pain. Without question, pain meds provide necessary, welcomed relief. And fortunately, psychotropic drugs are available to treat mental illnesses. But are medicines treating problems at their source, or are they primarily managing symptoms?

What some doctors fail to realize is that spiritual problems can be the source of both physical and mental illness. That's why holistic treatments

– ones that address the needs of body, mind, *and* spirit – prove effective in so many cases. Going a step farther, renowned psychiatrist Carl Jung suggested, "After age 35, *all* problems are spiritual problems." Jung was a pioneer in recognizing that spiritual work promotes healing on all levels. His breakthrough discoveries formed the foundation for today's twelve-step programs. In other words, there are times that, if we want to be healed, we must be willing to do spiritual work. We must be willing to love and to forgive. And we must be willing to work on the spiritual pain which stems from our unconscious belief that humankind was disobedient and God shall never forgive this original sin.

Some people ask: Is God punishing those who are sick? In response to that question, consider this: How does a god who intentionally makes someone sick reconcile with a God who *is* love? How does a god who *causes* illness reconcile with a Creator who wants each of his children to live joyously? What's more, Jesus was a healer. His ministry focused on alleviating pain, not promoting it. And other questions arise as well. What does it mean to be cured? Is healing simply a state of mind? Is emotional healing nothing more than achieving an underlying sense of wholeness? Is spiritual healing manifested as a profound and lasting inner peace?

And finally, there's a curious paradox: Healing takes time, but time itself cannot heal. Along with time, healing requires the added dimension of forgiveness. Just as love and forgiveness are inseparable, forgiveness and healing are also joined. Forgiveness *is* healing. In his ministry, Jesus healed broken bodies, broken minds, and broken spirits. Would it surprise you to learn that Jesus extended unconditional love and forgiveness at the very moment in which he offered healing?

In addition to practicing love and forgiveness, spiritual work includes prayer, worship, Bible study, meditation, counseling, support groups, and reflective spiritual reading. And energy work, like healing touch, is also in the mix of possibilities. A young woman named Mary was curious to learn more about healing touch. She enrolled in a series of classes sponsored by a respected hospital in Cincinnati. After finishing the training, Mary and her classmates were getting ready to practice their healing techniques on a group of volunteers. Suddenly, Mary sensed something extraordinary; something that was indescribable, yet palpable. Thinking there might be a problem with the room's ventilation system, Mary asked, "What *is* that I'm feeling?" Making no effort to stop what she was doing, or to even make eye contact, the instructor casually replied, "The angels are gathering."

Along with heavenly angels, God blesses us with another healing gift – a gift most high: grace. A gift in the truest sense, grace doesn't have to be earned. It flows from God's unconditional love. Divine grace is freely given, without the need to be deserved. For Christians, healing on the spiritual level requires two additional gifts: redemption – a deliverance from sin; and salvation – the promise of eternal life in heaven. And for those who embrace Christianity, redemption and salvation are found through Jesus Christ. Christians believe it was an act of grace for Christ to willingly accept the pain, suffering, and humiliation of crucifixion. His sacrifice was for the redemption and salvation of others. His sacrifice expunged the errors of original sin. And his resurrection remains the ultimate gift – an assurance that life *is* eternal. Resurrection is the heart of sanctification, and it affirms that God is a *living* God whose love is everlasting.

Grace touches our lives in many ways. Once, there was a young servant whose primary task was to carry water for his master. Early each morning, the young boy would make a long journey to the water's source. A stout, wooden rod rested across his shoulders; and two large, clay jars were attached to the rod – one vessel hanging from each end. Upon reaching the well, the boy would fill both jars. This was enough water to last his master an entire day. By chance, one jar was perfect, while the other was not. The flawed vessel was cracked. It leaked water to the extent that, by the time the boy returned to his master's home, the jar was only half-filled.

One day, as the boy neared the end of his journey, the imperfect jar was despondent. It felt shame and guilt. Sensing this, the young servant said, "Knowing your flaw, I planted seeds along your side of the pathway. Look behind you and behold the beautiful flowers growing. They prosper because of your spilled water. And each day, my master's table is graced by the gift of these flowers. At last, the truth has been revealed: Your imperfection is a blessing."

In the human condition, every vessel is imperfect. There's no one who is unflawed. We are destined to make mistakes and to suffer from them. This reminds us how challenged we are in our mission to love and to forgive – in our mission to be healed. In terms of emotional and spiritual healing, most of us are works in progress. Yet if you allow him, God will teach you how to love. And by giving love, you shall receive love. If you welcome him, God will teach you how to forgive. And by offering forgiveness, you shall receive forgiveness. And if you ask him, God will teach you how to heal. And by healing others, you shall be healed as well.

★★★

Forgiveness isn't an opportunity to return to hurtful ways; it's an opportunity to return to God.

★★★

Forgiveness has elements of surrender and sacrifice. Specifically, you must surrender thoughts of revenge and sacrifice bitter feelings.

★★★

As you strive to promote God's will, the Holy Spirit shall guide you. And as you arrive exactly at the right place and time, the Holy Spirit shall help you perform miracles.

★★★

A miracle is anything that increases the awareness of God's presence in the world.

★★★

Christ's ministry revealed the glory of selfless service. In truth, Jesus showed us how to serve both God and humanity.

54. New Beginnings

Symbolic rituals and ceremonies can help people let go of the past and launch a new beginning. First, write down the details of past grievances, and write about the pain you've experienced. Take all the time needed to express your feelings about the hardships you've endured. Then, find an appropriate location for your ritual, a safe place to either bury or burn the written pages. If you wish, family and friends can witness the ceremony. Another option is to symbolically attach your despair to a balloon and allow it to literally fly away.

If you are mourning the loss of a loved one, you might create a remembrance garden. Or, if you prefer, you could plant a tree and place a memorial plaque at its base. While a young tree honors the past, it signals a new beginning as well. These types of rituals promote a fresh start to life.

★★★

Your book of life has countless chapters. As one chapter ends, a new one begins. As one journey concludes, a new one starts. And each new journey holds infinite promise.

55. Our Abundant World

And God said . . .

I urge my children to be faithful stewards of the earth. In fact, caring for the planet is a noble way to honor me. Clean air and water please me, as do your creative endeavors and thoughtful "improvements." By design, the universe recycles energy continuously. And my plan for you includes plenty of everything you need. Therefore, scarcity is an illusion; and so-called shortages typically result from manipulations by those searching for greater wealth and power.

Blinded by greed, some people allow food to rot in the fields while many go hungry. Hardened by selfishness, some people fail to distribute readily available medicine and aid to the sick and needy. These acts contradict my will. And yes, there are a few who plot to conquer the entire world. They want to vanquish every last one of their perceived enemies. They want to annihilate every last remnant of the world's beauty. Yet, I tell you the truth: Their psychotic fantasies shall crumble. Despotic empires may rise, but they are destined to fall. Lacking my love, oppressive rule is certain to wither.

Individual life forms are transient and temporal. Yet by its very nature, *life* is unsusceptible to extinction. And though earthly resources may appear, in some instances, to be limited or unsustainable, such is not reality. My steadfast love shall lead men and women to make inspired new discoveries, including bold advances in technology.

To those who seek me, I have already promised ample food and water, clothing and shelter. Indeed, they shall have these things and infinitely more. My command is this: Love me; and love your neighbor as you love yourself. Rejoice in my covenant of sustenance. Go forth in love, and celebrate my everlasting abundance.

★★★

I am never the cause of unthinkable tragedies. Yet, I make sure that incredible good shall come from them.

56. Redefining Life's Meaning

As your health declines, you may feel physical, emotional, or spiritual pain. When you're unable to do the things you once could do, you might begin to think: "I don't want to be a burden on anyone." Or you might ask, "Why am I still alive? What does God have planned for me?" These are tough questions, because everyone's life is one-of-a-kind;

each person's pathway is unique. Yet, common threads weave through the tapestry of life; and among them is this reality: Everyone born of this world must, by death, leave it.

As you start to feel more dependent and vulnerable, it's normal to experience anxiety. It's normal to be wary of an uncertain future. Everybody wants to have a sense of control in life. But at some point, we learn that our control is limited. And as our health weakens, we face the prospect of losing even more control. So again, you might ask, "What *is* God's plan for me? How could my life have meaning if I can't get out of bed?"

While God's plan isn't always clear, there's one thing you can know for sure. When you welcome Christ's love into your heart, you become a light of the world. And when you are a light of the world, your light shines on others. Think of it this way. When a pebble is dropped into a pond of still water, it creates a series of ripples that extend outward. Those ripples travel farther and farther. In time, they stretch to the horizon and beyond.

In a similar fashion, the light in your heart extends outward. It touches each person who comes near you. Your light may shine on a family member or a friend. It may touch a doctor, a nurse, a new acquaintance, or a complete stranger. It's up to God to make those connections. And because your light stems from divine love, it illuminates, uplifts, inspires, encourages, and affirms all who are touched by it. And yes, the people touched by your light, go on to touch others; and those people touch still others; and so on, like ripples in a pond. It's the miracle of love.

Now, the truth is revealed. You can serve God and help countless people, without ever leaving your bed. And your light in this world leaves an ongoing legacy. In closing, reflect on this new possibility for life's meaning: With Christ's love in your heart, you are a light in the world – a light that shines on everyone you meet. Your light brings peace to those who are touched by it. And your legacy is one of lasting love and joy.

★★★

Rather than mourn what you can no longer do, give thanks for what you can still do. Rather than dwell on what you no longer have, celebrate what you still have.

★★★

No one can go back and make a brand new start. But anyone can start from now and make a brand new ending.

57. The Prayer of Saint Francis

Lord, make me an instrument of your peace.
Where there is hatred, let me sow love;
Where there is injury, pardon;
Where there is doubt, faith;
Where there is despair, hope;
Where there is darkness, light;
And where there is sadness, joy.

O Divine Master, grant that I may not so much seek
To be consoled, as to console;
To be understood, as to understand;
To be loved, as to love.
For it is in giving that we receive;
It is in pardoning that we are pardoned;
And it is in dying that we are born to eternal life. Amen

58. A Mildly Curious Mind

Have you ever wondered why so many people struggle to recognize reality? As it turns out, there may be a surprisingly simple explanation for much of our confusion. The human mind, it seems, would benefit from a larger dose of curiosity. Here's why. After discovering something new, there's a sense of excitement and the mind demonstrates a keen interest. This initial burst of natural curiosity, however, tends to wane rather quickly. As a result, the mind concludes, much too soon, that there's nothing more to learn. In other words, everything is just as it appears to be – there's no need to dig deeper.

So if you're exploring a jungle and stumble upon something never before seen, curiosity will compel you to examine it. Then, a few mental notes are taken. Let's say, for example, you're inspecting an oddly curved object about three feet long. It's very sturdy, comes to a point, and has an off-white color. With absolutely no idea of its true nature, your mind names it a tusk. And once something is labeled, ownership quickly follows.

From this moment forward, the mind perceives itself as an authority on the new subject of tusks and, sadly, the story ends here. Rarely is there enough interest – that is, adequate curiosity – to prompt further study. Thus, we don't connect the dots. We fail to recognize that our newfound object is actually part of something much greater; that a tusk is, in fact, just a small part of an undiscovered creature that might one day be named an elephant. Until we are ready to dig deeper, our mind will be completely unaware of the elephant's existence. What's more, we shall remain oblivious to the fact that even an elephant is just a tiny part of truth and reality.

★★★

Though it may have killed the cat, intellectual curiosity illuminates our pathway to truth. And if you believe that everything real must have a name and a shape, then pause and think again. Otherwise, God may appear to be nonexistent.

59. Voices and Choices

Whether it's recognized or not, most people face a daily struggle – an ongoing conflict between their two inner voices. The human mind is relentless. It creates an endless stream of thoughts and self-talk, with much of it negative and dispiriting in nature.

The mind's voice is always loud and it's frequently angry. It's this voice which suggests that you are a victim, and that the people you believe are responsible for your suffering deserve to be punished. This is your ego-driven voice of jealousy, fear, and retribution.

Yet everyone has a second voice, a guide which does not originate from the mind. But you must listen very carefully, for this counselor speaks in a softer tone. Fortunately, its voice is kinder and gentler in nature. And its source is your heart. This is your spirit-driven voice of love, compassion, and forgiveness; a voice of gratitude, praise, and thankfulness.

Each day presents lots of opportunities to make empowering choices. As your day unfolds, which voice will you listen to? Whose guidance will you seek? One leads to never-ending turmoil, while the other brings inner peace. Your ego screams, *Don't be a loser, listen to me!* And your heart whispers, *God is love, trust in Him.* As always, the choice is yours.

★★★

While in the presence of his grandson, a Cherokee elder talked about an ongoing battle that was raging inside him. He said, "My son, it is a struggle between two wolves. One wolf is evil. It displays anger, jealousy, greed, arrogance, resentment, violence, and self-pity. The other wolf is good. It displays love, peace, hope, humility, kindness, compassion, and joy." The grandson thought about this for a minute, and then asked his grandfather: "Which wolf wins?" The Cherokee elder smiled and replied, "The one I feed."

★★★

The ego creates a problem. Then, it brags about finding a clever solution. But is the problem real? Is the solution truly helpful? Perhaps that is why history keeps repeating itself.

★★★

First, the ego screams that you are God's gift to the world. Next, the ego shouts that you are worthless. Neither extreme is helpful, and neither is true.

★★★

Even people driven primarily by anger and rage can have breakthrough moments of kindness and compassion. It is, after all, their true nature.

60. The Unity Prayer

The love of God enfolds us.

The light of God surrounds us.

The power of God protects us.

The presence of God watches over us.

Wherever we are, God is! Amen

61. Contemplations of a Monk

Theologian, author, scholar, and pacifist Thomas Merton was born in France on January 31, 1915. At age twenty, Merton moved to New York City where he earned undergraduate and graduate degrees from Columbia University. After converting to Catholicism, he became a Trappist monk and joined Kentucky's Abbey of Gethsemane in 1941. This cloistered, Roman Catholic Order practices stability, fidelity, obedience, silence, and contemplation. The monks produce handmade goods that are sold to support the monastery.

Merton garnered critical acclaim for his essays and his bestselling autobiography *The Seven Storey Mountain*. This success enabled him to travel the globe and advance his chosen causes of social justice and world peace. Later in life, Merton was deeply influenced by the meditational teachings of Zen Buddhism. He wrote: "The problem of my salvation is, in fact, a problem of finding out who I am, of discovering my true self."

Merton also wrote about love: "When you love someone, you forget about yourself and serve the other person; and if the love is mutual, the other person is serving you. In a loving relationship, each one forgets his own interests. You live without care or concern for anything of yourself."

In March of 1958, Thomas Merton had a transforming vision at the busy corner of Fourth and Walnut Streets in Louisville, Kentucky. These are his words: "Suddenly, I was overwhelmed with the realization that I loved all the people around me. They were mine and I theirs. I realized that we could not be alien to one another even though we were total strangers. I understood that the belief of a separate existence is an illusion." On December 10, 1968, Merton died from an accident that happened during a visit to Thailand.

★★★

The following contemplations are representative of Merton's Christian beliefs.

O God, through Christ we have been made one with you. Fill us, then, with love and let us be bound together with love. And let us witness the ultimate reality that is love.

Christ lives in us and leads us, together, as we build the kingdom of God.

The resurrection is the life and action of Christ himself. By the Holy Spirit, it is part of us.

An encounter with Jesus liberates a power we didn't know we had. Christ gives us hope, resilience, and an ability to bounce back when we thought we were completely defeated.

The clumsy beauty of this particular colt on this April day in this field under these clouds is a holiness consecrated by God.

The wildflowers that nobody notices at the edge of the road are saints looking up at the face of God.

Sin starts from a false sense of self.

Contemplation is spontaneous awe at the sacredness of life and being.

Every moment of each person's life plants a seed in his soul.

The Christian in whom Christ is alive dares to think and act differently from the crowd.

You are not a Christian if you say with your lips that Christ has risen, but secretly believe he is dead.

To be born again is not to become someone else, but to become one's true self. It is to rise above the level of individual ego.

The rebirth of spirit which Jesus spoke of is not necessarily a single event. It happens many times in a person's life as he or she passes through successive stages of spiritual growth.

The born again Christian must renounce his own desire and will to dominate, and let the Holy Spirit act in and through him.

Despite all differences, love unites us.

62. Tragedies

In Oklahoma City, on April 19, 1995, a bomb explodes. 168 lives are lost, including nineteen children. A community is shattered and a nation is stunned.

In Colorado, on April 20, 1999, teenage shooters enter Columbine High School. Bullets fly and thirteen are killed. Neighborhoods grieve and a nation prays.

In New York City, on September 11, 2001, Twin Towers collapse and thousands die. On that day, the same planned attack claims lives at the Pentagon in Washington, D.C. and in a field southeast of Pittsburgh, Pennsylvania. Cities weep and a nation rebuilds.

In Newtown, Connecticut on December 14, 2012, a gun blazes. Six adults and twenty schoolchildren perish. Families are broken and a nation mourns.

People ask: *Why?*

And God asks: *Why would insanity ever make sense?*

People ask: *Is there a loving God?*

And God asks: *When will my children learn to love one another?*

People ask: *God, how can you let these things happen?*

And God asks: *Have you forgotten my promise of free will?*

People ask: *God, where were you during these tragedies?*

And God asks: *Was I not there inspiring the heroes? Was I not there encouraging the first responders? Was I not there comforting the injured? Was I not there calming the caregivers? Was I not there healing the broken? And was I not there offering heaven's peace to the innocent who were dying?*

63. Turning to the Psalms

When looking for rest, repeat these words: "I will lie down and sleep in peace; for you alone, O Lord, make me dwell in safety." (Psalm 4)

When trying to calm a busy mind, reflect on these words: "Be still, and know that I am God." (Psalm 46)

When feeling sad, recite these words: "The Lord is close to the brokenhearted and saves those who are crushed in spirit." (Psalm 34)

When you are frustrated, ask these words: "How long must I wrestle with my thoughts, O God, and every day have sorrow in my heart?" (Psalm 13)

When looking for protection, reflect on these words: "For God will command his angels to guard you in all your ways. They will lift you up in their hands." (Psalm 91)

When seeking forgiveness, repeat these words: "Create in me a pure heart, O Lord, and renew a steadfast spirit within me." (Psalm 51)

When you feel distant from God, recite these words: "If I rise on the wings of the dawn, if I settle on the far side of the sea, even there God's hand will guide me; his right hand will hold me fast." (Psalm 139)

When looking for courage, reflect on these words: "God is my refuge and strength, an ever-present help in times of trouble." (Psalm 46)

When searching for safety, repeat these words: "The Lord will keep me from all harm; he will watch over my life. The Lord will watch over my coming and going, both now and forevermore." (Psalm 121)

When seeking comfort, recite these words: "The Lord is my shepherd, I shall not want. He makes me lie down in green pastures; he leads me beside quiet waters; he restores my soul." (Psalm 23)

And when you feel thankful, proclaim these words: "Shout for joy to the Lord, all the earth. Worship the Lord with gladness; come before him with joyful songs." (Psalm 100)

64. Inner Perfection

Within an untouched monolith, the sculptor's creation awaits its unveiling. The marble is already perfect. There's nothing missing or anything to add. Yet, inspiration compels the artisan to remove every last speck of unwanted stone. And only then will his masterpiece be visible for all to celebrate!

On a similar note, everything is already perfect within your Scared Heart. There's nothing missing or anything to add. Yet, God inspires you to chip away at your mind's illusions; those self-indulgent distractions which obscure God's truth and reality. And after removing every last speck of unwanted ego, a divine masterpiece is revealed. Then, all of heaven celebrates!

65. Spiritual Healing: A Guided Imagery

You are about to travel to a restful setting. Your imagination can take you anywhere in the world. Perhaps you will choose to lie on a sandy beach and listen to the sound of breaking waves; or maybe you will visit a tropical forest and smell the sweet fragrance of exotic flowers; or perhaps you will travel to the summit of a rugged mountain and feel a cool breeze on your face; or maybe you will simply choose to snuggle in the familiar blankets of your own comfortable bed. The choice is yours. Now, go to that special place. Allow your mind to create a picture of your new surroundings. Safe in this restful environment, you can stay focused on the present moment. Your body is relaxed. Your breathing is calm and steady. Nothing can harm you. It's peaceful, and there's an underlying sense that all is well.

Now, you feel a holy presence. There's an extraordinary sensation of unconditional love. Amazingly, this feeling of God's love transforms into something you can actually see. It appears as a gentle, white Light. This heavenly Light silently approaches. First, your head and face are touched by the soft Light. Moving downward, your shoulders, arms, hands, and fingers are now wrapped in Light. The Light envelops your chest and stomach as well. Finally, your legs, feet, and toes are embraced in Light. Now, your entire body is surrounded by the sacred Light. In truth, you are receiving a gift from God. For this gentle, heavenly Light eases pain. This soft, holy Light promotes emotional and spiritual healing.

To your surprise, an angel appears – a special attendant sent just for you. Before your eyes, heavenly fabrics of purple and lavender mingle with the white Light of God's love. Ever so gently, you are cradled in the arms of your angel. You feel safer and more secure than you've ever felt before. Now, you have an inspired thought. You know that, if you choose, you can invite the healing white Light to flow *within* you. Extending your arms outward, God's Light enters your heart. Feel this pure Light as it flows through you. Feel its warmth. Feel its energy and healing power. Your entire being – body, mind, and spirit – bathes in divine, unconditional love. Sensing a profound closeness with your Creator, you revel in this moment, hoping it will last forever. But ours is a world of beginnings and endings. And with gentleness beyond description, your angel returns you to the wonderful resting place you've chosen. As your heavenly attendant prepares to leave, all remnants of the sublime Light find a permanent home within your heart.

There is no sense of disappointment, for you know God's love dwells within you. And because of that, you feel an indescribable inner peace. You feel whole. You know you've been touched by mercy and grace. You know that God is helping you heal emotionally and spiritually. And it's understood that you can welcome God's Light into your heart anytime you desire – anytime you feel sadness or anxiety; worry or regret; anytime you feel the sting of fear, guilt, or unworthiness. Indeed, the sacred Light shall always be in your heart. And yes, it *will* connect you to God. It *will* illuminate your pathway. Now, you offer a short prayer: O Glorious God, thank you for your loving presence. Thank you for always walking at my side. Thank you for your angels who watch over me. And thank you for the gift of your healing Light. Amen

66. Life Lessons

It's seldom helpful to compare your life to the life of someone else. Often, such comparisons will have you thinking that your life is too harsh and your trials are unfair. Does this sound familiar? Don't be fooled by misguided conclusions. Each hardship addresses a unique, individual need. Every challenge offers an occasion to master a specific life lesson.

Hardship, in fact, provides a perfect chance to grow closer to God. By design, each obstacle in your path presents an opportunity to make choices; and in turn, every choice produces meaningful consequences. As it happens, you learn and grow by *experiencing* the direct consequences of your choices, both wise and foolish ones.

There's no limit to the type of scenarios or the number of chances you may have to learn a life lesson. Thankfully, once a particular lesson is truly mastered, there's no need to experience further turbulence – that is, until a new assignment comes your way. So the next time you face a grueling challenge, don't make the mistake of comparing your life to your neighbor's. Instead, gather your courage and composure. Then look upward and proclaim, "I bless this opportunity to learn and to grow!"

★★★

Experience is a tough teacher. You always have to take the test before receiving the lesson.

★★★

As you endure challenges and overcome hardships, you experience God's love in a deeper, more meaningful way.

67. Stubbornness

Once upon a time, there lived a man named George. His neighbors described him as a bit stubborn, but a nice man nonetheless. George had built his house next to a river and spring rains always brought the threat of flooding. One year, the seasonal rains were particularly heavy and the river was rising fast. As George listened to the radio, he was warned: People living close to the river should evacuate immediately. But George thought, "I'll stay here. God will lower the water and keep me safe."

As the river spilled over its banks, George heard someone knocking at his door. A fireman pleaded with him to leave the house right away. But George replied, "I'll stay here. God will lower the water and keep me safe." Yet the rain continued and the river rose higher and higher. Soon he was perched on the rooftop, the last safe place above the surrounding floodwaters. Suddenly, a distinctive sound came from the sky. As George peered upward through the pouring rain, he saw the outline of a helicopter. A rope ladder was dropped onto the roof, but George cupped his hands and shouted, "I'll stay here. God will lower the water and keep me safe!"

A short time later, George stood at the gates of heaven with a puzzled look on his face. When Saint Peter approached him, George asked, "Why didn't God lower the water and keep me safe?" Saint Peter, trying to hide his exasperation, answered: "Do you really think God has forsaken you? First, he talked to you through the radio. Next, he knocked on your door. And finally, he sent you a helicopter. It isn't God's fault that you died!"

★★★

By becoming too headstrong, we may fail to see God's helping hand.

★★★

When our expectations are not aligned with God's will, we are likely to be disappointed.

68. Teachers and Students

In the United States, about one in every 700 babies is diagnosed with Down syndrome. As they grow up, these children confront a myriad of developmental and cognitive disabilities. They have facial features and other bodily characteristics that are outside the norm. Moreover, young adults with Down syndrome have, on average, an IQ of 50 compared to a typical 100 IQ. They have a lower life expectancy as well. Oh, and there's one more thing: They love unconditionally.

Have you ever known someone with Down syndrome? Though they may have special needs, they've never met a stranger. Everybody is greeted by a warm smile that's likely to be followed by a big hug. Of course, there are times of anger, frustration, and sadness because people with Down syndrome are, after all, human. Their innocence allows them to cry when sorry or hurt. And for the most part, they live in the present moment – the only possible time to experience unbridled joy.

Their spirit shines brightly. Life isn't dissected, intellectualized, or trivialized. It's honest, transparent, and sincere. Quite simply, life *is*. Unfulfilled dreams are as rare as broken promises. Their past holds few regrets, and their future has no worries. They don't chase wealth or status. And they seldom doubt that God is real.

Those with Down syndrome and other types of disabilities often require special help. As a result, caregivers have opportunities to serve, to learn, and to grow. Finally, the truth is revealed: People with special needs are not life's students, they are life's teachers. And once again, we're reminded that ours is a topsy-turvy world.

★★★

Is it possible for exceptional intelligence to be both a blessing *and* a burden? There's plenty of upside to having a Mensa-worthy IQ. Yet, a brilliant mind often attaches great importance to itself. And in this sense, exceptional intelligence may be a handicap. Here's why. Brilliant minds tend to dismiss that which cannot be seen, touched, or proven by science. What's more, a high IQ often leads to an inflated ego. And an ego-driven mind invariably attacks whatever questions its judgment or threatens its supremacy, hence the resistance to trust in God and to grow in faith. Each person's spiritual path has countless obstacles and one-of-a-kind challenges. Are you allowing a whip-smart mind and an oversized ego to be barriers to your spiritual growth?

★★★

It's common knowledge that every person on the planet is born with an Intelligence Quotient, or IQ. But many people don't realize that we're also born with a Spiritual Quotient, or SQ. Because life is ever-changing, IQs and SQs are subject to change as well. Research has shown that a person's IQ is elevated as he or she "exercises" the brain. So it makes sense that our SQ will soar to new heights as we grow in love and faith. Life, after all, provides countless opportunities to express love and kindness. What's more, a cognitive disability may not hinder someone's spiritual growth. So take a moment to answer this question: What changes can you make to raise your SQ?

69. Life, Death, and Hope

In times of sickness or decline, we want to feel safe and loved. In times of pain or distress, we seek to learn more about life's meaning and purpose. And in times of loss or sadness, we strive to maintain hope. These existential truths are found in every corner of the world, and they resonate within the very core of our human psyche. When facing a crisis, people of faith reach out to God. And while they may not be free of suffering and doubt, people who ask for God's guidance and help – those who embrace their spiritual essence – are well-equipped to confront an uncertain future.

★★★

If you were to approach the edge of a deep canyon, you might strain your neck and cautiously peer downward for a few seconds. Those who stare too long into the canyon's depths may begin to feel dizzy. Then, their gaze must focus in a new direction. Otherwise, they risk falling. In a similar way, most people confront thoughts of death for just brief moments at a time. Otherwise, they risk feeling overwhelmed. Yet people who summon the courage to face death's certainty – those who find the strength to examine and to accept their mortality – sometimes receive an unexpected gift: a renewed joy for living. Often, they choose to drink more fully from the cup of life for whatever time they have left in this world.

Like a potter shaping clay, a writer shapes his thoughts. Perhaps the following thoughts by poet Kahlil Gibran will create a sense of calmness:

What is it to cease breathing but to free the breath from its restless tides; to free one's breath so that it may rise and expand and seek God unencumbered?

Only when you drink from the river of silence shall you begin to sing.

Only when you reach the top of the mountain shall you begin to climb.

And when the earth shall claim your limbs, only then shall you begin to dance.

★★★

There is one thing certain about the past: It is not here now, so it can no longer harm you. And there is one thing certain about the future: It is not yet here, so it cannot harm you now. You are safe in this present moment. We appear to live in a dualistic world, a world in which many things seem to have an opposite: past and future, up and down, hot and cold, black and white. So it's understandable to instinctively conclude that life and death are opposites. But in truth, death is the counterpart to birth. Birth and death are polarities in nature's realm of cycles. Yet life has no opposite; for life is eternal and rises above the transitions and limitations of this world. Is the earthly body your true identity? Or is it your soul, your spirit? Saint Paul wrote, "Fix your eyes not on what is seen, but what is unseen. For what is seen is temporary, but what is unseen is everlasting."

★★★

Death is but a gentle awakening, a passage which takes us from the shadows to the light.

★★★

We've not yet unraveled the sublime mysteries of sleep. However, there's one thing doctors know for sure: Sleep deprivation causes chronic fatigue. A lack of sleep may eventually lead to more serious health problems or, in rare cases, death. Almost everyone endures the occasional restless night. We toss and turn and simply cannot fall asleep. And when we finally doze for a bit, we're trapped in a dream cycle. We awaken only to feel more exhausted.

In order to be rested and energized in the morning, we must have a period of deep sleep, a time when the mind is completely free of thoughts and dreams. Just as there's a spiritual side to wakefulness, our sleeping hours have a spiritual dimension as well. In that realm of absolute silence and stillness, we commune with God. We connect with an infinite, divine presence. In truth, it's a time of healing, a time to experience the peace of heaven as we once knew it. Then, we awaken refreshed and renewed.

★★★

Fatigue makes us confront enemies that were vanquished long ago.

★★★

Everyone's history, their life story, has highs and lows. Whenever you find yourself immersed in negative thoughts; or if you are sad, worried, or fearful; or if you can't fall asleep, pause for a few minutes and count your blessings. Redirect your thoughts to whatever it is you are thankful for. Choose to focus your mind on the positive aspects of life. And if you wish, you can offer a prayer thanking God for the gifts and blessings you've received. Right now, take whatever time is needed to identify the things in your life – from the past and the present – which you are most grateful for. Do your blessings nurture a sense of hope?

70. Turn to Me

And God said . . .

There are times when you do not turn to me. Why? Perhaps you believe your problem is too small to bring to me. Maybe you think that, by coming to you, I must abandon all others. Or perhaps you feel unworthy of my time and attention – that you're undeserving of my help. Yet, none of these concerns have a speck of merit.

First, anything which disrupts your inner peace is important enough to bring to me. Problems are never too large or too small, for there are no hierarchies of worldly troubles. I don't compare one problem to another. Nor do I rank problems or attach degrees of difficulty to them. Although you do these things, such judgments are foreign to me.

Next, I am not confined by time and space. Unlike you, my presence is everywhere at every moment. There is no place or time where I am not. Therefore, each person who reaches out will, in truth, connect with me. Only those who do not ask for my help will go without it.

So I ask: Why do you feel unworthy, undeserving? Does a loving father not provide for his children? Does a watchful shepherd not tend to his flock? My child, you are deeply loved. Turn to me for healing. Reach out to me for comfort. And come to me for help.

★★★

As you face a daunting task, ask me for strength and guidance. Ask me for courage and calmness; and let your heart rest easy.

71. Thoughts and Words

In a single day, human minds generate countless thoughts. Some are inspired, but most are not. Many of them are formed within the conscious mind, but there are subconscious thoughts as well. Yet thoughts, regardless of their nature, can wield great power. And words can carry enormous power too. As your thoughts and words stream forth into the universe, it's possible to ask for something and not even realize it. And on the flip side, it's possible to receive something and be completely unaware that you asked for it.

★★★

Jerry is a project manager for a busy construction company. There are three other project managers – Lisa, Bob, and Don – who work with Jerry. But a series of unexpected events, a perfect storm of calamity, has Jerry feeling sorry for himself. Lisa is on leave, providing care for her mother who's recovering from a stroke. Bob is off work because of injuries suffered in a car accident. And this morning, Don injured his back at a jobsite. He can't work and has no idea when he might return. Suddenly, Jerry's not only taking care of his own job, he's doing the work of three others. His mood becomes dark. He thinks: *Why am I the only one working? It's not fair!* That evening, Jerry complains to his wife, "I'm doing the work of four people. When will *I* get to take some time off?"

Three days later, Jerry is finishing a quick lunch break. He has to drive to a meeting. But on his way there, Jerry experiences severe nausea. He also feels a sharp pain under the right side of his ribcage. Instead of attending the meeting, he's being examined by an ER doctor. It's learned that Jerry's having a gallbladder attack. Within an hour, he's admitted to the hospital. Jerry will not be returning to work this day. Nor will he be able to go back to his job anytime soon.

★★★

Jerry didn't ask to become sick. Hardly anyone does. Or at least, no one ever *consciously* asks to be sick. Yet, Jerry did ask for some time off work. Has this illness fulfilled his wish? Could it be that Jerry's gallbladder attack, and its timing, were just a coincidence? Or did his thoughts and words help manifest this event?

★★★

By design, the universe is like a mirror. What is sent forth is what returns. You harvest what you plant. And while there's no need to panic, it may prove helpful to dismiss negative thoughts as they arise, and to develop a more disciplined, positive mindset. You can choose to let go of fear, anger, frustration, and self-pity. It's always your choice to make. And of course, it's wise to be mindful of what you wish for, and to be thoughtful of what you pray for.

72. A Pledge

Empowered by choice, I pledge to be more easygoing, forgiving, kind, and loving towards life in all of its expressions, including myself. I pledge to be helpful and to respect everyone I meet, without exception.

I trust the love, mercy, and wisdom of God – the all-knowing God who understands that I have limitations and that I make mistakes. I place my faith in an infinite, all-forgiving Creator whose grace has no boundaries. I release my fears of judgment and condemnation. I will transcend negativity by making positive choices. With the discipline which stems from my passionate commitment, I no longer view negative thoughts and behaviors as viable options.

73. The Story of Job

The Old Testament includes the story of Job, one of the wealthiest and most prominent men of his time. Over the years, Job had amassed a great fortune which included vast areas of productive land, herds of prized animals, and many other treasured possessions. He loved his family, and he also loved God. Then, a series of tragedies occurred. Job's valuable sheep were killed. After this, his camels, oxen, and donkeys were stolen. Next, his sons and daughters died in a terrible accident. And finally, Job was plagued by painful sores which covered his entire body, from the soles of his feet to the top of his head.

At first, Job remained true to God. But soon, Job became fixated on why these things had happened. Stunned by his horrific losses and wracked with excruciating pain, he thought: *What have I done to offend God? Why have I been punished?* In other words, Job began to live in the past. He felt that life was unfair. He wallowed in self-pity and cursed the day he was born.

Job received counsel from three close friends. They offered comfort and gave Job advice on how he might regain God's favor. Yet, nothing improved. No one could provide the insight needed to end Job's pain and suffering. Life had lost its meaning. Job was miserable and without hope. Ultimately, he gave up. He surrendered to God's will. Job told the Lord: "I know you can do all things; that no plan of yours can be thwarted." At last, Job allowed God to determine what was good for him. He chose to trust God unconditionally and to let go of the past. After forgiving his hardships and letting go of past grievances, Job started living in the present – the only time in which he could feel God's peace. What's more, the present moment is when God offers his gifts and blessings; the only time new doors of opportunity are opened.

Shortly thereafter, Job's health was restored; and as time passed, he gained an even larger fortune. He was blessed with beautiful children and found a renewed sense of hope. No longer complacent in his relationship with God, Job became more eager to grow in love and faith. And with Job, God was well pleased.

★★★

When Job hit rock bottom, he finally surrendered to God. Exhausted and exasperated, he stopped making judgments. He allowed God to decide what was good and what was bad. Job perceived the world differently and allowed God's plan to unfold at its own pace. As he began to follow his heart, Job's pain subsided. By giving up so little, he gained so much. And from that moment forward, his blessings grew exponentially.

★★★

In due course, the scales of justice are destined to be balanced. Yet, there are periods of time when the scales are *not* balanced, times when we must be patient, and times when surrendering to God's will is our only way to experience peace.

★★★

If you choose to let go of the past, God shall bless you with new ways to grow in love and faith. And as your love grows greater and greater, you will see the glory of God.

★★★

God offers new gifts when past wrongs have been forgiven, and God offers new blessings when minds and hearts are focused on living in the present.

★★★

God is never the source of our pain. Still, if something happens, then it's meant to happen; and if it's meant to happen, then it serves the greater whole in some way. Yet, we may never know exactly how life's tragedies are serving humankind. Therefore, these unsolvable mysteries constantly test our faith and resolve.

★★★

Hardships help us gain a deeper understanding of life. And as we gain a deeper understanding of life, we appreciate it more and more.

★★★

Just as there are man's laws and God's laws; there is human justice and divine justice.

74. Perceptions and Choices

The year was 1939 and a teenager named David Hawkins had an after-school job delivering newspapers in rural Wisconsin. He used a bicycle to travel the rigorous, seventeen-mile roundtrip. One day on his route, something happened that forever changed David's life. Decades later, he described his experience this way.

"On a dark winter's night, I was caught in a twenty-below-zero blizzard. My bicycle fell over on the ice and the fierce wind ripped the newspapers out of the handlebar basket, blowing them across a snowy field. There were tears of frustration and exhaustion, and my clothes were frozen stiff. To get out of the wind, I broke through the icy crest of a high snow bank, dug out a space, and crawled into it. Soon, the shivering stopped and there was delicious warmth; and then a state of peace beyond all description. This was accompanied by a glowing light and the presence of infinite love which had no beginning and no end. My body and surroundings faded as my awareness was fused with this all-present, illuminated state. My mind grew silent; all thought stopped. An infinite, divine presence was all that was or ever could be, beyond all time or description."

"After this sense of timelessness, I suddenly felt someone shaking my knee. Then my father's anxious face appeared. There was great reluctance to return to my physical body and all which that entailed; but because of my father's anguish, divine Spirit nurtured and reactivated my body. There was compassion for my father's fear of my death; although at the same time, for me, the concept of death seemed absurd."

David Hawkins went on to graduate from medical school. As a respected psychiatrist, his private practice grew to be the largest in New York City. He managed fifty staff members and treated over two thousand patients a year. Hawkins provided care for people with debilitating mental illnesses. But after years of witnessing profound human suffering, Hawkins felt exhausted, depleted, and overwhelmed. It was as though he had begun to experience the pain of his patients. Starting to doubt the existence of a loving God, Hawkins was engaged in a serious crisis of health and faith.

Hawkins took an extended leave of absence from his medical practice. And during this time, he was gravely ill. Though never fearing death, he nonetheless shouted, "If there is a God, I ask him to help me now! I surrender to whatever Higher Power there might be." That moment signaled the start of an incredible spiritual journey. Like many philosophers and theologians before him, Hawkins began asking questions: How could a God of love allow such intense human suffering? After a period of reflection, Hawkins mused: Is it possible that one of the primary reasons we are in this world is to grow spiritually? And if this is so, what things in life afford us the greatest opportunities for spiritual growth?

Pain is rarely welcomed. Yet, we often draw closer to God during difficult, stressful, and even tragic times. So perhaps we should rethink our judgments about the challenges we face. Maybe they shouldn't be viewed so harshly. That's not to say we should deny our feelings, or that our pain isn't real. But a shift in perception might be warranted. In the end, Hawkins persevered. Both his health and his trust in God were restored.

David Hawkins became an acclaimed author and teacher. His breakthrough research on human consciousness and brain chemistry led him to work collaboratively with Nobel laureate, Linus Pauling. Hawkins lectured and hosted spiritual workshops around the world until his death in 2012. He believed that a mature faith eventually leads to a complete surrender to God's will. Here, surrender is not an act of weakness or cowardice. It's a demonstration of acceptance, trust, courage, and strength. Placing complete trust in God will nurture a sustained sense of safety, well-being, and peace. And it's a liberating journey. Why? Because when we surrender to a Higher Power, there's no longer a desire to control or micro-manage our lives. There's no longer a reason to worry about the future. There's no longer a need to singlehandedly save the world. All of these daunting tasks are left to God. And the result is a confident feeling that all is well.

Still, there are empowering choices we can make. Chief among them is the willingness to adjust our perception of the human experience. *A Course in Miracles* suggests that sometimes a miracle is nothing more than a shift in perception. The story of the Mongolian stallion is a classic example of shifting perceptions. A struggling family lives near a remote border of Mongolia. One day, a stallion magically appears. It helps them with many of their farm chores. The horse is good. Then, while riding the stallion, the oldest son is thrown and breaks his leg. The horse is bad. Soon after, a government official arrives to claim the family's oldest son, so that he may fight in a bloody war. However, with his leg broken, the oldest son is honorably excused from combat. The horse is good. A few weeks later, the stallion unexpectedly disappears. Now the family is left with nothing. The horse is bad. But after several more weeks, the stallion returns, this time accompanied by five mares. The horse is good.

While we may be unable to choose what happens, we can always choose how to *perceive* what happens. Indeed, it's a blessing to be able to choose how personal experiences and the world at large are viewed. As a result, we can choose to see peace, rather than conflict; love, rather than fear; abundance, rather than lack; and instead of seeing random acts of chaos, we can choose to recognize a divine plan at work in our lives and in the world.

Abraham Lincoln is credited with saying: "Most of us are just as happy as we make up our minds to be." Like Sam, an eighty-year-old man who has lived alone since his wife, Doris, died two years ago. Though he still misses Doris, Sam is comfortable. He enjoys living independently, in a spacious, familiar place. And he's happy. But Sam's health is declining. He struggles with bathing and preparing meals. Then one fateful day, Sam fell. Though his injuries weren't serious, his children urged Sam to move into an assisted living community, where he could be helped whenever it was needed. Sam agreed to the move.

A few weeks later, his son, Thomas, drives Sam to his new home. In a voice tinged with anxiety, Thomas explains, "Dad, you're going to notice some changes. The room is small, and you'll be sharing it with a roommate." Sam replies, "I like my new room *and* my roommate." Looking puzzled, Thomas exclaims, "But Dad, you haven't seen your room or your roommate yet!" Sam answers, "That has nothing to do with it. I can decide to be happy in advance. Happiness doesn't depend on my room or the person I share it with; it depends on how I choose to see them. In my mind, I've already decided I like them."

Spiritual teachers have long suggested that happiness has little to do with what "happens" to us. Yes, we can find temporary excitement in what we do; we can find fleeting pleasure in things we own; and we can find welcomed love, comfort, and support from close relationships. Yet, none of these leads to *lasting* happiness. Joy does not originate from an external source; it comes from within our heart. Happiness is an empowering choice that each of us, like Sam, can make.

In a similar way, you can choose to be kind and compassionate to the people you meet as each day unfolds. You can choose to forgive. You can cling to anger, fear, jealousy, and guilt, or you can choose to release them. And in terms of your identity, you can choose to be a victim or a victor. In the journey ahead, will you decide to *accept* the future, and dismiss its uncertainty? Will you decide to *accept* change, and let go of its pain? Will you choose to surrender *all* judgments to God? Will you turn to your Creator as a Source of courage, strength, wisdom, and guidance? And finally, will you trust God and ask that his will be done?

★★★

The idea of surrender is foreign to our human nature. It causes us to worry. It defies our desire for control. But look at it this way. What things can we really control? Do we truly control our body? Our safety? Our emotions? Our relationships? So if we choose to surrender to God's will, are we really giving up anything of importance? Or are we simply giving up a misguided thought; a mistaken belief that we had control in the first place?

★★★

Awareness and consciousness are often thought to be one and the same. However, Eastern religions draw distinctions between them. Hinduism, for example, teaches that human awareness is timeless, changeless, and indivisible. Awareness is independent and absolute, without beginning or end. Consciousness, on the other hand, is tied to life's content. Therefore, human consciousness is relative to individual and collective experiences. While consciousness is ever-growing and ever-changing, awareness is life's calm and silent backdrop.

★★★

In his groundbreaking research, David Hawkins demonstrated that consciousness not only drives human behavior; it influences our perceptions and emotions as well. As a result, an individual's level of consciousness shapes his views on life and God. A terrorist, for instance, functions at a very low level of consciousness. He lives in a state of despair. His life is tragic and his God is vengeful. But someone who functions at a higher level of consciousness might, for example, live in a state of optimism. For this person, life is harmonious and his God is merciful. And someone functioning at a higher level still – someone who has grown even more in love and faith – may live in a perpetual state of peace. For this person, life is meaningful and his God is one of unconditional love.

★★★

While on earth, Jesus inspired his followers. His mere presence filled their hearts with hope. Today, his teachings continue to uplift and to comfort. And Christ's resurrection has elevated the consciousness of humanity at large.

75. That Was Then

Lying in a hospital bed, a man began to think: *Just six months ago, I was strong and healthy.* Then, he heard a voice whisper, "That was then, this is now." Next, the man thought: *Just three months ago, I still had a job.* Again, a voice whispered, "That was then, this is now." Before long, the man's thoughts turned to his finances: *Just a few weeks ago, I had money in my bank account.* And once more, a voice whispered, "That was then, this is now."

There is a straightforward moral to this story. Because life is ever-changing, today may bear little resemblance to yesterday. When looking for that which is changeless, turn to God's love. And when searching for that which is timeless, turn to the present moment. The present is the only time you can experience the peace of God; the only time you can receive God's blessings. And if your mind and thoughts are focused on the past, then you are ill-prepared to welcome new gifts.

★★★

Worrying is a bit like going back and forth in a rocking chair. It gives you something to do, but it doesn't get you anywhere.

★★★

Anger actually carries a great deal of energy. The next time you are angry, redirect your rage. Channel it into a committed effort to make a positive change in your life.

76. Workings of the Mind

Human minds have two parts. Like the visible tip of an iceberg, the conscious mind is the smaller part. And like an ominous mountain of ice cloaked beneath the sea, the unconscious mind is the larger part. Everything said or done or witnessed is placed into a storage vault within the unconscious mind, including feelings of anger, fear, and resentment. As it happens, these unhealthy feelings resurface in situations which trigger painful, subconscious memories. Negative feelings can be tied to events going all the way back to childhood.

Forgiveness will cleanse and heal the mind of past grievances and the mental anguish attached to them. Unfortunately, many people avoid their pain and deny it at all costs. When this happens, their anger and fear are repressed. People try to bury their pain, but it remains alive. People try to elude their pain, but it can't be outrun. Eventually, something will happen and – in an instant – the anger and fear return. The tears and torment are reborn.

★★★

Dreams are expressions of the unconscious mind, and they often include symbols of repressed fear and guilt. Psychotherapists will sometimes explore the messages and meanings hidden in a client's dreams, especially recurring dreams or nightmares. This helps identify the underlying cause of the client's problem.

★★★

You visit someone. And before long, you are upset by something they say or do. Quite often, your annoyance has nothing to do with the person you are visiting. You may, in fact, be upset because the other person has reminded you – subconsciously – of something you don't like about yourself. In part, that's what Jesus meant when he said, "Why do you look at the speck of sawdust in your brother's eye and pay no attention to the plank in your own eye?"

★★★

What is forgiveness? Forgiveness is letting go of the past. It's releasing a burden. It's having a clean slate and a fresh start. It's looking at someone who has hurt you and seeing the face of Christ. Forgiveness is reclaiming your freedom. Therefore, it is a gift given to oneself.

★★★

How long will you wait to let go of your anger? Do thoughts of forgiveness frighten you? Will you lose your identity by forgiving the past? If you let go of your anger, how will your life be better?

★★★

When something disturbing happens, simply bless it; release it; and be free.

★★★

Tears are the words of a broken heart.

77. Going Home: A Guided Imagery

When work is finished, people say, "I'm going home." Actually, they are *returning* home. And this, of course, implies they've been there before. Ideally, your home is a sanctuary – a calm, peaceful place where you can safely rest. Hopefully, your home is welcoming and comfortable; and you feel that you belong there. Upon entering your home, you start to relax and let go of any stress. It's an opportunity for renewal. So it shouldn't be surprising that, as death approaches, someone might say, "I'll be going home soon." These words suggest that heaven is somehow familiar, that it's a sacred sanctuary to which they are *returning*. And Scripture seems to support this view.

God said to the prophet Jeremiah, "Before I formed you in the womb, I knew you." And in reference to heaven, Jesus assured his disciples: "You know the way to the place where I am going." Could these words mean that your soul has already heard the sweet sounds of angelic harps; that your spirit already knows the fragrance of heavenly roses; and that your Sacred Heart has already seen the radiant face of God? Could it be that our transition from this world to the next is, in truth, a homecoming? Do we intuitively know what it's like to be welcomed into paradise? And if this is so, are we not equipped to overcome the fears and anxieties sparked by our physical mortality? Are we not prepared to face a natural death with greater clarity, acceptance, and understanding?

★★★

According to an ancient Japanese proverb, no matter what road you travel, you're going home.

★★★

Listen and try to remember a sacred song you knew so long ago, one loved more than any melody you've cherished in this world. Now, form these images in your mind. Beyond the sun and stars, past everything you've seen, and yet somehow familiar, there is an arc of golden light that stretches within a great and shining circle. Your eyes see the entire circle as it fills with light. The edges of the circle gradually disappear, and the light that was inside it, is no longer contained at all. This golden light expands and shines on everything. It extends to infinity, forever shining, with no break or limit. Everything touched by the radiant light is joined in perfect continuity. Nor could anything be excluded, for there is nowhere that the light is not.

This is the vision of the children of God, a vision you know well. Here is the sight and the source of those who know their Father. Here is the memory of what you are; a soul embraced in divine Light; forever joined to all, as surely as all is forever joined to you. Accept *this* vision of who you are, and not an earthly body. You know the ancient song, and know it well. Nothing will ever be as dear to you as this eternal song of love, a timeless melody that God's children sing to their Father still. And the song offered as praise to the Creator honors his creations as well. Now the blind can see. For what miracle is greater than this remembrance? And who is there in which this memory sleeps not? The light in your heart awakens the song in another. As the song awakens in another, you remember it yourself. And by remembering it yourself, the song awakens in everyone.

Adapted from *A Course in Miracles*

78. A New Way to Perceive the World

The human mind relishes every opportunity for judgment. Our minds judge the past, the present, and the future. Our minds decide what's good and evil, right and wrong, fair and unfair. It's the mind which separates weak from strong and bright from dull. It judges who is friend or foe, kin or stranger. Our minds are most comfortable in an environment which has no gray, only black and white. In other words, human minds create rigid structures which promote an artificial sense of control. As a result, your mind embraces dualism, the belief that our world has many opposites. And at first glance, it appears that we *are* living in a dualistic world, a domain of polarities. After all, is there not a night and day; an east and west; a hot and cold?

Your mind's linear thinking categorizes the world into an endless series of finite, straight lines. One line begins with sweet and ends with bitter. Another line begins with healthy and ends with sick. Yet another starts with love and stops with hate. And of course, there's a line that begins with life and ends with death. You might ask, "Is there a problem with this kind of thinking?" Actually, there *is* a problem, because linear thinking is inaccurate and misleading. It's inaccurate because linear perceptions are illusory. And it's misleading because people who perceive their lives in polarities tend to see a separated world rather than a connected one.

Next you may wonder, "Are there really no opposites in the world?" Take a closer look. On earth, the western hemisphere's day blends seamlessly with the eastern hemisphere's night. And without fail, night's darkness slowly surrenders to the light of a new day. On our planet, north gradually joins with south, which meets again with north. And polar cold stretches to touch tropical heat, only to merge once more with numbing cold. Next, consider the seasons. Spring ushers a summer; that leads to an autumn which heralds a winter; that yields to another spring. Soon, it's clear that ours is not a simple world of separate lines, it's a complex world of interconnecting circles. This divine reality is significant because, unlike lines, circles are perfect and unbroken. As it is with God, circles are the alpha and the omega, without beginning or end.

This illuminating shift in perception helps us see a more innocent and connected world. Suddenly, it's easier to marvel at earth's wonder and beauty – a world that, by design, cannot be snuffed out; a world whose splendor and abundance cannot be erased by greed or jealousy, fear or hatred. From this new perspective, how could love have an opposite? Moreover, how could God's children be anything but brothers and sisters? For in truth, love is an everlasting circle. Love is a sacred, eternal, and universal bond which cannot be broken by a tragic accident, a brutal crime, a painful disease, or an untimely death. Finally, understand that life, too, has no opposite; because in the circle of life, endings are actually beginnings. And each beginning holds promise beyond our wildest dreams.

79. Living for Today

Today, I am in awe of the one Spirit
And the diverse creations born of the one Spirit

Today, everything and everyone belong
And I forgive what I cannot understand

Today, I teach love and compassion
Kindness and helpfulness

Today, my childlike eyes see only innocence and perfection
Beauty and abundance

Today, I feel an infinite divine presence
As I choose to follow my heart

Immersed in this moment, I am humble and grateful
Jubilant and triumphant!

80. Glenda Green

Glenda Green is an accomplished portrait painter and spiritual artist. With her work displayed at the Smithsonian Institution and the Museum of the City of New York, critics have praised Green as a distinguished American realist painter. Her oil paintings are marked by intuitive spirituality, evocative color, and elegant craftsmanship.

Green completed her undergraduate degree in Art at Texas Christian University and earned a Master's in Art History from Tulane University.

In her lauded career, Green has received hundreds of commissions, primarily to paint angels and other religious artwork. Yet, her most famous piece is a portrait of Jesus which she named *The Lamb and the Lion*. Started in November of 1991, the painting took four grueling months to complete. But Green's labor of love – when it was finally unveiled – generated a huge outpouring of public interest. In response, she travelled through five states and displayed the painting at more than eighty Christian churches.

Then, in preparation for the portrait's display at St. Francis Episcopal Church in Willow Park, Texas, a catastrophe unfolded. Green and a small group of parishioners watched in disbelief as a heavy floodlight fell from a tripod and crashed into the painting. Green describes what happened next. "As we repositioned the painting on the easel, everyone present observed the extent of its damage: a four-inch dent in the canvas with a one-inch tear at its center. I passed my finger completely through the incision! I knew right away that the dent would always protrude, and the tear, though it could be patched, would always be noticeable."

Green compared the accident to the fate of nursery rhyme character, Humpty Dumpty. That is to say, you can put the pieces back together but they will never be whole again. The St. Francis viewing was, of course, cancelled; and Green's trembling hands placed the damaged portrait back into its travelling case. She decided to examine it again in the morning and then schedule repairs with a professional conservation studio.

Although she endured a restless night, Green stayed true to her plan. She got out of bed the following morning and removed the painting from its case. To her utter astonishment, the damage was gone. She cautiously ran her fingers across the painting. There was no dent, no cut, and no loss of paint. Flipping the portrait over, she looked closely at the weave of the canvas. It was as tight and strong as the first day it had been stretched.

Green recounted it this way: "Holding the portrait up to a window, there wasn't a single pinhole of light. Nor was there even a fleck of missing paint. My examination of the canvas through a high magnification lens revealed that no fibers were torn. What I was seeing was nearly as disturbing as the original accident." St. Francis Church has written testimonials from those who witnessed the event and saw the damage firsthand. Moreover, there's no indication that the painting has ever been repaired.

Not only is Green an acclaimed artist, she's a respected author as well. There are those who believe that the repair of Christ's portrait is a miracle, while others dismiss it as a hoax. Likewise, some believe that Green's Christ-centered writing is divinely inspired, while others do not. Nevertheless, her work remains popular among spiritual seekers; and her crowning achievement *The Lamb and the Lion* is permanently displayed in a chapel owned by the Christ Truth League of Fort Worth, Texas.

★★★

God has never stopped talking to us. His guidance didn't end at the conclusion of the Old Testament. Nor did his counsel stop with the closing words of Revelation. And though there can never be a new book comparable to the Bible, today's authors are writing inspirational material for those who have an open mind – helpful books produced by Spirit-guided men and women. And if you ask, God will lead you to them.

81. The Attraction of Opposites

Everyone has heard that opposites attract. But a closer examination suggests this common belief could be misleading. In truth, there are lots of reasons why you prefer to spend time with certain people more so than others. Common interests, for example, bring people together.

A mutual enthusiasm for travel, sports, or a special hobby creates an attraction among individuals. Similar career paths and shared employers bring us together as well. Those attending the same college will form an allegiance. And personalities play an important role too. At a large party, for instance, introverts often seek the quiet company of one or two familiar faces, while extroverts may mingle with outgoing strangers.

Of course, shared life experiences – such as groups of mothers raising young children – create mutual attractions. And people with racial or cultural ties are naturally drawn together. Even people with the same disease form lasting bonds. In fact, it's our commonalities which join people, rather than our differences. Lasting relationships are usually built on the foundation of common ground. So, do opposites really attract? Sometimes, but magnets aside, polar opposites are seldom a happy pairing.

There's still another reason why you're drawn to certain people. As it happens, every person on the planet functions at a particular level of consciousness and self-understanding. It's a characteristic as unique as a fingerprint. Are you surprised, then, that people who've reached similar levels of spiritual growth are attracted to one another? Yet, because it's a hidden phenomenon, most people are unaware of this very real attraction. It's also notable that someone with a low level of consciousness tends to be suspicious, even fearful, of a person having a significantly higher understanding of truth and realty. This explains why there were some who felt threatened during Christ's earthly ministry; why some were afraid of Jesus and his "radical" teachings.

★★★

Neither IQ nor wealth is an indicator of consciousness. And certainly, a high level of self-understanding doesn't make one person inherently superior to another – any more than one fingerprint could possibly be better than another. Most importantly, God's love isn't tied to the consciousness of his creations. What it does mean, however, is that the more conscious person has a better grasp of reality. And as such, this person offers a better example of how God wishes us to live; for they are more receptive to Spirit guidance and empowerment.

★★★

Like the invisible Creator who makes all that is seen, consciousness is a paradox; for it's an unseen power visible in all that you do.

★★★

Consciousness drives human behavior. This reality explains why our world is plagued by crime, poverty, inequity, and war. Furthermore, it helps us understand why money, government programs, and diplomacy – though well intended – will *never* end these problems. Only spiritual growth can change the world. Life is not static; we are always growing. And in the afterlife, we continue to grow in love and faith. Jesus affirmed this as he talked about his miracles: "Anyone who has faith in me will do what I have been doing. He will do even greater things than these."

★★★

In heaven, saints gather with the saints. In hell, misguided souls seek out those who are equally lost and hopeless. Ultimately, it is love which joins and binds us; and sadly, not everyone is ready to receive God's love.

★★★

The Light of Christ is helping our world evolve to higher levels of love.

82. Divine Judgment

It's the elephant in the room that we seldom talk about: judgment. Even for people with a mature faith, thoughts of divine accountability and judgment are unnerving. Feelings of guilt and unworthiness are usually responsible for this underlying anxiety. And often, the foundation of these feelings was formed in early childhood. Perhaps we didn't compare favorably to a sibling. Or maybe we were overlooked during tryouts for the basketball team or the school play.

Everyone, it seems, has heard that inner voice of doubt; the whisper that suggests you're not good enough, smart enough, or pretty enough. Then again, maybe people have unleashed verbal assaults which imply that you are unworthy; that no one could ever love you. With this in mind, we can turn to Scripture for a better understanding of judgment, both human and divine.

In Matthew 7:2, Jesus spoke about human judgment: "Do not judge, or you too will be judged." And in John 8:15, Jesus said, "You judge by human standards; I pass judgment on no one." It's clear that people are not equipped to judge either themselves or others. Quite often, human judgment is simply an excuse to blame somebody else for a self-created problem.

As for divine accountability, Matthew 12:36 hints that our words are woven into the fabric of the universe, where they remain for all of eternity. And Galatians 6:7 suggests that every single day is a day of divine judgment; that each new day is a harvest of seeds planted long ago. Therefore, we really *do* reap what we sow. And yes, there really *are* consequences for hurtful words and hateful behavior. But that doesn't mean we should live in fear of God's judgment.

Think of it this way. Divine judgment is like breathing in and out. It is part of every moment of your life, yet it stays in the background. And just as you are at peace with taking a breath, you can be at peace with God's judgment. There's neither a courtroom nor a stern, robed judge. And there's never a time when the accused must stand and tremble while awaiting his fate. Assurance of this is found in 1 John 4:16-17: "And so we know and rely on the love God has for us . . . Whoever lives in love, lives in God; and God in him. In this way, love is made complete among us so that we will have confidence on judgment day . . . ."

Remember, God offers his love and grace without conditions. Moreover, God never demands perfection or questions your worthiness. God simply asks you to love him. And as you do this, all of heaven smiles upon you.

★★★

Humankind's fall from paradise has caused considerable pain. Thankfully, we cannot fall from God's grace.

★★★

It has been taught that you needn't fear a judge whose eyes see only innocence.

83. Innocence Lost

An innocent child is born into the world.

The child learns that he is separate from his mother, and he struggles with loneliness.

The child learns that he makes mistakes, and he deserves punishment.

The child learns that some people do not approve of him, and he hides his guilt and shame.

The child learns that some people cannot be trusted, and he is introduced to fear.

The child learns that some people do not love him, and he bears the burden of unworthiness.

The child learns that people become sick, and he tries to be strong and brave.

The child learns that people die, and he copes with pain and sadness.

His childhood is a journey which leads to lost innocence.

And yet, his only sin is the pursuit of joy and happiness.

★★★

Are there sounds more vibrant and pure than those of young children on a playground?

★★★

Children who are sick do not blame God for their illness. They do not identify someone else as the source of their troubles or the cause of their pain. Nor do children view themselves as victims. This indicates that we're not born with an instinct to project anger and blame onto others. We're not born with the notion that life is unfair. Sadly, it's something that we learn and come to believe.

★★★

Women travelled great distances and brought their babies in the hope that Jesus would touch and bless their beloved children. Christ's disciples tried to prevent these women from getting too close to their teacher. But Jesus said, "Let the children come to me, for the kingdom of God belongs to ones such as these. I tell you the truth: Anyone who will not receive the kingdom of God like a little child will never enter it."

★★★

Could it be that humanity's only sin is the pursuit of happiness? Isn't it starkly evident that we do what we *think* will bring happiness? Of course, misguided choices lead to a broad range of results, from benign disappointments to stunning catastrophes. Still, is there not an underlying innocence to it all?

84. An Existential Lens

Humans are the only creatures in the world who perceive their existence as an intriguing set of problems. And this singular mindset has spawned existentialism, a philosophy which examines some of life's most perplexing mysteries. Specifically, existentialism explores issues such as freedom, oppositional forces, isolation, meaninglessness, guilt, and death. The conflicts tied to these topics are a source of anxiety for men and women around the world, regardless of race or culture.

Of course, anxiety is normal, even for those who are exceptionally healthy and well-balanced. Still, excessive anxiety can be debilitating. Stress and anxiety may grow to the point where people completely withdraw from the world. Like the population at large, some existentialists believe in a Higher Power, while others do not. This spiritual reflection doesn't weigh existentialism's merits or flaws. Rather, its humble objective is to introduce an alternative view of the human experience. With this in mind, let's explore some of the compelling problems identified by existential philosophers.

FREEDOM

Freedom is generally considered a positive aspect of one's life. Yet, existentialists view freedom as a condition which produces anxiety. The reason, they say, is because freedom ultimately leads to greater responsibility. Here's why. In a state of freedom, each and every act involves the need to make a choice. And the very process of decision making produces stress.

What's more, someone who's free to make choices is, by definition, accountable for the consequences of those choices. Freedom, therefore, disallows victim status. That is, we cannot project blame onto others when things go wrong. So the greater our freedom, the more choices we must make. More choices bring greater responsibility, and greater responsibility leads to – you guessed it – increased stress and anxiety.

Irvin Yalom, a respected existential psychotherapist, once had a patient who announced, "It's not my fault when things go wrong! After all, my behavior is controlled by the unconscious mind." After a moment of reflection, Yalom replied, "Perhaps, but *whose* unconscious mind is it?" For existentialists, the essence of freedom is simply this: You, alone, are making choices. And you, alone, are responsible for their consequences. When things go badly, don't point the finger of blame towards anyone other than yourself.

And finally, existentialists have discovered what is sometimes called the freedom paradox: Although we are free to choose, we never chose to have the freedom of choice. We are, as French philosopher Jean-Paul Sartre observed, condemned to freedom.

OPPOSITIONAL FORCES

Existentialist philosophers posit that our lives unfold in a state of tension produced by opposing forces. In other words, we are caught in an endless web of attractions between the secular and the spiritual, the physical and the metaphysical, the darkness and the light, the finite and the infinite, and most significantly, between life and death. The conflicts created by these opposing forces are yet another source of human stress. Hence, we are destined to experience anxiety.

ISOLATION

Existentialists believe that each person's life is, fundamentally, a solitary and individual journey. Yalom explains it this way: "There's an unbridgeable gulf between oneself and any other being. The frightening truth is that we enter life as an independent being, and we take leave of life alone." Therefore, it isn't surprising for people to feel lonely and to struggle with maintaining happy and wholesome personal relationships.

Existentialism urges people to connect as deeply as possible with others, while at the same time acknowledging separateness and individuality. Yalom suggests that we build "need-free" relationships. Meaning, we should offer friendship and love without promoting a personal agenda;

and we must acknowledge the other person's independence of mind and thought. Such relationships, according to Yalom, make both parties feel more alive and engaged in life.

MEANINGLESSNESS

Classic existential questions include: What is the meaning of life? What is the purpose of *my* life? And the typical existentialist would answer: Life has no inherent meaning, so it's up to you to invent or discover one. Furthermore, it's up to you to find the *purpose* of your life as well.

Yet, existential psychiatrist Viktor Frankl held a somewhat different view. His perspective was shaped by the hardships he witnessed and endured while imprisoned in a Nazi concentration camp during the Second World War. Frankl believed that human beings possess a basic instinct to seek and find life's meaning and purpose. Frankl also proposed that meaning *does* exist, but each person has the responsibility to identify and define it. And finally, Frankl emphasized that purpose is not found through a preoccupation with oneself. Rather, we must look beyond individual self-interest.

Existentialists agree on a number of possible paths which lead people to discover meaning and purpose. They include:

- Altruism – serving others through unselfish kindness and compassion.
- Dedication – promoting a cause such as world peace, clean air, curing a disease, etc.
- Creativity – producing original music, art, literature, etc.
- Self-Transcendence – setting aside materialistic goals to pursue selflessness.
- Suffering – facing hardships with optimism, dignity, and integrity.
- Religion or Spirituality – serving one's God or Higher Power.
- Hedonism – embracing worldly joys and sorrows with equal and unabashed enthusiasm.
- Self-Actualization – maximizing personal improvement and potential.

GUILT

Most people have occasional feelings of unease with themselves. Accordingly, most existentialists accept that the human condition invariably leads us to experience guilt. First, we are deeply indebted to life itself. Additionally, we believe that we're always capable of being a better person, of being more patient, more helpful, more tolerant, and more loving. Thus, we are destined to feel the pangs of guilt, just as we are destined to have periods of anxiety. We carry the baggage of disappointing others and ourselves. And the *awareness* that we are not living to our fullest human potential – that we are disingenuous – inevitably brings guilt, self-pity, and feelings of unworthiness.

DEATH

Existential philosophers acknowledge that life is fraught with pain and suffering. Actually, existentialism suggests that pain doesn't stop entirely until death. Still, it is a philosophy which attempts to promote hope, not despair. Existentialists believe that life should be lived to the fullest, and that human struggles should be faced head-on.

Research has shown that denial is the most common way people choose to cope with death. Yet, existentialists propose that as we accept the certainty of death in the future, we may experience a greater zest for life in the present. Yalom explains it this way: "Existence cannot be postponed. Many cancer patients report that they live more fully when focused on the present moment. They no longer postpone living until sometime in the future. They realize they can live *only* in the present. The present cannot be outlived. Indeed, the present – not the future – is the eternal tense." Because there's no benefit to adopting a morbid preoccupation about the future, existentialism encourages people to live in the now, as individuals empowered by the freedom of choice.

Terminal illness triggers profound change. Perhaps for the first time, someone is reflecting on death's finality. Maybe for the first time, someone is learning that his chosen defense mechanism for death – denial – has lost its effectiveness. And anxiety is sure to follow. This holds true for his loved ones and perhaps his caregivers as well; for they, too, may have dismissed previous thoughts of their own mortality. Then, the issues become: How can those who are fearful, angry, or depressed about death provide genuine comfort to the sick? How can those who haven't confronted their own mortality offer effective care and support to the dying?

★★★

There's a common goal shared among all professional caregivers: building relationships. In fact, trust-based relationships form the foundation of effective care. The doctors and nurses who make an effort to build trust are the ones most appreciated by their patients. Counselors understand that creating a safe, nonjudgmental, and "need-free" relationship with each client is the very essence of psychotherapy. And respected psychologist Carl Rogers encouraged everyone to offer acceptance and "unconditional positive regard" in their interactions with others.

★★★

Many Native Americans believe that life unfolds between the light and the shadows. When a loved one is troubled or depressed, tribal members gather to offer their support. They form a circle, and a tobacco-filled pipe is shared by those assembled. Because the tobacco is rooted in the soil and the smoke rises above the clouds, the pipe ritual symbolically connects the earth to the heavens. Then, a talking stick is passed among those sitting in the circle. Only the person holding the stick is allowed to speak. Yet, everybody receives an opportunity to encourage and affirm the one who suffers in the shadows. The kind words bring healing. Indeed, the talking continues until their troubled brother returns to the light.

★★★

The Buddha taught that all fear stems from our worries about poverty, sickness, old age, and death.

★★★

"Death is *not* an empty void; it is the room of creation. Nature goes to exactly the same place to create a galaxy of stars, a cluster of planets, a rainforest, a human body, or a thought. Not only does God continuously create new universes, he becomes them." Deepak Chopra

★★★

"Death is a primordial source of anxiety. It whirs continuously beneath the membrane of life and exerts a vast influence upon our experience and conduct." Irvin Yalom

★★★

"I am the resurrection and the life. He who believes in me will live, even though he dies; and whoever lives and believes in me will never die." Jesus of Nazareth

85. Reaching out to God

Is it possible that, even after death, a relationship with God can be improved? Among Christian religions, the Roman Catholic Church, the Anglican–Episcopal Church, and conservative Orthodox churches teach that, when someone dies, his soul may need purification prior to its heavenly reception. In Catholicism, purgatory is closely linked with purification. Purgatory is the soul's resting place, a realm between death and final judgment. It's viewed as a period of sanctification through grace. So the need for purification implies that some souls are not quite ready to receive God's love. The question, then, is what happens as one's soul is made ready to meet the Holy Father?

In the Bible, quite a lot is written about hell, little is written about heaven, and purgatory receives no specific mention at all. The Bible states that, while there's no sense of suffering in heaven, hell has plenty of anguish. Scripture suggests that the fires of hell will burn forever. But does this mean that the souls which taste the torments of hell must remain there for all of eternity? Or think of it this way. Was Christ's ministry focused on lessons of everlasting damnation?

Jesus said, "My Father's house has many rooms." In other words, there are countless experiences within God's heavenly kingdom. This means that each afterlife journey is one-of-a-kind, just like each person's life on earth. Moreover, there's no evidence that God's promise of free will shall ever be nullified! Therefore, each soul may have an opportunity to shape its afterlife experiences. Purification, then, could be largely self-determined and still remain wholly within God's plan for salvation. Yet, questions remain. Does God's plan include possibilities of pain and despair? Is torment found in some of the "rooms" available for the soul's purification?

Near-death or out-of-body experiences may offer insights into the afterlife. Near-death occurrences commonly include one or more of the following themes: feeling a profound inner peace; seeing a brilliant white light; experiencing an intimate connection with God; feeling weightless; meeting a "dead" family member; or receiving a message that it isn't the right time for a heavenly welcome. Yet, some near-death events are vastly different, and Howard Storm's narrative – although it has a few classic characteristics – is a stunning departure from the norm.

Storm was a self-proclaimed atheist who took delight in ridiculing those who believed in a Higher Power. Storm now admits he was angry, bitter, hateful, and rude during those years. Here's his story. While vacationing in Europe, Storm became violently ill. He was diagnosed with a perforated stomach, a life-threatening condition accompanied by excruciating pain. Confined to a hospital bed, Storm was alarmed to suddenly realize that he was no longer living within his body. Instead, he was hovering above it. And what happened next was anything but peaceful.

Storm entered a realm of bleak darkness. Within seconds, demons began taunting and torturing him. He endured intense pain for what seemed to be a very long time. Storm desperately wanted to end this suffering, but he couldn't escape the grip of his tormentors. For some reason, he began to recall early childhood memories, thoughts of when he attended Sunday school. Then, Storm remembered the words and melody to a song learned long ago: *Jesus loves me, this I know; for the Bible tells me so.* He started singing, softly and tentatively. To his surprise, the demons began backing away. Emboldened, he sang louder and with greater gusto. Soon thereafter, his persecutors vanished.

Though relieved, Storm was still hurting and vulnerable. He had no idea what new, horrific monsters might emerge from this pitch-black hell. Storm was a broken man. And at that moment, he asked Jesus to help him. Storm recounts that, almost immediately, a tiny point of white light appeared in the distance. The light grew larger as it got closer and closer. Soon, he was totally engulfed by a brilliant, white light. Storm remembers experiencing an indescribable, unfathomable love. But at the same time, he was overcome by deep feelings of guilt and shame. Sobbing inconsolably, he recalled his disdain for people of faith. He remembered his cursing the very notion of a living God.

According to Storm, it seemed as if oceans of time had passed when, finally, his crying subsided. Held in the arms of Jesus, Storm experienced the full force of unconditional divine love. He felt the joy of purification and the peace of grace. Storm's destiny was to return to his earthly body. Eventually, he recovered from his serious illness; but he was completely and permanently transformed. His new life of faith bore no resemblance to his past. Storm's book *My Descent into Death: A Second Chance at Life* offers additional details about his near-death experience and the transformation which resulted.

So, must suffering always be everlasting? Do people who turn their backs on God's Light, those who choose to dwell in a world of self-created shadows, endure unthinkable despair for all of eternity? Theologians hold differing views. Some insist the anguish of hell – the pain caused by one's separation from God – lasts forever. Yet, other biblical scholars embrace a more merciful Creator; a Heavenly Father who adds hope to suffering's equation. Could it be that, even after death, the soul can choose once again? That, in truth, there is still a chance for redemption? Might this be the perfect plan of a God who *is* love?

Universalists believe that everyone receives opportunities for salvation. Mormons and Unitarians, among others, also embrace this theology. Perhaps you've heard the story about a spiritual seeker who encounters a fork in the pathway to enlightenment. He stops and studies the two signs in front of him. The first sign announces *This Way to Heaven* and the second sign beckons *This Way to Learn How to Enter Heaven*. It's a comical scenario that just might contain an element of truth.

From a global perspective, Eastern religions view reincarnation as the means by which one's soul prepares to join with God. Sikh gurus, for example, teach that every soul embarks on a spiritual journey which lasts eons of time and includes hundreds of incarnations. Hindus also believe in reincarnation, while rejecting both divine judgment and eternal punishment. And as more and more Christians gradually adopt a wider range of beliefs, theological conflicts are sure to follow. For instance, most Christians believe that everyone must face divine judgment. Yet, there's a flip side. It's grossly arrogant for *any* person to place arbitrary boundaries on God's grace.

In closing, reflect on these questions. How may God's grace be expressed in an eternal afterlife? What might happen to the souls not yet ready to accept God's love? And finally, could salvation be found in the afterlife?

★★★

Is it ever too late to reach out to God's unending love? Is it ever too late to receive God's infinite grace?

86. Contemplations of a Master Teacher

Sri Nisargadatta Maharaj was born in the spring of 1897 in a rural area outside of Bombay, India. His parents were poor farmers and

Nisargadatta's childhood was devoted to tending cattle, driving oxen, and working the fields. Eventually, he became a successful shopkeeper, a vocation which he kept for several decades. Nisargadatta's world, however, was turned upside-down by an unexpected epiphany: the realization of his own immortality.

After this spiritual awakening, he became a seeker of truth; and years later, a spiritual teacher. Nisargadatta's lessons, though heavily influenced by Hinduism, rise above ideological and religious boundaries. As a teacher, his mission was to mitigate suffering by prompting his students to reflect on their true nature and to abandon all false identities. He believed that understanding leads to freedom. Nisargadatta said, "Spiritual work is timeless. It was the same thousands of years ago and will remain the same for thousands of years to come. Progress is measured by diminished anxiety, a greater sense of joy, a deeper peace within, and a greater energy without."

Nisargadatta lived alone in a tiny, unpretentious home and was humble and gracious to all visitors. Those who knew him said that he was uneducated, but imminently wise; he was poor, but immensely rich. His students claimed that he was warm-hearted, humorous, fearless, and genuine. His seminal book, *I Am That* is a spiritual classic which has remained in print since its first publication over thirty years ago. Deepak Chopra proclaimed, "It's the one book I always carry with me." Nisargadatta died in Bombay on September 8, 1981 at age 84.

★★★

The following contemplations are representative of his spiritual beliefs.

The highest form of human intelligence is to observe oneself without judgment.

To have an open mind, you must dismiss judgment. And to dismiss judgment, you must detach from your mind's stream of thoughts which are based upon the past.

Time is all that separates the saint from the sinner. The saint once sinned, and the sinner will be sanctified.

The river of life flows between the banks of pain and pleasure.

Your world is manufactured, subjective, fragmentary, temporary, personal, and hanging on the thread of memory. It has little to do with reality.

Ideas of suffering are all in the mind. Just as you don't have to worry about digesting food, I don't have to worry about suffering. For in my mind, nothing goes wrong.

You want pleasure because you suffer. Yet the search for pleasure is the cause of your pain. It's a vicious circle.

To mistake appearance for reality is a grievous sin and the cause of all calamities.

You are eternal and infinitely creative. Don't forget what you are.

Reality is neither the mirror nor the image reflected in the mirror.

Nothing the mind can visualize and want is of much value. To let go of desire is the highest bliss.

Each event is the effect and expression of the whole and is in fundamental harmony with the whole.

Meditation will help you find your bonds, loosen them, and untie them. When you are no longer attached to anything, you will have done your share. God will do the rest.

Reality is wholly independent of the world. Whatever is real is changeless and timeless. Since your body is dependent on the existence of the world, it cannot be what you truly are.

Seeking out the "cause" of something is a pastime of the mind. There is no duality of cause and effect. Everything has its own cause. Or if you prefer, there is but a single cause: God's will.

Desires are often painful, but not all desires. The desire to be compassionate, for instance, is never painful.

In a lucid mind, desire is goodwill, compassion, and the urge to make happy rather than be happy.

It is not life that needs the body; it is the body that needs life.

In seeking reality, you will discover that you are neither the body nor the mind. And the love of the self in you is actually the love of the self in all.

By forgetting who you are and imagining yourself as a mortal creature, you create so much trouble for yourself that you have to wake up, as from a bad dream.

The universe does not need improvement, only your way of looking at it.

God is not only true and good; he is also beautiful. He creates beauty for the joy of it.

True happiness is spontaneous and effortless.

Whatever is received blissfully is beautiful.

Because your mind is not focused on your true self, you lose your sense of well-being.

See the world as it is, not as you imagine it to be. In my world, the weather is always fine.

God does not create one thing to serve another. Each is made for its own sake.

87. The Lost Son

Jesus often directed his teaching to the religious leaders of that time. Christ recognized that many church officials were, at best, lacking in compassion; and at worst, they were hypocrites. After local clergy had accused Jesus of eating with "sinners" he responded with a parable: *The Lost Son*. This lesson is sometimes called *The Prodigal Son*, whereby prodigal means extravagantly wasteful.

Here's an overview of Luke 15:11-32. There lived a young son who yearned to experience the world. So the son approached his father and asked to receive his inheritance early. Though the father was saddened, he granted his son's request. Upon reaching a distant land, the son eventually spent his entire inheritance on wild living. Having neither food nor shelter, the son longed for the luxuries enjoyed by his father's servants. So the son chose to return home. He would beg his father to take him back as a servant. Yet, seeing his son on the horizon, the father was filled with joy. When they were face to face, the father hugged and kissed his son. And when the son began to proclaim his unworthiness, the father disregarded those remarks. Indeed, the father told his servants, "Bring my son the finest robe. Put a ring on his finger and sandals on his feet. Slaughter the fattest calf and let us have a feast and celebrate. For this son of mine was lost, but now is found."

Biblical scholars believe that the story's father is symbolic of God, and the father's compassion and forgiveness represent God's love and grace. And yes, the lost son personifies the imperfections of virtually every human being who has ever lived. By worldly standards, the son was a dismal failure. He abandoned his father and squandered his inheritance. He debauched and caroused. The son made countless mistakes and poor choices. Yet, the father didn't chastise or punish him. Nor did the father care about what his son had done while away from home.

With this parable, Jesus provides an illuminated view of divine love and grace. The story's message heralds the very nature of Christian faith: God *is* love. So perhaps Jesus is asking: Why are you fearful of

God's judgment? Why would you expect something less than a jubilant celebration as you approach heaven's gates? In truth, God has never asked you to earn his love, and he's never questioned your worthiness.

★★★

Could it be that our personal mistakes and poor choices bring much of life's pain? Are we not responsible for many of our own relationship problems, financial hardships, and mental anguish? And are we not accountable for our neediness and lack?

★★★

How does God's unconditional love and grace affect your salvation? Is salvation something more than a personal choice? The lost son chose to return home. Ultimately, he chose to trust his father and to embrace his father's love and forgiveness. Will you not make the same choice? Will you not choose to receive God's love and grace? Like the lost son, can you not be more trusting of God? And if this is salvation's essence, can you not be more accepting of death? Do this, and your heart shall be filled with peace, hope, and great expectation.

★★★

This parable also includes a secondary lesson, for the father had two sons. And unlike the irresponsible younger son, the father's older son remained faithful and righteous. But the older son was jealous over the lavish homecoming that his wayward brother received. The elder son lamented, "Father, you never honored me with a feast like this!" And the father replied, "My son, you are always with me and everything I have is yours. But today, we are celebrating because your brother, who was dead, is alive again." This lesson reminds us that only God is equipped to pass judgment. Furthermore, when we already have ownership of God's greatest blessings, why be jealous of a gift that God gives to another?

★★★

Is there ever a bad time to reach out to God?

★★★

We can hope that it's never too late to say: "God, help me."

88. Togetherness

Death is nothing at all,
I have only stepped into the next room.
Whatever we were to each other,
We are still.

Call me by my old familiar name,
Speak to me in the easy way you always did.
Laugh as you always laughed
At the little jokes we enjoyed together.

Play, smile, think of me, pray for me.
Let my name be the household word it always was,
Let it be spoken without effort.

Life means all that it ever meant,
It is the same as it ever was.
There is absolute, unbroken continuity.

Why should I be out of your mind
Just because I am out of your sight?
I am but waiting for you, for a short interval;
Somewhere very near, just around the corner.

Nothing is past, nothing is lost,
One brief moment and all will be as it was before.
Yet better, happier, and forever;
As we shall be together with the Lord.

Adapted from a sermon by Henry Scott Holland (1847-1918)

89. Love and Holy Relationships

Our lives unfold through relationships. And holy relationships, those sacred unions blessed by God, are always founded on love. For it is love which joins and holds people together. Always remember that God *is* love. And as a child of God, made in his image, love is the very essence of who you are. Nevertheless, love is a mystery, for it cannot be fully defined. It cannot be entirely explained or understood. You know intuitively that love, though it may be predicted, cannot be controlled or manipulated. You know instinctively that love might be suppressed, but never extinguished.

Though it bends, love does not break. And in your heart, you know that love is nurtured through forgiveness. Having no true opposite, love unveils the illusion of polarities. Yet, there is a paradox; for love is both the lamb and the lion; it is the rose but also the thorn. Love is both the storm and the calm; the bitter and the sweet. Love is exquisitely free, yet it flourishes in bonds of devotion. Love never punishes; yet it's the foundation of all justice. Love is a witness for truth; yet it doesn't judge. By never condemning, love remains innocent. Love conquers by surrendering, and it rules by lifting up.

Holy relationships belong to God, to be empowered or dissolved according to his will. This ensures that someone's life cannot truly be owned by another. By God's design, freedom, equality, kindness, and respect are the ultimate hallmarks of our interactions with others. Each holy relationship honors the universal bond shared by all living things. Each loving union honors the kinship between creation and Creator.

By divine will, a relationship built on innocence and purity is our greatest human expression. When love is nurtured within a sacred sanctuary, there's reason to hope for a better world. And when anointed by God, a holy relationship brings heaven to earth. Understand that as your love grows, your faith grows as well. So in the end, there is but one rule to follow: Simply *be* the love that you are. Then with you, God shall be pleased!

Adapted from the teachings of Glenda Green

90. Contemplations of a Holy Man

Tenzin Gyatso is better known as the fourteenth Dalai Lama, the spiritual leader of Tibet. Because Tibetans are ruled by an oppressive and unwelcomed Chinese government, the Dalai Lama lives in exile. Most of the time, he resides in one of his two compounds located near Dharamshala, India. Yet, he maintains an ambitious travel schedule which has taken him around the world many times over. He's an unofficial ambassador of his country and his Buddhist faith tradition. With the Dalai Lama's responsibilities becoming more and more ceremonial, he has openly wondered if he might be the last person to hold this time-honored title.

For his humanitarian contributions and efforts to promote world peace, the Dalai Lama has received both the Albert Schweitzer Award and the Nobel Peace Prize. In addition, he's written several books on Buddhist philosophies, which are pacifist and non-theistic. The fourteenth Dalai Lama is a bright, jovial man who charms people with his warm smile and practical wisdom.

★★★

The following contemplations are representative of the Dalai Lama's spiritual beliefs.

Pleasure relates to the body and its senses, while happiness relates to the mind and heart.

One of the keys to happiness, mental discipline empowers you to dismiss negative thoughts and maintain a positive state of mind. Mental discipline is the essence of Buddhist practice.

As you train your mind, you are cultivating happiness. Self-discipline promotes wholesome behavior, and wholesome behavior promotes happiness.

Human beings inherently possess the potential to be kind, gentle, and compassionate. It is our nature.

If you consciously decide to be more kind, gentle, and compassionate and if you work earnestly to achieve that goal, then the rest of your life will be profoundly changed.

To help promote a feeling of empathy for someone, be mindful of what you have in common: birth and death; a body and a mind; the need to eat and drink; and a desire for more happiness and less suffering.

Compassion urges you to serve others with a sense of commitment, responsibility, and respect.

Compassion will compel you to extend warmth and kindness to others and to alleviate their suffering.

If you can adopt a mindset which *accepts* worldwide human suffering, it will help counteract feelings of unhappiness and discontent.

We add to our suffering by overreacting to minor things and by taking things personally.

Much like birth and death, pain is a natural part of life.

Just as blood is constantly flowing, life is ever-changing. No matter how pleasurable or painful a moment might be, it will not last. Change is one thing we can count on.

Don't allow regret to degenerate into self-hatred and self-induced suffering.

Try to look at life in a holistic way. Realize that every situation is the culmination of countless events.

Remember that all situations have hidden meaning and significance, including situations which appear to be very negative.

What we have done in the past determines the circumstances we face in the present. Yet karma is an active process, and we are not destined to be victims. The initiatives we take in the present will shape our future. And because each day's choices make a difference, we are never helpless or hopeless.

As you practice looking at painful situations from a different perspective, you can develop a calmness of mind. What at first seems overwhelming can become manageable.

Do not be caught by the hook of hatred. Those who hurt you are your teachers. If there were no rivals or enemies, how could you practice patience and tolerance?

Personal suffering provides an opportunity to develop greater compassion.

If there *is* a solution to your problem, then there's no need to worry. And if there is *no* solution to your problem, then there's no sense in worrying about it.

Positive thoughts are the antidotes to fear and anger.

91. Bodies, Names, and Roles

In his first letter to the Corinthians, Saint Paul wrote that an earthly body has one kind of splendor, but a heavenly body has splendor of a different kind. In other words, God has created both organic bodies *and* spirit bodies. So while earthly bodies are made of bone, flesh, and blood, there's reason to believe that heavenly bodies are comprised of spirit, light, and love.

Picture a realm of indescribable beauty, a joyful and peaceful sanctuary, a place absent of worldly burdens and stress. Imagine a paradise where there are no stereotypes or discriminations. Could it be that, in heaven, we relinquish worldly names and roles? Perhaps it will no longer be Bob, the husband and father; or Susan, the wife and mother. Instead, imagine heaven as a spiritual realm where you will answer to your God-given name and will be known simply as a beloved child of the Holy Father. Yet, not only will you keep your individual identity, you will also enjoy an intimate, eternal connection with everyone whom you've known and loved.

★★★

For his role in Christ's arrest and crucifixion, Judas has been reviled. Yet, was his part not needed? And was there another man or woman to play his role?

★★★

Saint Paul taught that when this earthly tent we live in is taken down – when we die and leave these bodies – we will have a home in heaven and an eternal body made for us by God.

★★★

Oh death, where is thy sting? Oh grave, where is thy victory?

92. A Course in Miracles

In June of 1965, Dr. William Thetford was a Professor of Medical Psychology at the Columbia University College of Physicians and Surgeons. He and colleague Dr. Helen Schucman, an Associate Professor of Medical Psychology at Columbia, were working as consultants to a research project at Cornell University. Their weekly meetings and collaborations with Cornell researchers had become uncomfortably contentious. In a fit of exasperation, Thetford said to Schucman, "We're using the wrong approach. There must be another way!" According to Schucman, her colleague's proclamation triggered a long series of visionary experiences, including what she later described as receiving messages from an "inner voice."

Schucman told Thetford that hearing this new "inner voice" made her uncomfortable. But Thetford encouraged her to write down the messages she received. Thus began a seven year journey of taking notes. This was followed by another three years of organizing, editing, and publishing headed by another colleague, Dr. Kenneth Wapnick. First released in 1976, *A Course in Miracles* includes a 669 page text and a 488 page workbook. The spiritual messages introduce a new way to perceive the world with an emphasis on love and forgiveness. Interestingly, its non-dualistic paradigm was completely foreign to Thetford, Schucman, and Wapnick, the principal collaborators.

Schucman's claim of hearing an unfamiliar inner voice adds an element of controversy. Critics wonder if she was forthright about the book's authorship. Still, millions of readers have chosen to set aside their doubts and simply accept the spiritual wisdom on its own merits, rather than questioning its source. *A Course in Miracles* is nearing its fortieth consecutive year in print and is available in thirty languages.

★★★

The following contemplations are representative of the lessons offered in *A Course in Miracles*.

Teach only love, for that is what you are.

Those who see themselves as whole make no demands.

The Holy Spirit's voice is as loud as your willingness to listen.

No evidence will convince you of the truth you do not want.

I will find heaven. Everything else shall fall away.

The strain of constant judgment is virtually intolerable.

Today belongs to love. Let me fear not.

Where two have joined for healing, God is there.

What I see reflects my thinking. And my thinking reflects the choice of what I see.

Holiness created me holy. Perfection created me perfect.

No one can fail who seeks to reach the truth.

As a light of the world, forgiveness is my function.

Let me be still and listen to the truth.

Joy and peace abide in me.

I will step back and let God lead the way.

God is but love. Therefore, so am I.

Forgiveness ends all suffering and loss.

I choose to spend this day in perfect peace.

I will not be afraid of love this day.

I seek a future different from the past.

I need but call and God will answer.

I am not asked to make a sacrifice to find the peace of God.

Awake and be glad, for your sins are forgiven.

There is no time or place where God is absent. There is nothing to fear.

Forgiveness is the only gift I must give.

Creation's gentleness is all I see.

Nothing real can be threatened, nothing unreal exists. Herein rests the peace of God.

93. More about Angels

Yes, there is evil. And yes, there are malevolent, ethereal beings. Nonetheless, long and brutal wars fought between good and evil within the spirit realms are largely a human construct. Though they may be warriors, angels use only love to overcome those who threaten or obstruct them. For in truth, love *is* mightier than the sword. Love is the supreme power, the very essence of life. Nothing is greater. At first, this seems counter-intuitive. But that's because power is misunderstood. Most often, power is confused with force.

Force is used to conquer and oppress, while power is used to liberate and illuminate. Just as God is love, God is a Higher Power as well. Accordingly, power is a derivative of love. Love is the *source* of power, while force is driven by fear. Love is a divine attribute, but force is a manipulative tool of the ego. Demons rely solely on force during confrontations. Yet, heavenly angels wield the higher power of love. Hence, they always prevail.

Remember that fallen angels have already chosen to turn away from love. They dwell in shadows and fear is their primary source of strength. By abandoning love, fallen angels have lost much of their former power. So while evil spirits are a real danger to humans, they pose no serious threat to God's legions. Love and power are, indeed, God-like attributes. When overwhelmed by divine love, demonic creatures are temporarily immobilized. Heavenly power renders them as harmless as a sleeping child.

There is a hierarchy among angels: the greater their love, the higher their rank. Because archangels have the greatest love, they hold the highest rank and power. When in harmony with God's will, the love of a single archangel can change the course of our entire planet. Note that it was Gabriel who visited a young virgin named Mary. Like people, angels have a wide range of gifts and talents. And they, too, have individual levels of faith and consciousness. Therefore, God chooses just the right angel, or group of angels, for each assignment.

Having no wants or needs, God cannot be tempted. And as love's exclusive Source, God has no rivals. So could a castaway Satan and his warring minions actually threaten an omnipotent Almighty Creator?

Though it's the stuff of legends, only human minds can create an epic drama from such a mismatched battle.

★★★

Soldiers were guarding the tomb in which Christ's body had been placed. An angel of the Lord appeared, and the guards ". . . became like dead men." (Matthew 28:4)

★★★

As a child of God, it is your birthright to summon his heavenly angels. In other words, you can call out to angels and direct them to serve you or a loved one. But the commands must come from your heart, and they must be in harmony with God's will. For instance, you might say aloud: "In the name of the Holy Father, I command his angels to protect and watch over me." Or you might proclaim: "In keeping with God's will, I command his angels of mercy to guide and comfort my daughter, Jenny."

94. Parting Gifts

Jane's cancer had begun to spread, and curative treatments were no longer an option. Her oncologist suggested hospice care. And soon after, Jane had the services of an entire team of caregivers: a doctor, a nurse, a nurse's aide, a massage therapist, a social worker, and a chaplain. Each one was a specialist in providing comfort and support. A hospital bed was placed in Jane's living room, which was easier to reach than her second floor bedroom. For now, she was comfortably settled in her own home, exactly where she wanted to be.

But Jane couldn't help thinking about the future. Her physician had warned that, as the disease progressed, she might experience intense pain. Jane wondered if she could endure it. What's more, she didn't want to be a burden to her daughter, Sarah. Yet Jane understood that she would soon need someone to prepare meals and help her with bathing and toileting. And later, she might require around the clock help. Jane thought: *I'm so embarrassed. After all, I'm the mother, the nurturing one. I raised Sarah and comforted her when she was sick. I'm the one who always takes care of people when they need it. But now, Sarah insists on helping me. It's all so different, so strange!*

Just as she was feeling overwhelmed, it occurred to Jane that she could ask God for guidance, that she could seek wisdom and courage through prayer. She whispered the following words before falling asleep: "Dear God, help me make wise choices during this time of change. Let me know what I can do to show Sarah how much I love her. And tell me how I can serve and honor you during the trials which lie ahead. Please let me feel your presence, and allow me to experience your peace. Amen."

The next morning, Jane felt rested and renewed. But more importantly, she had a clearer vision of how her future would unfold. A proclamation poured from her heart, and she wrote the following promises on a piece of paper: First, I refuse to feel sorry for myself. Instead of counting my troubles, I'll count my blessings. I will stay positive and upbeat! Next, I will be a model patient. I'll trust hospice to manage my pain. I know that my hospice team will always be there for me. And I'll welcome Sarah's help as well. I will let her know how much her help means to me. By looking after me, my daughter will become a wonderful caregiver. It's a gift I can offer her. And finally, I'll try to be calm as I face death. With God's help, this shall be my last expression of love to Sarah. I'll show her that goodbyes, while they may be very sad, can be said without fear or regret. I will teach my daughter how to die with grace and dignity.

Jane kept every one of her promises. She *was* a model patient. As expected, her hospice team was there for Jane; her pain was well-managed, and she was comfortable. And Sarah was there for her, too. Jane received all the help and support she needed. She remained strong and calm until she died peacefully in her home, exactly where she wanted to die. By witnessing her mother's love and faith, Sarah became a compassionate caregiver and felt appreciated.

As she witnessed her mother's grace, Sarah learned how to die with dignity. And as she received her mother's parting gifts, Sarah was transformed. By sharing this true story, we honor Jane's legacy. And as we admire her determination, we're reminded that God gives everyone the opportunity to be extraordinary.

★★★

If you knew that you only had one month or one week to live, what would you change? If you knew today was the last time you would see your loved ones, what would you do? What would you say to them?

★★★

Sometimes we help the dying; and other times, they help us.

95. More about Hope and Faith

Hope and faith have helped men, women, and children overcome bitter hardships and achieve extraordinary things. But are there examples of hope and faith in the animal kingdom as well? Are animals simply creatures of habit? Is instinct the only explanation for their epic journeys and complex behaviors? Or could it be that, on some level, hope and faith abound in nature? Consider the following facts.

- Gibbons, wolves, prairie voles, swans, French angel fish, turtle doves, Canadian geese, and bald eagles are among the known species that mate for life.

- Each year, many whale species migrate to cooler waters in the summer and to warmer waters in the winter. The gray whale travels the longest distance, a route of roughly 12,000 miles.

- The cliff swallows of San Juan Capistrano appear annually on March 19th after making a 6,000 mile journey from Argentina. This incredible phenomenon has endured for centuries.

- Nearing the end of their life cycle, salmon leave their ocean home to travel inland. It's a perilous, upstream journey that can stretch up to 900 miles. Salmon climb to elevations reaching 7,000 feet. Along the way, they hurdle twelve-foot waterfalls and pass through gauntlets of hungry bears. A large number of salmon fail to reach their final destination. Many die from exhaustion. Yet, enough survivors return to their mountain birthplace to spawn and ensure the future of their species.

- And monarch butterflies rule the insect world. Their unparalleled transcontinental and transatlantic migrations are the stuff of legends, requiring up to four generations of butterflies to complete a single round trip.

96. The Book of Revelation

Ministers preach about it. Dissertations are written on it. And seminary courses probe its mysteries. Indeed, the Book of Revelation, the last book of the New Testament, is a challenging read. Maybe its cryptic clues cannot be deciphered. Perhaps its enigmas shall remain unsolved. In any event, Revelation is a compelling prophecy; and no one knows when its drama will unfold. The author, Saint John, had a series of apocalyptic dreams that were chronicled in graphic detail. His warlike visions included a fiery red dragon, a sea beast with seven heads, scorpion tailed locusts, and lion–headed cavalry.

Biblical scholars continue to debate the meaning of Revelation's vivid symbolism. Nevertheless, Saint John's prophecies clearly herald the dawn of a new world, and they warn that our planet's rebirth will include periods of intense strife and suffering. Yet, perhaps the demons and their battles will be confined to the domain of human minds. Perhaps spiritual pain will be the cause of our scars.

In the war preceding our new world, maybe humankind shall conquer dualism and vanquish the ego. Maybe our rebirth will include epiphanies of greater awareness and self-realization, and the new dawn will bring an elevated spiritual consciousness and everlasting inner peace. Is it possible that genocide, exploitation, persecution, oppression, murder, and hatred are the monsters to be slain? Is it destined that love shall be the ultimate victor? Is it ordained that salvation is the prize, and heaven on earth shall be the victors' spoils?

97. Toby and Malaya

Toby's family was tight-knit, and he was still very young when stricken with pneumonia. His devoted mother, Malaya, stayed at Toby's side. She stroked his head and comforted him. She tenderly cared for him. But it wasn't enough, not on this day. And after Toby had taken his final breath, Malaya screamed and moaned. His death shocked the entire family. While they gathered and mourned, Malaya kept her vigil. She groomed Toby one last time, as if he still had somewhere important to go. Yet, at a moment like this, who can be sure what feelings are coming from a mother's heart? At a time such as this, who can be sure what thoughts are crossing the mind of an African chimpanzee?

★★★

Expressions of grief are widespread in the animal kingdom. And some groups of animals, especially primates, observe post-death rituals. Why have these behaviors evolved? What is their purpose? Do some animals use rituals as a way of saying goodbye? Or could it be that certain animals instinctively prepare their dead for an afterlife?

Adapted from a story by Lisa Miller

98. Plato's Cave

Could it be that human perceptions are often in conflict with reality? Are there illusions in our world? The following vignette is an adaptation from Plato's book *The Republic*, written in 360 BC. Socrates is teaching a lesson to a young student . . .

[Socrates] Let me show you how some perceptions of reality are more enlightened than others, and how truth can set us free. Imagine a small group of men living in a cave. They have been imprisoned in this cave since childhood. Because their bodies are chained and their necks are restricted, they can look only straight ahead. Located behind the men and near the cave's ceiling is a blazing fire; and between the fire and the prisoners is an elevated stage, not unlike the kind of stage used for a puppet show.

[Student] I see.

[Socrates] The stage features a parade of animal figures sculpted from stone. These carved objects are positioned in such a way that, as they move across the stage, the fire casts their shadows onto the wall facing the prisoners. The chained men see only the shadows of the various stone figures located on the stage behind them.

[Student] Yes. If they could not move their heads, the prisoners would see only the shadows moving across the wall of the cave.

[Socrates] You and I know that the prisoners are seeing an illusion of reality. Yet, if the men were to talk to one another, would they not give names to the shadow figures which appear before them?

[Student] True, they would.

[Socrates] The prisoners' reality would be nothing more than shadowy images of the actual carved figures. Yet, each shadow would soon be known by a name – a word assigned by the group of men.

[Student] No question, it would be so.

[Socrates] By using names to identify and to define the different shadows, the prisoners are now *thrice* removed from reality; for they have assigned names and meaning to shadows – shadows which were cast by stone figures that, in truth, were mere images of actual animals.

[Student] I see what you mean. Indeed, this is a very strange way to perceive reality.

[Socrates] Next, imagine that one prisoner is released. He will stand up, turn around, and see the blazing fire. Its brightness will blind him. But after a while, his eyes will adjust and he will see the stone figures used to create the shadows he previously viewed. Still, he will not recognize these figures at first. If the freed prisoner is told that the shadows he viewed were just illusions, he will be confused. For will he not believe that shadows are more real than carved images? To better understand the carved images, the former prisoner's eyes will need more time to adjust.

[Student] Yes, that is so.

[Socrates] Now, let us suppose the former prisoner is escorted outside of the cave. As he steps into the sunlight, would his eyes not, once again, be blinded by the brightness?

[Student] Of course, they would.

[Socrates] After a while, the man's eyes will adjust. But will he see the sun as the source of life? Will he recognize anything that *we* have found to be a more enlightened reality?

[Student] No, certainly not.

[Socrates] If he's told that the sun is the source of life, the former prisoner will disagree. In his ignorance and vanity, the man will argue that *he* is the source of life. After all, did he not name the shadows? But given more time for his eyes to adjust, the man will eventually conclude that the sun *is* the source of life. This more enlightened perception of reality will raise his consciousness. Then, would the man not want to share his new reality with the remaining prisoners?

[Student] Yes. He would want to do so right away.

[Socrates] So let us suppose the liberated man returns to the inside of the cave. Now he stands before the remaining prisoners and tries to teach them a more enlightened reality. But, would he not be mocked and ridiculed?

[Student] Indeed, he certainly would be.

[Socrates] And would the remaining prisoners not feel frightened or threatened by this man's new perception of reality? Were they able, might not the remaining prisoners attack and kill him?

[Student] I see what you mean.

[Socrates] Yet, the former prisoner is not bothered by ridicule; nor is he worried about being attacked and killed. For by now, the man's eyes have had even more time to adjust; and at last he understands that *God* is the true Source of life. With a perception of reality that is more enlightened still, the liberated prisoner has elevated his consciousness once again. The man isn't afraid to die because he sees that death is but another awakening, a passage which will take him from the shadows to the light. Moreover, he accepts the fact that each remaining prisoner must make his own one-of-a kind journey to discover the true Source of life. Then one by one, every deceptive shadow will dissolve in the timeless light of divine reality.

99. Living Your Faith

For thousands of years, historians have recorded the details of fierce battles and bloody wars. A significant number of these conflicts were religious wars, fought in the name of God. And while wars to end oppression are, at times, a justifiable part of the human condition, can we truly glorify our Creator by maiming and killing his children? Or is a *holy war* the ultimate oxymoron? Today, many people remain intolerant of religious views which differ from their own. Maybe that's one of the reasons why a growing number of young adults are rejecting organized religion. Yet, most people still believe in God. And surveys confirm that more and more adults are placing a high value on spiritual growth. So, is it really possible to glorify God without attending a formal worship service? And finally, how can people grow spiritually if they choose to dismiss religion?

First, understand that, as you become more loving, you become more Godlike. So perhaps the best way to honor and glorify God is to *live* your faith, to express greater love in what you say and do. The wonderful part of living one's faith is that everybody can choose to do it. In other words, it's not a question of money, health, or age. It doesn't matter if a person has gained social status or lives on a park bench. The seeker could be a stay-at-home mom or the president of a large corporation. Every person, regardless of individual circumstances, can choose to be more kind and helpful, to be more caring and compassionate, and to be more loving and forgiving. And by making a committed choice to live your faith – to *live* and *be* the love that you are – you will grow spiritually as well.

★★★

Nationality and culture aside, life's purpose is the same for everyone: to grow in faith and love. Our shared purpose is to elevate human consciousness. However, life's meaning is defined by each individual. Moreover, life's meaning is evolutionary; whereas humanity's collective purpose remains changeless. As people make choices and attach value to their behaviors, roles, and activities, every single day holds the potential for spiritual growth.

★★★

Growing pains are a natural part of the journey, yet some pathways are smoother and more direct than others. Spiritual growth is forever linked, as it must be, with divine reality. Indeed, our lives unfold on the stage of timeless truth, and God's plan serves as the world's backdrop. Woven into the tapestry of creation, this universal scenario is unaffected by human ignorance or denial, arrogance or disdain.

★★★

Spiritual work helps tame the human ego. By practicing love and forgiveness, a ravenous grizzly bear can be transformed into a harmless teddy bear.

★★★

Those who denounce God or deny his existence are, in truth, asking for divine help and healing.

★★★

In organized religion, covenants and traditions unite people, while doctrines and laws divide them.

100. Immortality

And God said . . .

First, look at life. Have you ever tried to extinguish life? Waste no effort trying. By my design, it cannot be done. For every life form that's threatened with extinction, countless others are born.

Next, look at love. Have you ever tried to capture love? Waste no effort trying. By my plan, it cannot be done. For each heart that's imprisoned, countless others are freed.

And finally, look at spirit — that which I breathe out. Have you ever tried to cripple spirit? Waste no effort trying. By my will, it cannot be done. Though it may be transformed, spirit is invulnerable. Though it may move from here to there, a soul can never be harmed.

Bring me the sword that slays love. Show me the arrow that kills spirit. And so I ask: How could you be anything but immortal?

★★★

Once, there was a time before you were. Yet, there shall never be a time when you are not.

★★★

If you believe your one life lasts forever, isn't it childish to think there is never-ending injustice?

101. Bedside Vigils

Imagine that your mother is nearing death. She's lying in a hospital bed, unable to speak. You approach her bedside. Sitting quietly, you create a calm, sacred space. Knowing that touch is important, you gently hold her hand and stroke her hair. Her muscles relax and her breathing eases. Your quiet presence is making a difference. Perhaps there's no need to say anything at all. Or maybe your heart will urge you to talk, to share a special memory one last time. Your mother hears every word, and your voice is a source of comfort.

Perhaps you will softly sing her favorite song. Or maybe there's something important to say about the past. Do you need to forgive your mother? If so, can you offer forgiveness at this very moment? Turn to God for courage. Then you might say, "Mom, I forgive you." Or perhaps you are seeking forgiveness. And if so, can you ask her to forgive you right now? Turn to God for strength. Then you might say, "Mom, I'm sorry. Please forgive me."

At the bedside, long periods of silence are natural; and they needn't be awkward. Yet, at just the right moment, you could instinctively lean close to her ear. And choosing your words carefully, you could whisper, "Thank you for being my Mom, for always taking care of me. I love you and will always miss you. But I want you to know that I'll be alright. It's okay to let go." Is there love more genuine than this? Is there a greater gift you can offer?

★★★

As you spend time with a loved one who is dying, it isn't helpful to deny what is happening. Nor does it help to deny your feelings about what is happening. Instead, try to accept the truth that nothing can be done to prevent a natural death; just as nothing can be done to stop a natural birth. Try to accept that you're not in control. By surrendering to this reality, you'll become more calm and strong. As you gain a sense of peace with impending death, your loved one will receive even more comfort from your presence. And your heart will remind you that words aren't always necessary within a sacred space.

★★★

As someone you love draws closer to death, questions arise. Why is he holding on? Is there unfinished business, something that must be said or done? Yet, such questions often bring angst and frustration; for the answers are beyond human reach. Follow your heart and do as you are led to do. Tell him that he is safe, and he is loved. Remind him that God shall never forsake or abandon him. Offer him a silent prayer; ask God's angels to gather around him, to guide and protect him. But remember to welcome each moment of life as the blessing and mystery it truly is. And accept that only God can know the day and hour of your loved one's final breath.

★★★

Mary, mother of Jesus, remained at the foot of the cross. There was little she could do but wait patiently. There was little she could do but be present with him. It was then Mary learned that waiting is the worst of times. Yet, the moment Christ died, his suffering was over. At last, he was free of pain. His sacrifice had ended; his legacy of hope had begun. And it was then Mary learned that waiting is the best of times.

102. Angel Helper: A Guided Imagery

O Merciful Father, we are grateful for your loving angels. We are grateful for their kindness and protection. And we are thankful for your guiding angels, the angels who offer comfort as we travel to our heavenly home. Amen

★★★

On your mind's artistic canvas, you are creating an image of a beautiful angel. This angel is compassionate yet strong, tender yet confident, majestic yet humble. It is remarkably agile and swift. Each movement is an inspired expression of grace. Use your mind to form a picture of this heavenly angel.

It is not by chance that this angel has appeared before your eyes; for at this very moment, he is searching for a helper. God uses this special angel to guide souls from earth to heaven. And in just a moment, you will witness one of those sacred journeys. As a helper, you will be right next to the guiding angel. You realize this opportunity is a wonderful blessing, and you have no fear or anxiety. You are calm, but there's also an eager anticipation.

And so, the journey begins. To your surprise, it's quite easy to travel at the angel's side – effortless, in fact. It's as if the two of you are attached by a magical tether. Your weightlessness keeps you in perfect harmony with every angelic motion. And the pathway is spectacular: celestial colors blending with cosmic pulsations, unworldly beauty merging with mind-blowing vistas. There are no edges or corners, ups or downs. You see the similarities between the unthinkably small and the unimaginably large. You hear primordial sounds and rhythms which are both alien, yet familiar. In awe of God's creations, you lose all sense of time and distance.

Now, a brilliant, swirling light appears. The guiding angel is leading you to an illuminated opening, a special gateway. Picture this alluring, white light. You are drawn to it. You feel its uplifting energy. Now you are travelling inside a connecting passageway, embraced by brilliant light. Here, your sensation of wonder is replaced by a feeling of peace, a peace so profound that *only* God could be the Source. Indeed, you are sensing a presence beyond description, a love that could only come from a God who *is* love. Heaven is very near.

The guiding angel pauses, and so do you. There's no need to go any farther. From here, heaven-bound souls are already immersed in songs of praise. From here, each precious soul is safe; its homecoming celebration has begun. Thus, your journey ends. As promised, you were the witness to a sacred crossing. You will, of course, take this pathway one more time: when *your* soul travels to eternity.

At just the right moment, you will approach heaven's threshold. At the appointed time, Jesus will extend his arms to greet you. And after Christ's healing embrace, God himself shall wipe away your tears. Until then, there's nothing to fear. There's no cause for worry. If it's helpful, you can return to this celestial pathway as often as you like. You can be an angel's helper over and over again. By doing so, you will come to know the journey well. And when you finally accept the certainty that you are safe and loved, you will feel the peace of God.

★★★

Where the mountain and the grain of sand are joined as one, where there is no difference between them, there you shall see the face of God. And if you choose to search for this holy place, then start the journey within your Sacred Heart. Look inward, and the truth shall set you free.

★★★

Spiritual work paves the way for a peaceful transition from this world to the next.

103. The Afterlife: A Realm of Unlimited Possibilities

The human experience includes both joys and sorrows. Though we celebrate great triumphs, we also endure bitter disappointments. Indeed, pain – whether it's physical, emotional, or spiritual – is an ongoing dimension of the human condition. Most of us are born into this world as students. We grow, we mature, and ever so slowly, we learn. Fortunately, teachers are born into this world as well; teachers who show us how to live and how to love; special men, women, and children who show us how to persevere; Spirit-guided teachers who show us how to forgive; and God-chosen leaders who inspire hope.

Jesus used both words and deeds to teach us how to live. He told his followers that there's no reason to worry about worldly things. He assured them, "Your Father knows what you need before you ask him." Jesus also said, "Seek the kingdom of heaven, and your earthly needs will be given to you as well." He reminded believers that there's no reason to be fearful of an uncertain future. He comforted his disciples by telling them, "Let not your hearts be troubled. Trust in God and trust also in me." Then Jesus said," In my Father's house are many rooms. If it were not so, I would have told you." Finally, he promised, "I am going there to prepare a place for you." By saying *let not your hearts be troubled* Jesus is teaching that when we have faith, there is no cause to worry; that when we choose to trust God – to invite his love into our heart – there is nothing to fear.

Christian theologians agree that *my Father's house* refers to heaven. And heaven's *many rooms* suggest a countless number of rooms. And in contrast to those found in man-made buildings, each heavenly room may be infinite in size. In truth, the vastness of God's creation is beyond our comprehension. Many rooms equate to an endless array of afterlife experiences. It suggests heavenly colors and beauty never before seen by human eyes. It hints of music and praise never before heard by human ears, and it promises joys unimagined by human minds. And will we not be able to shape our heavenly experiences? Made in God's image,

159

we are inherently creative. In this world, creative instincts are expressed through endeavors such as music, art, literature, and architecture. Yet, heavenly expressions hold the potential to be exponentially more creative. In heaven's realms, love and free will are manifested through acts of creation.

The afterlife is timeless. There are no clocks or calendars. And like the vastness of creation, eternity is beyond human understanding. In this world, people are invested in time. Our lives unfold in chronological order and include a past and a future. But instead of a horizontal timeline, picture a vertical line where time is not; where the past, the present, and the future are eternally joined as one. This image offers insights into heaven's timeless realm. And clearly, someone's life on earth – even if it lasts one hundred years or longer – is less than an instant compared to forever.

After telling his followers that God's house has many rooms, Jesus declared, "If it were not so, I would have told you." With this statement, Jesus is saying he would never teach something that isn't true. Next, he promised, "I am going there to prepare a place for you." Not only are his words a profound message of hope, it also means that each person's afterlife is a one-of-a-kind journey. Then he added, "Your Father has been pleased to give you the kingdom." In other words, heaven doesn't need to be earned. It's offered as a gift – a gift which flows from God's grace. In the Bible, we are promised there will be a day when there's no more death or mourning or crying or pain; and that God himself shall wipe away all tears. Heaven, then, is a realm of oneness, wholeness, and perfection. There's an intimate connection with all whom you've ever known and loved. There's no sense of worry, lack, or separation. There's no sense of fear or conflict, disappointment or guilt. And your heavenly body will be everlasting. It will be a body that never grows old or weak, sick or tired. In heaven, minds are lucid and bodies are perfect, for there are no betrayals in paradise.

Searching for words to describe the ineffable, God is both the Yin and the Yang, whole and complete. God is the Alpha and Omega, with neither beginning nor end. And he understands that everyone makes mistakes. So there's nothing that you can think or say or do that is beyond God's forgiveness. His love and grace have no boundaries. What's more, you are worthy of God's love. Think of it this way. If God really believes his children are unworthy, then why did he send a Savior? And where is the loving father who believes his children are undeserving of grace; undeserving of joy? Christ's victory over death is your divine assurance that life is eternal. The resurrection of Christ transformed the cross, an instrument of torture, into the ultimate symbol of hope. Scripture teaches that God *is* love and his presence is with you always. You are never truly alone, even for a moment. Ask God to help you experience his peace. Ask God to let you feel the comfort of his angels as they watch over you. Then, look upward and bathe in the healing Light of Jesus Christ.

★★★

In a timeless realm, can it ever be "too late" to invite the love of Christ into one's heart?

★★★

What is your vision of heaven? What will your heavenly room be like?

104. Suicide

On some level, we've already agreed to face the daunting challenges this world has to offer. Deep within each soul, there's an implicit understanding that pain is part of our earthly journey. That's why Saint Paul, in 1 Corinthians 10:13, has written about the promises God makes to his children. First, you will never be asked to learn a life lesson which is not required of everyone. Furthermore, God will not allow you to be tested beyond your strength. And finally, God always provides a way out, so that you can endure every trial and hardship which comes along.

But these divine promises raise profound questions. If there's never a situation which cannot be overcome, why do people commit suicide? Why does someone choose to take his own life? Individual motives for suicide are uniquely complex. Perhaps some people see it as a way to regain control, a way to ensure a self-determined future. But collectively, there's a common denominator among those taking their own life: the desire to escape pain. And unfortunately, pain comes in many forms. For example, someone might perceive himself as a burden to his loved ones, and the subsequent guilt and mental anguish might spark suicidal thoughts. Others become despondent over social rejection or broken relationships. Substance abuse and unexpected setbacks in health or finances can lead to thoughts of suicide. And as for people confronting physical pain, some have a higher tolerance for it, and less fear of it, than others.

Excruciating pain may cause an immediate desire to die. Moreover, people suffering from extended periods of mental and emotional pain – like fear, shame, despair, and hopelessness – can also lose their will to live. It happens more often than you might think. Of course, it's been documented that mental illness, including chronic depression, can trigger suicidal ideation as well. And spiritual pain is yet another source of self-destructive thoughts. There are times we become dispirited and lose our connection with God. We feel unloved, unworthy, and abandoned. We feel lost, broken, and disheartened. We lose our faith. And though periods of sadness are normal, it's never normal to begin making plans to take your own life.

Should you have persistent thoughts of suicide, or if you start working on a plan to carry it out, seek professional help immediately. Call the national suicide hotline at 800-273-TALK or dial 911. Know that God doesn't expect you to remain alone or isolated when facing tough times. In truth, God often inspires doctors, counselors, and other professional caregivers and works miracles through them.

Divine blessings include effective treatments for mental illness and potent medicines which mitigate pain. Heavenly aid may come from compassionate counselors or Spirit-guided clergy. And when you ask for guidance, God may lead you to inspirational teachers or uplifting support groups. Pray for help and wisdom. Pray for strength and courage. Remember that you needn't be alone. And finally, realize that problems are seldom as formidable as you perceive them to be. It's easy to become confused, especially when you're feeling sad. It's easy to conclude that your troubles are insurmountable when, in fact, they are not. And by asking for God's help, it will be possible to prevail over any challenge which comes your way.

★★★

Suicide has been called a permanent response to a temporary problem. Suicide is always a choice. It's a way out. But is it ever a wise choice? Is it ever the best way out?

★★★

Suicide is devastating to surviving family members and friends. Added to the normal grief which stems from losing a loved one, other issues arise. Things like: Why did it happen? This isn't natural. How could I have prevented it? I've never known anyone who has taken their own life. Will I see them in heaven? It doesn't make any sense to me. Where was God when this happened? And finally, someone will say: It's my fault. The resulting torment makes it more difficult for family and friends to heal and attain a sense of peace. And there's a stinging irony as well. While suicide takes only a moment, it leaves a lasting legacy of unanswered questions and inconsolable sadness.

★★★

Every choice has consequences. And there's an undeniable accountability to God for even the most desperate decision made during a dark time of weakness. Yet, perhaps human consequences needn't be eternal. If divine love has no limits – if God's grace is truly without boundaries – then maybe those who commit suicide will ultimately be able to find salvation. Each person's afterlife includes an infinite array of one-of-a-kind experiences and opportunities. We never stop growing. And with countless heavenly rooms, would Jesus not prepare a special place of healing and atonement for someone who has taken his own life? Could a Loving Father deny comfort to his child, broken in spirit?

★★★

When entrenched in a valley of darkness and despair, we must find the courage to shout, "God, help me!"

105. Unfinished Business

There are many ways to prepare for death. Some people focus on taking care of unfinished business. By making a Living Will and naming a Power of Attorney, people are able to maintain a sense of order and control. They thoughtfully bequeath their assets and personal property, and they appoint an Estate Executor to carry out their wishes. Quite often, people choose to write a legacy letter to their loved ones. Or perhaps a series of letters might be written, with certain ones to be opened and read at some point in the future. Another option is to create an audio or video legacy, a remembrance which can be heard or viewed by future generations. And yet, a review of unfinished business may initiate an entirely different journey: the pursuit of reconciliation.

★★★

People with terminal diseases commonly lose their appetite. They simply have no desire to eat. At that point, spiritual nourishment may be more important than food.

★★★

Based on the narratives of coma survivors, we know that people hear much better as other body functions slow down. As a result, there's seldom a need to shout at a loved one who's dying. A calm, quiet voice offers greater bedside comfort.

106. Relationships, Grief, and the Miracle of Healing

RELATIONSHIPS

Relationships: We're born into them, we seek new ones, and we learn so much from them. Complex by nature, relationships may include a mix of love *and* fear; a blend of selflessness *and* exploitation. As a result, relationships teach us how to be, and how not to be. It's true that relationships often come and go. Sometimes they end in anger, pain, and sadness. Then, we call them failed relationships. Yet if we've grown from the experience, could they really be failures?

Relationships that stretch over a long period of time usually provide our best opportunities for personal growth. Long-term interactions with family, friends, and life partners give us a chance to build character. There's a simple explanation for why we grow through relationships: They require work. Through them, we learn how to love and how to forgive. In healthy relationships, we learn how to put the needs of others ahead of our own. In balanced relationships, we learn kindness, compassion, and patience. In loving relationships, we learn how to hope, to trust, and to persevere. And each time a close relationship comes to an end, we grieve.

GRIEF

Today's psychologists widely agree that change – along with our perception of change – is the primary source of grief. Typically, we view change as a threat or a loss. Whether it's about a job, our health, our finances, a relationship, or that new stain on our favorite pair of jeans, each change that we face triggers a grieving process – a period of time when we assess the damage and sort through our feelings. And depending on someone's perceptions and choices, a single grief event may last anywhere from a moment to a lifetime. In reality, the mind can only assimilate tiny bits of change at a time. When too much change comes too quickly, we feel overwhelmed. We're literally stunned and unable to think clearly.

And of course, a loved one's death sparks our greatest sense of loss. Death is the transition from this world to the next, while grief is the pain felt by those left behind. When a friend, a life partner, or a family member dies, we miss their presence. We grieve, and the pain is very real. Death unleashes an emotional mix of anger, fear, guilt, and sadness. Sometimes, we're overcome by sorrow. We realize that our lives will never again be the same. During our darkest periods, we try to cope one day at a time – or perhaps just minute by minute. Although each path is different, common themes are found within mourning. Dr. Elisabeth Kubler-Ross was among the first to recognize that, as we grieve, there are usually periods of denial, anger, and sadness. And Kubler-Ross realized that as healing unfolds, it's possible to arrive at a place of acceptance – a moment when we choose to embrace a different life; a life that has a *new* normal. Understand that every journey, regardless of its length, begins with a first step. There's never a need to deny your feelings. There's never a need to be embarrassed by your pain. And there's no reason to feel guilty when a moment of happiness breaks through.

People make judgments about death. It's part of human nature. So for those who are old and suffering, death is merciful. But for the young, death is unfair. When parents bury their children, death is untimely. And if it's caused by a tragic accident or a criminal act, death is wrongful. Yet, arbitrary judgments may prolong someone's pain. They build barriers which prevent healing. As perceptions of injustice are reinforced, those who grieve run the risk of adopting a new, but negative, identity: the innocent victim. This disempowering self-image creates even more obstacles to healing.

When a life partner dies, people are particularly vulnerable to the hazards of obstructive judgments and perceptions. There can be added worries about safety, financial security, or personal well-being. And yes, identity issues persist as well. A woman may think, "I was a wife for such a long time, now I'm a widow. How does this change my life?"

Or a man might say, "When my wife was alive, I took good care of her. Now, there's no one who needs me." Ultimately, grief's pain cries out for healing; it cries out for a miracle.

THE MIRACLE OF HEALING

Spiritual teachers have suggested that healing requires a miracle. But if this is so, then why don't we see more evidence of miracles? Maybe the truth is hidden in plain sight. In other words, perhaps miracles are misunderstood. Most people believe that miracles happen rarely, if ever. It's also thought that miracles only occur on a grand scale, something so spectacular – such as Moses parting the Red Sea – that divine intervention is the only explanation. But are there other kinds of miracles too? Is it possible that miracles are happening all around us, but without any fanfare? Could God's healing work be so subtle as to go unnoticed?

Consider this scenario. Someone you know has recently died and a family member, Laura, is hurting from this loss. Though you didn't attend the funeral, two weeks later you happen to run into Laura at the grocery store. Out of kindness, you offer condolences and empathetic listening. Several minutes later, you and Laura hug and say goodbye. Was this a chance encounter? Either way, it's one that you soon forget. Yet, perhaps something else is happening, something you're unaware of. Over the next few weeks, other people run into Laura as well. And they, too, extend kindness and compassion. As a result, Laura is uplifted. Her pain is fading a bit, and she's beginning to feel better. She's starting to heal. And your kindness – your random encounter – has played an important role. Why? Because kindness brings comfort; comfort awakens love; love nurtures forgiveness; forgiveness promotes healing; and healing sparks happiness. Is this not a miracle? And is it not likely that similar miracles are happening all over the world, each and every day?

Make no mistake, emotional and spiritual healing requires work; work like prayer, meditation, counseling, support groups, and so on. Still, genuine healing cannot occur without forgiveness. Forgiveness *is* healing, and it requires introspection and mindfulness. Forgiveness might mean asking someone to forgive you, including your loved one who has died. It could mean asking God to forgive you, or it could mean forgiving God — if you believe that a Higher Power has caused your pain. Forgiveness might mean letting go of grievances and forgiving people who are no longer in your life. And always, you must be willing to forgive yourself. Each step promotes healing. Each one lessens your pain and sadness. Most importantly, each step requires a decision, an empowering choice that only you can make.

Quite often, forgiveness needs a catalyst — a gentle nudge to get things started. So in this sense, every act of kindness is a reminder that it's okay to forgive. Moreover, each time someone chooses to forgive, they affirm their earlier choice to seek healing. It's another example of the paradox that healing takes time, but time itself does not heal. Healing needs both time *and* forgiveness. After a loved one dies, you might benefit from other work as well. For instance, pause to redefine who you are. Stop to reassess life's purpose and meaning. Identify the things in your life that remain important to you. And consider assigning greater value to things in life that are less transient; things that can't be taken from you, like volunteer work.

After a long string of gray, dismal days, it's easy to forget that — hidden behind the sky's thick clouds — the sun is shining brightly. In truth, the sun always shines, even when dense clouds are blocking its light. Grief is like a formidable barrier of dark clouds, clouds that stand between you and God's love. Day after day, you feel tired, sad, and lonely. Obscured by clouds of grief, God seems so distant, so far away. Yet, forgiveness will lift your clouds of despair. One by one, they will drift away. Aided by time, forgiveness will remove all of the barriers which stand between you and God's love. Like the sun, divine Light is always shining. Know that God shall never abandon you. He has not left you, and he never will.

★★★

We come into this world with family. Then, we seek and connect with those who are familiar.

★★★

Grief and healing journeys are one-of-a-kind. The Kubler-Ross model includes stages of denial, bargaining, anger, sadness, and acceptance. Yet, these stages may occur in any sequence. And while some stages might be skipped entirely, others could be experienced numerous times.

★★★

Albert Einstein said, "There are two ways to live. You can live as if nothing is a miracle, or you can live as if everything is a miracle."

★★★

During a contemplative moment, Elizabeth Kubler-Ross wrote: Should you shield the canyons from the windstorms, you would never see the beauty of their carvings.

107. The ten Boom Family

Casper and Cornelia ten Boom were horrified by the Nazi persecution of Jews during the Second World War. They were Dutch Christians who lived their faith and taught God's Word to their children, including daughters Corrie and Betsie. The ten Booms welcomed scores of Jews into their home, offering them food and shelter and helping them avoid the death camps. When German soldiers finally discovered what the ten Booms were doing, the entire family was imprisoned. Corrie and Betsie were separated from their parents and transported to Ravensbruck Concentration Camp, where conditions were dire. On one occasion, they watched as a woman was brutally beaten by a guard. Corrie noticed that, in the midst of this savage assault, Betsie started praying. Later, Corrie whispered to her sister, "I saw you praying for that poor woman." And Betsie replied, "Yes, I was praying. But my prayers were for the guard."

★★★

Shortly before dying at Ravensbruck, Betsie assured Corrie, "There is no pit so deep that God is not deeper still."

★★★

Surmounting incredible circumstances, Corrie ten Boom survived her incarceration. She spent much of her life helping concentration camp survivors and teaching lessons of forgiveness. Corrie wrote several books as well, including her bestseller *The Hiding Place.*

108. Gloria Patri

Glory be to the Father, and to the Son, and to the Holy Spirit;

As it was in the beginning, is now, and ever shall be;

World without end. Amen

Early Christian liturgy, author unknown

109. Eternal Suffering

God doesn't change, but our perception of him changes. Dante wrote that the gate to hell has a warning which reads: *Abandon hope, all those who enter here.*

★★★

Hell has been described as a separation from God's presence; an everlasting state in which God's love cannot be experienced.

★★★

What happens to the souls of those who spurn God's love?

★★★

If God *is* love, then love is omnipotent, omniscient, and omnipresent.

If love is all-powerful, all-knowing, and ever-present, then love has no boundaries.

If love has no boundaries, then love is timeless.

If love is timeless, then love is changeless.

If love is changeless, then love has no exceptions.

If love has no exceptions, then love excludes no one.

If love excludes no one, then there's no divine intent for love to be withheld.

And if there's no divine intent for love to be withheld, then is hell self-imposed?

Lacking God's intention to withhold love, there's no theological foundation for eternal suffering. In other words, there isn't a reason to *not* experience God's presence, except as a personal choice. This opens the door to an everlasting hope of atonement and salvation. Could the afterlife hold opportunities for lost souls to be sanctified and to *choose once again?*

★★★

Although hell might be a product of the mind, it's a real place nonetheless.

110. Ways of the World

Dreams: Align your dreams with the world in which you live. For instance, if you live in a free society and your dream is to be a shopkeeper; and if you hope to provide for your family by that means, then you'll need to offer quality goods at a fair price. Your shop must have a polite, helpful staff. Your business must be stocked with items that people need or want. You should choose a suitable location and keep regular hours. And finally, your shop must generate a profit. Without an appropriate business model, your dreams may be crushed. Freedom guarantees opportunity, not success. Thus, it pays to be wise in the ways of the world.

★★★

Economies: Free societies and free enterprise are as compatible as fresh air and sunshine. A free market elevates the standard of products and services, and it promotes affordable prices too. Competitive, unregulated commerce maintains a helpful balance among supply, quality, and cost. Therefore, the poor and disadvantaged benefit from a free market economy more so than any other demographic.

★★★

Money, Science, and the Golden Rule: Congruent with the ways of the world, those who possess the gold shall rule; money is never a problem unless you don't have it; and scientists are not immune to the influences of arrogance, vanity, and greed.

★★★

Politics: Most politicians, like everyone else, are doing the best they can. Still, it's an arena which obviously attracts those seeking power and authority. Thus, there's always the possibility of corruption. In a representative government, for instance, politicians face the temptation of placing self-interest above the common good of their constituents. The governmental policies of a democracy, of course, should promote personal liberty and equality. What's more, a smaller, less intrusive government tends to be more efficient than a larger, more controlling one. In a perfect world, governments will help people with disabilities or special needs. This kind of help should be life-long, if necessary. And governments, ideally, will provide assistance to individuals and families recovering from catastrophes as well. Yet, there's a fine line between aid and dependency. Programs leading to long-term entitlement among able segments of the population may actually hinder the pursuit of a meaningful life. Sometimes, such programs come from good intentions gone awry. Other times, politicians discretely gain power by supporting burdensome programs which, in truth, help no one. Either way, oppression and exploitation defy God's will. In free societies, beneficent governments add a helpful degree of structure and order. However, the political leaders of socialist, communist, Marxist, fascist, and totalitarian societies maintain and expand their control through force and by enacting laws which stifle freedom and opposition. Fortunately, it is God – not government – who stands as the ultimate protector of liberty and equality.

★★★

Religion: On one hand, religion has long been abused by individuals seeking personal glory. But on the other hand, religion has inspired and uplifted countless men and women in every corner of the world. As always, atrocities are committed by people, not by churches, temples, mosques, synagogues, or ashrams. And obviously, the world religions that promote love and kindness are the ones which honor God.

★★★

Ministry: Nearly everyone has the opportunity to engage in a ministry. At their most fundamental level, ministries express love. A ministry can be as simple as offering a friendly smile. It can be as unassuming as being a good listener. There are ministries of presence and touch; encouragement and helpfulness; kindness and compassion; and ministries of respect, humility, and selfless service. And yes, there are high profile ministries as well – ones that reach out to every continent and culture.

However, ministries which attain a grand scale are not inherently more important than their smaller counterparts. Ministries of all types and sizes find favor with God.

★★★

Love *vs.* Sex: Love is an expression of the heart, not the mind. And sex is an expression of the mind, not the body. Love is pure and innocent giving – a gift that's freely offered without conditions or concern for oneself. Within a holy relationship, consensual sex is a manifestation of love. Promiscuous sex, however, is entirely self-serving. Actually, immoral behavior is a substitute for something which the unconscious mind thinks is missing. Most often, the missing "something" is a meaningful relationship with God.

★★★

Causes can add meaning to life, and they give people the feeling that they're making a difference. As it happens, people really do make the world a better place by extending kindness and helpfulness through worthy causes. Ideally, a cause will promote love, not fear.

★★★

Taxes are firmly entrenched within governmental rule of law. Jesus acknowledged this by saying, "Give back to Caesar what is Caesar's, and to God what is God's." However, in a perfect world, governments will be held accountable for their stewardship of tax revenues. And finally, free societies shouldn't allow taxes to become an unbearable burden.

★★★

Death: On the physical plane, death is final, absolute, and often tinged with sadness. It is nature's counterpart to birth. Yet, mortality applies only to the body. For on the spirit plane, death is a transition – the end of one chapter and the start of a new one. While endings are bittersweet, beginnings are filled with joyful expectations.

111. Doxology

Praise God, from whom all blessings flow;

Praise Him, all creatures here below;

Praise Him above, ye heavenly host;

Praise Father, Son, and Holy Ghost. Amen

Christian liturgy by Thomas Ken (1637-1711)

112. The Story of Joseph

Many experts, including secular critics, point to the Bible as the greatest book ever written; and the story of Joseph is one of the reasons why. It has all the ingredients of an epic drama: wealth, power, injustice, irony, faith, suffering, wisdom, mercy, God, and destiny. Joseph's compelling riches to rags to riches journey has both a happy ending and a moral. And it chronicles key events in the history of God's chosen people, the Israelites. Joseph's father, Jacob, was the patriarch of the twelve tribes of Israel. King David descended from this lineage, and Jesus, as prophesized, was of the Davidic line.

Here's an overview of this compelling story found in the closing chapters of Genesis. Joseph was a young man blessed with many talents, and he had a remarkable faith as well. His father, Jacob, was the son of Isaac and the grandson of Abraham, founder of the Jewish nation. Jacob recognized that Joseph was special and stood apart from his other children. But Jacob's love for his gifted son sparked jealousy among several of Joseph's brothers. Ultimately, his enraged brothers kidnapped Joseph and sold him into slavery. Next, they convinced Jacob that his beloved son had been killed by a wild animal. And while Jacob mourned, the brothers were certain they would never see Joseph again.

Against his will, Joseph was taken to Egypt and was imprisoned there. But if Joseph was indeed shocked or angered by his new circumstances, he didn't show it. He never wallowed in self-pity. Among his many gifts, Joseph had the ability to interpret dreams. And much like today, the people of those times were keenly interested in dreams and their hidden meanings. Even the prison guards could see that Joseph was a wise and clever man. And his reputation as a dream savant eventually led to an audience with the most powerful man in Egypt.

The pharaoh was deeply troubled by a recurring dream, and none of his advisors were able to determine its meaning. So Joseph, a humble prisoner, was summoned to the royal palace. The pharaoh said, "I had a dream, and no one can interpret it. I understand that you can tell me its meaning." Joseph replied, "I cannot do it, but God will provide the answer you desire."

After listening to the details of the dream, Joseph offered his interpretation – the message God was sending to the pharaoh. Joseph explained that Egypt would have seven years of abundance followed by seven years of famine. Then, he advised the pharaoh to appoint a trusted person to manage his land and his harvests. Joseph said that by saving a portion of crops during the plentiful years, Egypt's people would not starve to death during the years of famine.

With his insightful response, Joseph gained favor with the pharaoh. The king, in fact, appointed Joseph to oversee the ambitious plan needed to avert disaster. Instantly, the former prisoner had become a respected commissioner. And soon thereafter, Joseph was wealthy and powerful. His authority was second only to the pharaoh's. Yet, Joseph was uncertain of what the future might hold. He had no idea that God was planning a family reunion.

An unlikely sequence of events brought Joseph's brothers to Egypt. And though Jacob still believed that Joseph was dead, the jealous brothers learned of Joseph's rise to prominence. After returning home, the devious brothers had little choice but to tell their father that Joseph was alive. Jacob, thrilled by the news, travelled to Egypt. And there, father and son were joyfully reunited.

The story ends with Joseph's contrite brothers bowing down to him and pleading for mercy. But Joseph told them, "Don't be afraid. Am I in the place of God? You intended to harm me, but God intended it for good; for the saving of many lives. So, fear not. I will provide for you and your children."

★★★

Abraham, Jacob, and Joseph were blood relatives. But what else did they have in common? How did they gain favor with God? Why were Moses and the prominent leaders of this era chosen above all others? What does it mean to have God's favor? And finally, can anyone become a servant of the Lord, or is it just for "special" people?

First, look at the attributes shared by Moses, Abraham, Jacob, and Joseph. Each man loved God profoundly. Each one had a deep and abiding faith. Each man trusted God; and each one was willing to do God's work. To say it another way, every one of these men gained favor with God because they loved him, trusted him, and had an unwavering faith. They were uniquely suited to promote God's will. Bear in mind that during biblical times, most people were still worshiping pagan gods. Very few believed in one Supreme Creator. And even fewer believed they could have a personal relationship with God.

Finding favor with God is, in truth, having the qualities needed to be one of his "special agents." God doesn't love some of his children more than others. He simply calls on those who are most able and willing to serve him. He picks just the right person for every assignment. And yes, as we grow in love, each one of us can be a faithful servant of the Lord.

★★★

177

As for the twelve tribes of Israel, some prospered while others did not. The tribes which lacked faith were lost to the temptations of the secular world.

★★★

Physician and scientist Robert Lanza isn't afraid to think outside the box. He believes that the things around us exist only during the moments in which we observe them. Actually, it isn't so much the observer; it's the observer's consciousness. In other words, Mount Rushmore exists only when there's a tourist – and his consciousness – visiting a particular location in South Dakota. Lanza suggests that wherever you find consciousness, you will find things like soil, rocks, water, clouds, and so on. And there will be grass and flowers and trees as well. Indeed, he believes our entire universe is the product of consciousness.

As it turns out, Lanza's radical theory is backed by sound reasoning. Remember, everything we can see and touch – both the animate and the inanimate – is comprised of tiny, vibrating strands of energy. And those infinitesimal strands of energy continuously go back and forth between our physical universe and somewhere unknown. They are neither here, nor there. That is, until someone is observing them. Then they stay fixed in our world. It's a key principle of quantum physics. And it's important to note that observers are interchangeable, their personal identities appear to be irrelevant.

So Mount Rushmore, the one-of-a-kind sculpture of four U.S. Presidents, will be seen by each person and every group of people standing at that spot. This reality offers strong evidence that human beings are truly interconnected. Because if we were not, then one tourist may see a mountain sculpture, but the next person might see a barren desert, and the person after that might see ocean waves breaking on a shore. Yet, our interconnectedness goes far deeper than this.

If, for example, there are sheep grazing in a field; and if a shepherd and a wolf happen to be nearby, then both the shepherd *and* the wolf will see the same sheep. What's more, each individual lamb will see the same shepherd and wolf. Indeed, every living creature in the vicinity – by means of its consciousness – will see the same grazing sheep, the same shepherd and wolf, and the same grass, flowers, insects, birds, trees, and clouds. And while each life form may view the world from an entirely different perspective, *all* organic life is interconnected on some level. Therefore, life and consciousness clearly have individual *and* collective dimensions.

★★★

Dr. Lanza's theory proposes that *life* has created the universe, not the other way around. And perhaps this paradigm shift will help scientists connect the dots which lead to God.

★★★

It seems as though modern physics and the Bible really do share common ground. For people of faith, the world's interconnectedness brings new meaning to the mission of caring for our brothers and sisters. This universal connectedness, or synchronicity, sheds new light on what it means to be good stewards of our planet, and what it truly means to love our neighbors. And the complex relationships we have with God's creations help us understand that *love* is what connects us. Love is what joins and binds us. That, indeed, love is *all* there is.

PART TWO

INSPIRED MEDITATION

PRELUDE TO MEDITATION

Meditation and prayer are closely linked, and Christians have practiced the art of meditation for centuries. It's believed that Jesus meditated regularly, especially when he was alone and removed from the rigors of his ministry. Quite simply, meditation is spiritual work which helps us grow closer to God. And by establishing a stronger connection with God, we reach a greater understanding of divine truth and reality. Thus, we're better prepared to help others and ourselves; and we're better equipped to serve the Lord. Meditation provides the tools we need to cope with the trials and hardships that are sure to come our way.

While meditation doesn't change what actually happens, it changes our *perception* of what happens – a giant step forward as we strive to maintain our sense of well-being and inner peace. Meditation promotes spiritual growth, which in turn empowers us to distinguish between the meaningful and the meaningless. What's more, it leads us to look inward for God's love, rather than outward.

The reflections in Part One have built the required spiritual foundation to move forward in your journey. Part Two contains 365 meditations, enough to last an entire year. They are written from God's point of view – or from the perspective of Jesus, if you prefer. Of course, you could read all of the meditations in a single day. But if you do this, consider reading them again. Otherwise, their effectiveness will be greatly diminished. Think of these meditations as daily devotions if you wish. And to gain optimal benefit, follow the guidelines suggested below.

First, read the day's meditation. Next, pause for a few minutes to reflect on its meaning. A meditation, much like a parable, typically has multiple levels of assimilation and application. Then, reflect on the benefits of this lesson if you were to apply its spiritual concept. How might this new idea be helpful on a day-to-day basis? How could this new insight improve your life? Morning is the perfect time to do this work and set the stage for a day of learning. It should take only fifteen minutes or so.

Next, it's time to integrate the meditation into your daily routine. As the day unfolds, apply the spiritual concept to every situation you face, without exception. Continue to remind yourself of the message and its meaning, and remain vigilant in its application to each conflict or problem that arises.

Around midday, read the meditation again. Reflect once more on its meaning, helpfulness, and integration. Remember to apply its lesson to every circumstance which comes your way that afternoon and evening. This follow-up reading and reflection should take only five minutes or so.

As you approach the day's end, read the meditation one last time. Reflect on its meaning and pause to look back on the day's events. Were you able to apply its message to every situation without exception? Why or why not? Did the integration of this spiritual lesson provide the benefit you had hoped for? Why or why not? The evening review and evaluation should take only ten minutes or so.

These Christian-rooted meditations are, by design, brief and to the point. Therefore, you can invest as little as thirty minutes to complete each day's readings, reflections, and concluding evaluation. And while there are other kinds of meditations and different ways to practice them, this recommended approach will nurture a favorable outcome. You will also find that many of the lessons share similar themes. So there are, in fact, a number of chances to learn and apply each spiritual concept. The bottom line is that spiritual lessons must be integrated if they are to be life-changing.

Don't be too hard on yourself during the end-of-day introspection and review. Spiritual growth, by its very nature, is a work in progress. Sometimes it takes weeks, months, or even years to achieve significant breakthroughs. Most often, progress is gradual; and results, though very real, are difficult to measure.

Each morning, ask God to provide the strength, wisdom, and guidance needed to achieve the successful outcome you desire. With Jesus at your side, you will never be alone in your journey. Moreover, those who complete their one year commitment to meditation will, with God's help, experience a profound transformation. And as you embrace and bless every trial which comes your way – as you endure life's storms and keep your faith – heaven shall look upon you and rejoice!

MEDITATION ONE

Your mind cannot distinguish reality from illusion when both are presented with equal conviction. That is why reality is the heart's domain. I tell you truly: Your heart will counsel you to express love and kindness in every situation. Today, follow your heart in all that you say and do.

MEDITATION TWO

I ask you to be in the world, but not of it. Therefore, strive to maintain an inner peace, even as you face hardship. Strive to keep a sense of calmness, even as you face persecution. Rise above the world's relentless drama. Work on this today.

MEDITATION THREE

By my design, you are uniquely creative; and by my will, you have a loving nature. By my design, you are a light in the world; and by my will, you have an immortal soul. Today, remember how I have made you. Today, remember who you truly are.

MEDITATION FOUR

My perfection surrounds you. Look at the world and behold my beauty. Look at your life and see my glory. Today, your life is sufficient proof of my existence and my love. Today, you have ample evidence that I shall never forsake you.

MEDITATION FIVE

Why let worldly troubles diminish your love? Today, your smile will welcome the people who approach you. Your friendliness will uplift the people close to you, and your courage will inspire the people around you. Today, allow your love to shine forth in dazzling brilliance!

MEDITATION SIX

The world is filled with things that come and go. Yet, you needn't be alarmed; for what is real is shapeless and timeless. Believe me when I say: Spirit is your true identity. And as you place greater faith in the unseen, you will receive my gift of peace. Work on this today.

MEDITATION SEVEN

I am the Comforter who walks at your side. I am the Protector who is with you always. Today, you are safe and you are loved. Accept this reality and be free at last!

MEDITATION EIGHT

My creations are formed in innocence, for how could it be otherwise? Today, look upon all people and all things, and judge them not. As the day unfolds, your eyes will see only innocence. And then, you may rest easy.

MEDITATION NINE

A false reality cannot solve your problems anymore than a serpent can be your Savior. I am the way and the truth and the light. Today, trust is the solution to all of your problems. Today, my love is your salvation.

MEDITATION TEN

Denigration and exploitation only lead to despair. Believe me when I say: Morality is a better choice. As the day unfolds, make sure that your choices express righteousness. Treat others as you would have others treat you. Work on this today.

MEDITATION ELEVEN

My children are uniquely individual, yet equally loved. Outward appearances mean nothing to me. So hear the truth: Unity celebrates the things which are shared, and it respects the things which are different. Today, honor humanity by looking beyond the superficial.

MEDITATION TWELVE

You are obsessed with control. Yet, can you stop the sun from rising? Can you keep the tides from coming in and going out? Believe me when I say: You have no idea what you really need. Therefore, trust the One who loves you more than any other. Surrender to the One who truly knows your needs.

MEDITATION THIRTEEN

I see your times of sadness and your days of despair. So listen to the truth: The past can no longer harm you. Let go of your pain, and I will wipe away your tears. Let go of your suffering, and I will hold you in my arms. Reflect on this today.

MEDITATION FOURTEEN

Some days may seem boring. Other days may seem uneventful or mundane. But instead of complaining, use this time to rest and gain strength. Welcome these calm waters as a needed respite. And when the next storm arrives, you will persevere. Remember this today.

MEDITATION FIFTEEN

Is wealth measured by what you steal? Is charity defined by what you keep? As the day unfolds, focus on giving. For as you give, you receive. And as you give to others, you give to me. Reflect on this today.

MEDITATION SIXTEEN

Just as a carpenter needs many tools, a teacher needs honesty, gentleness, patience, and compassion. Be my faithful servant this day. Keep an open mind and an open heart; for today, you are a teacher of love.

MEDITATION SEVENTEEN

At times, the world seems foreboding. At times, the world seems dark and gloomy. But this is a new and different day! Today, my light shines upon you. Today, you have nothing to fear.

MEDITATION EIGHTEEN

Why do you value self-reliance? Why do you cling to an illusion? Trust me when I say: You are completely dependent on me. Today, reflect on what this means.

MEDITATION NINETEEN

Whisper my name and take my right hand. Together, we will explore everything the world has to offer. Together, we will climb to unimagined heights. Today, we are inseparable. Today, we are joined as one.

MEDITATION TWENTY

Call out to me, and I will help you. Reach out to me, and I will guide you. Come to me, and I will protect you. Do these things today, and walk with confidence.

MEDITATION TWENTY-ONE

Why travel far and wide in your search for wholeness? Why journey here and there in your search for contentment? Today, come to the One who heals like no other. Today, turn to the One who gives heavenly peace.

MEDITATION TWENTY-TWO

My light will guide you from the temporal to the eternal. And my truth will lead you from illusion to reality. So I ask you to do one simple thing: Look closely at those who come your way. Look into their eyes and their hearts. Do this today, and you shall see love in all its glory!

MEDITATION TWENTY-THREE

Why stray from the One who comforts you? Why wander from the One who keeps you safe? Today, my mercy is your armor; so be not afraid. Today, my grace is your shield; so be not worried.

MEDITATION TWENTY-FOUR

Why do you wish to be a judge? I tell you the truth: The strain of endless condemnation will surely exhaust you. Today, see the world through innocent, childlike eyes. Do this, and be humbled by the holiness around you.

MEDITATION TWENTY-FIVE

Honesty is a virtue of the saints. And believe me when I say: Honesty demands that you be true to yourself. As the day unfolds, remember that truth and love are indivisible. Today, choose to distance yourself from dreamers who attach little value to honesty.

MEDITATION TWENTY-SIX

Do you want to please me? Do you want to honor the One who has made you? Then, simply *be* the love that you are. Do this today; and with you, I shall be pleased!

MEDITATION TWENTY-SEVEN

The world is your classroom, and today's assignment is to grow in faith. Your homework is to be kind and helpful, loving and trusting. Did I not teach this lesson long ago? As the day unfolds, remember to be a happy learner.

MEDITATION TWENTY-EIGHT

Your mind screams: *Do something now!* Yet, your heart whispers: *Wait quietly for guidance.* Today, wait patiently for my counsel. Today, be still and know that I am God.

MEDITATION TWENTY-NINE

Kindness is seldom heralded, and compassion is rarely reported. Therefore, disregard cynical accounts of the world. I tell you truly: Love is more alive than you can imagine. Today, offer kindness to someone you do not know. Today, offer comfort to a stranger.

MEDITATION THIRTY

Only forgiveness can unbind the chains of unworthiness and guilt. Only forgiveness can unlock the shackles of heartache and pain. So walk with me today. And as you hold my hand, let go of the past. Do this; then celebrate your freedom!

MEDITATION THIRTY-ONE

I am the Source of inspiration. As you help someone, you needn't worry about what to say or what to do; for I will direct you. Today, be confident and self-assured as you look for opportunities to serve. And at just the right moment, I will whisper words of wisdom and guidance.

MEDITATION THIRTY-TWO

I am the Source of comfort. As you walk through the shadows of your darkest valley, even there you can reach out to me; even there, you can take my right hand. Make this the day you choose to trust me wholly. Do this one simple thing today. Then, rest easy.

MEDITATION THIRTY-THREE

Look at the parade of jugglers passing by. Observe the excitement. Watch the circus clowns as they mingle with the crowd. Yet, resist the temptation to join them. Today, choose to rise above the foolish masses. Choose to follow me.

MEDITATION THIRTY-FOUR

As the Source of gifts and blessings, I ask you to receive as generously as you give. In truth, both giving *and* receiving are expressions of love. They are, indeed, of equal value. Today, welcome all gifts and blessings which come your way. And remember to accept them cheerfully!

MEDITATION THIRTY-FIVE

Although you can change your mind, your mind cannot change you. Real change is the heart's domain. Lasting change is invariably heart-driven. Today, choose to make a positive change. Make any change you wish. But remember, it must be heartfelt.

MEDITATION THIRTY-SIX

The love I freely offer is sufficient for you to confront hardship. The grace I freely offer is sufficient for you to find peace. Yet, if you must have more, allow my promise of heaven to nourish your hope. Today, allow heaven's certainty to sustain you.

MEDITATION THIRTY-SEVEN

I am the Source of peace. I am the Shepherd who does not leave your side. Therefore, let not your heart be troubled. Today, I hold you in my arms. Today, your regrets are prayers of thanksgiving and your tears are songs of praise!

MEDITATION THIRTY-EIGHT

As the Source of hope, believe me when I say: Where my children join for safety, I am there. Where my servants join for comfort, I am there. And where the faithful join for healing, I am there. This day, my light shall brighten your path. Today, go forth with confidence.

MEDITATION THIRTY-NINE

There are those who wonder: *Why do I never receive the day I hope for?* But this is a new and different day! Therefore, make no decisions without my help. Be Spirit-guided in all that you say and do. Work on these things today, tomorrow, and on the days after. Make them part of your routine. And before long, you will realize: *Today, I received the day I hoped for!*

MEDITATION FORTY

Will you join with me in Spirit? It is easier to do than you may think. Can you celebrate a sunset? Can you marvel at a rose? Can you whistle a song? Can you swoon with a lover? Today, be earnest and creative as you join with me in Spirit.

MEDITATION FORTY-ONE

Worldly things are here for one moment and gone the next. Even a star will shine but a short time compared to forever. Yet, nothing that is holy can be threatened, and nothing that is sacred can disappear; for the holy and the sacred are eternal. Today, embrace the truth that your soul is immortal.

MEDITATION FORTY-TWO

Jobs and careers are transient. Even relationships come and go. But do not confuse change with failure. Every change is an opportunity to grow in love and faith. Each new beginning is a chance to draw closer to me. And as those who are wise have learned: Not every wanderer is lost. Remember this today.

MEDITATION FORTY-THREE

You seek approval from those around you. You want affirmation from those close to you. Yet, such things are not what you *truly* yearn for. Popularity is fickle, and words of praise quickly fade. Today, follow the Shepherd whose voice you know. Do this, and receive your heart's desire.

MEDITATION FORTY-FOUR

Each new day might offer an unexpected gift. Each new day might bring an unforeseen blessing. Sometimes, my gifts are recognized as blessings. Often, they are seen as obstacles. And at times, my gifts go entirely unnoticed. So hear the truth: Even a miracle can be difficult to see. Reflect on this today.

MEDITATION FORTY-FIVE

I am the Source of calmness. Indeed, the most turbulent waters are stilled by my presence. Therefore, as you confront hardship, pour your heart out to me. Hold nothing back. Tell me about your deepest fears and darkest worries. Today, confide and trust in me.

MEDITATION FORTY-SIX

As you grow in love, feelings of emptiness begin to wane. As you grow in faith, feelings of inadequacy start to fade. And as you grow closer to me, you will gain a steadfast confidence. Today, invite me to walk with you. Do this, and the world will be less daunting.

MEDITATION FORTY-SEVEN

I am the Protector who does not sleep. I am the Comforter who requires no rest. Never hesitate to say: *God, help me!* Today, you needn't be alone. Turn to me the moment you feel threatened. Reach out to me at the first sign of trouble. Do this, and be not afraid.

MEDITATION FORTY-EIGHT

At times, routines can be boring. One day is the same as another. And the following day is like the one before it. Yet, even on the most ordinary day, you might witness a miracle. So today, be prepared for something extraordinary.

MEDITATION FORTY-NINE

My nature is to freely offer gifts and blessings, and your nature is to gratefully receive them. Yet, I say: Those who dwell on past regrets are not ready to receive today's gifts. And those who dwell on future worries are not able to accept today's blessings. Choose to live this day in the present moment. Open your heart and your arms to me.

MEDITATION FIFTY

The world is filled with distractions; and at times, you push me aside. These are the moments when you feel sadness, frustration, anxiety, and disappointment. But this is a new and different day! Today, keep an open mind as you focus on me. And by remaining vigilant, you can expect moments of peace, happiness, contentment, and fulfillment.

MEDITATION FIFTY-ONE

Trust me, and I will take you to a breathtaking vista. Yet, remember that life is both the destination *and* the journey. Therefore, welcome your triumphs *and* your trials. Embrace your gains *and* your losses. Today, give praise to all that comes your way!

MEDITATION FIFTY-TWO

I see your moments of triumph. And I see your troubled times as well. So I ask: Why do you not come to me? Is there a provider more generous; a comforter more gentle? Is there a protector who's stronger; a counselor who's wiser? Today, reflect on our relationship. What does it mean to you?

MEDITATION FIFTY-THREE

I hear the rumblings. One will say: *My health would be perfect, if only* . . . . Another will think: *My job would be ideal, if only* . . . . And yet another will complain: *My marriage would be wonderful, if only* . . . . So I tell you: Bless all things just as they are! Then, ask for my help as you strive to make improvements. Remember this today.

MEDITATION FIFTY-FOUR

Do the best presents come in small packages? Are the most thoughtful gifts wrapped in pretty paper? I tell you the truth: My greatest gifts are sometimes wrapped in hardship. Look closely at your trials. Could some of those dark clouds have a silver lining? Reflect on this today.

MEDITATION FIFTY-FIVE

I have given you the freedom to make choices. Therefore, you can turn to me, or not. You can bow to me, or not. And you can pray to me, or not. Today, remember the gift of free will. And remember, too, that gifts carry responsibility. Choose wisely this day!

MEDITATION FIFTY-SIX

Whatever dominates your mind will become your god. Perhaps you have an obsession that appears to be harmless. Yet, I tell you: Today's obsession is tomorrow's obstacle. Obsessions lead to imbalance, and they disrupt our relationship. Is there an unrelenting god in your life? Reflect on this today.

MEDITATION FIFTY-SEVEN

Are your dreams aligned with my plan? Are your hopes in harmony with my will? Trust me when I say: My only wish is for you to have heaven on earth. How then, could your hopes and dreams conflict with mine? Today, love has joined us as one. Reflect on what this means to you.

MEDITATION FIFTY-EIGHT

As you pray harder, life gets easier. Therefore, make this a day of prayer. Pray for loved ones, and pray for adversaries. Pray for friends and strangers alike. Pray for the sick and the strong, the old and the young. Pray for the poor and the rich, the pious and the lost. Give thanks, offer praise, and ask for my gifts and blessings!

MEDITATION FIFTY-NINE

First, the ego will invent a problem. Next, the ego will brag about its clever solution. Yet, neither the problem nor the solution is real. Today, look closely at your worries. Are they real, or not? Dismiss the self-created conflicts. And for the remaining ones, I tell you this: Trust will solve every possible problem.

MEDITATION SIXTY

Accept this day as the precious gift it truly is. Explore its mysteries boldly; embrace its holiness reverently; and drink from its cup enthusiastically. Today, live your life to the fullest!

MEDITATION SIXTY-ONE

Erase your fear by accepting my love. Extinguish your worries by embracing my peace. Surrender your guilt by receiving my grace. Relinquish your pain by trusting my mercy. And dismiss your illusions by heeding my truth. Work on these things today.

MEDITATION SIXTY-TWO

There are many who struggle to make healthy changes in their lives. Yet, even the longest journey begins with a humble first step. Knowledge *is* the first step to change. Knowledge brings awareness; awareness brings conviction; conviction brings determination; and determination brings lasting change. Remember these steps today, as they will bring the change your heart yearns for.

MEDITATION SIXTY-THREE

There are days when life is one slippery slope after the next. At times, it is difficult just to keep from falling. So follow the Guide who will not let your foot slip. Believe in the One who will never leave your side. Trust me today and worry no more!

MEDITATION SIXTY-FOUR

Today, look closely at the world. Examine the small things which might otherwise go unnoticed. Observe the subtle interactions among the people around you. Wherever there is goodness, you behold my love. And wherever there is kindness, you see my face. Remember this as your day unfolds.

MEDITATION SIXTY-FIVE

There are many who turn their backs to my radiance. Some of them are busy collecting earthly treasures. Yet, they are never satisfied. They are never fulfilled. I tell you the truth: Only I can nourish the soul. Drink from *my* well. Do this now, and thirst no longer.

MEDITATION SIXTY-SIX

Those who are wise have learned to live one day at a time. Yet, during your toughest trials, try living from one hour to the next. And as you work through your most painful days, try immersing yourself in each present moment. Today, work on living in the here and now. Do this, and be at peace with the world.

MEDITATION SIXTY-SEVEN

If you love me, then spend time with me. If you cherish me, then make room for me. And if you trust me, then greet me with open arms. All I ask is that you love me with your whole heart and soul and mind. Work on this today.

MEDITATION SIXTY-EIGHT

Look towards heaven and offer me your pain. Look towards heaven and offer me your suffering. Today, come to the One whose love will heal all wounds. Today, turn to the One whose mercy will comfort your soul.

MEDITATION SIXTY-NINE

Ashamed of their mistakes, there are some who run from me. Embarrassed by their flaws, there are others who hide from me. So hear the truth: You needn't flee from the mercy that comforts you; and you needn't hide from the grace that cleanses you. Today, remember that I love you just as you are.

MEDITATION SEVENTY

There will be days when you feel tired. Yet, weakness cannot keep you from adoring me. There will be times when you are sick. Yet, illness cannot stop you from loving me. I tell you the truth: Hope is invulnerable to disease. And faith is impervious to fatigue. Reflect on this today.

MEDITATION SEVENTY-ONE

When overwhelmed by physical pain, your mind tells you to grit your teeth and clench your fists. Yet, such resistance only intensifies the pain. That is why the mind must yield to the heart, for your heart will tell you to relax your muscles and allow your body to be limp. Your heart will tell you to surrender to the pain, to bless it and release it. And your heart will remind you to stay calm, to whisper my name, and to ask for my comfort. Remember this always.

MEDITATION SEVENTY-TWO

I am the living One who *is*. And if you doubt, then show me what existed *before* my presence. And if you doubt still, then take me to the place where I am *not*. Therefore, hear the truth: I am your everlasting help during troubled times. Remember this today.

MEDITATION SEVENTY-THREE

By my design, the world adapts and grows. By my will, life unfolds and evolves. Therefore, embrace the changes which come your way. Welcome them as miracles, or accept them as mysteries. Either way, nothing is gained by resisting the inevitable. Work on this today.

MEDITATION SEVENTY-FOUR

Why are you worried? And why are you afraid? For as promised, I am with you always; to the very end of the age. Welcome this truth and reclaim your peace. Embrace this reality and regain your freedom. Work on this today.

MEDITATION SEVENTY-FIVE

I knew you before you were born. In truth, I knew you before placing you in the womb. I have already comforted and reassured you. I have already explored the innermost depths of your soul. So I ask: Do you not *know* how much I love you? Reflect on this today.

MEDITATION SEVENTY-SIX

Trust me, just for this moment. Then, trust me over and over again. Soon, your trust will become a habit. Before long, it will be as natural as breathing in and out. Eventually, your trust in me will bring you unfathomable joy. Therefore, make this a day of trust.

MEDITATION SEVENTY-SEVEN

I have no needs, but you have many. Therefore, come to me when you are lost and lonely. Offer me praise and thanksgiving. For I tell you: Praise will break your cycle of self-pity, and thankfulness will stop your stream of negative thoughts. Worship me today. Though I do not need it, you do.

MEDITATION SEVENTY-EIGHT

When you are sick, dismiss the voice which suggests that you have been abandoned. And when you are hurting, ignore the voice which hints that you have been forsaken. Today, my angels are watching over you. Today, you are safe and loved.

MEDITATION SEVENTY-NINE

Anxiety may develop as you become fearful of the future. Or, anxiety might occur when you want something to happen before its time has come. And finally, anxiety can develop when something happens sooner than expected. Each of these scenarios is a test of faith. And that is why life offers the lessons you need, not the lessons you want. Today, everything will happen at just the right time – not a moment too soon or too late.

MEDITATION EIGHTY

Can an angry judge be fair? Can a fearful judge be impartial? Should one man condemn the same rain which blesses his neighbor's garden? So I tell you: Defer to the One who *is* justice. Now is the time to let go of judgment. Work on this today.

MEDITATION EIGHTY-ONE

Gratefulness keeps you from becoming arrogant, and thankfulness protects you from becoming jaded. I tell you the truth: Complacency brings hardship and lack, while gratitude brings prosperity and abundance. So today, be grateful for all that you have; and be thankful for all that you hope to have.

MEDITATION EIGHTY-TWO

Perhaps you are hurting, but fiercely private. Perhaps you are frail, but stubbornly independent. Still, there are those who stand ready to serve you. So I ask: Can you not welcome their help? Can you not appreciate their service, yet keep your dignity? Today, make sure to accept every expression of love that comes your way.

MEDITATION EIGHTY-THREE

Drug and alcohol abuse is never a healthy choice. The goal is to *expand* your awareness, not shrink it. The objective is to *elevate* your consciousness, not diminish it. Make this a day of wise decisions. Ask for my help if you need it. And if you do not, then pray for those who do.

MEDITATION EIGHTY-FOUR

Why are you sullen? Why do your eyes not sparkle? Believe me when I say: Your soul is impervious to disease; your spirit is invulnerable to injury. There is nothing that can keep you from illuminating the world. So today, let your light shine forth. Bring joy to heaven and earth alike!

MEDITATION EIGHTY-FIVE

Gifts are never wasted, including the ones that are scorned or rejected. Even the gifts that go unnoticed make a difference. Still, in a perfect world, each precious gift would be welcomed and valued; for then, its love would provide optimal benefit. Today, treasure every gift that life offers. Accept each one as the blessing it truly is.

MEDITATION EIGHTY-SIX

As long as you are alive, your life has meaning. As long as you are breathing, your life has purpose. And while the details may remain a mystery, I have a magnificent plan for you. Therefore, place your trust in the One who shall never betray you. Today, have faith in the One whose love shall never fade.

MEDITATION EIGHTY-SEVEN

There are many who think the universe is the source of life, and that life is the source of love. Yet, trust me when I say: Love is all there ever was, is now, and ever shall be. The animate and the inanimate, the visible and the invisible – all are born of my love. Love was *before* nothingness. Reflect on what this means to you.

MEDITATION EIGHTY-EIGHT

Choose me as your Guide. Listen to my voice and follow my lead. Do this today, and you will be exactly at the right place at the right time. Then, simply be kind and helpful.

MEDITATION EIGHTY-NINE

Every single day, there are many who do extraordinary things; for I have not created ordinary people. Today, do something extraordinary. And remember what the wise have learned: Miracles are often just small things done with great love.

MEDITATION NINETY

Do you not hear me? Do you not know the sound of my voice? In truth, there is no other like it; for mine is the voice that beckons you to love. Mine is the voice that asks you to forgive. Today, listen to my voice above all others. As the day unfolds, make sure that your choices express love and forgiveness.

MEDITATION NINETY-ONE

Ask me, and I will refill your empty cup. And as it overflows with my mercy, there will be no room for sadness. Ask me, and I will replenish your empty heart. And as it overflows with my grace, there will be no room for despair. Reflect on this today.

MEDITATION NINETY-TWO

You needn't be alone in the world. If you ask, I will come to you. If you wish, I will walk at your side. And if you want, I will hold your hand and never let it go. Remember this today.

MEDITATION NINETY-THREE

I know your every hope and every dream. Yet, I tell you: Be patient, for each gift arrives at just the right time. Be at peace with the world as you wait for my next blessing. Work on this today.

MEDITATION NINETY-FOUR

You needn't try to solve your problems without my help. Ask, and I will guide you to a higher elevation. And from this new overlook, you will gain a clearer vision. From this place most high, you will find a fresh insight to your latest adversity. Remember this today.

MEDITATION NINETY-FIVE

In silence, you are better prepared to hear my voice. In calmness, you are better equipped to do my work. Therefore, set aside time to be quiet and still. Work on this today, and be my faithful servant.

MEDITATION NINETY-SIX

I encourage you to laugh and smile, for cheerfulness can ease your burdens. Today, look for humor in life's ever-changing circumstances. Look for reasons to smile. And remember to laugh at yourself, because it brings you closer to forgiveness.

MEDITATION NINETY-SEVEN

I know you more intimately than you may think. I know your mistakes and the shame you carry. And still, my grace pours out to you. I know your faults and the guilt you carry. And still, I love you wholly. Remember this today.

MEDITATION NINETY-EIGHT

I will help you face your toughest opponent. I will help you confront your fiercest adversary. Still, you may feel the sting of pain. And in frustration, you might ask, "How long must I endure my enemy's wrath?" And I shall reply, "Is death not already vanquished? Is victory not already won?" Reflect on what this means to you.

MEDITATION NINETY-NINE

Before condemning someone, pause for a moment. Neither say nor do anything until you hear from me. And if you ask, "How, Lord, will I recognize your voice? How will I know it is you?" I shall answer, "Mine is the gentle voice of forgiveness. Mine is the tender voice of love." Remember this today.

MEDITATION ONE HUNDRED

My mercy is personified by those who worship me. My grace is embodied by those who praise me. And my love is manifested by those who serve me. Today, place me above all others; and love me with your whole heart. Work on this as the day unfolds.

MEDITATION ONE HUNDRED ONE

There are some who find scarcity wherever they search. Others see limits wherever they look. Yet, I tell you the truth: Scarcity and limits are but worldly illusions. This is a new and different day! Today, you will gaze upon abundance; and there will be no end to what you can achieve.

MEDITATION ONE HUNDRED TWO

Even during violent storms, an ocean's depths remain calm and unchanged. In a similar way, the love found deep within your heart is unchanged by hardship. And the peace found deep within your soul is unaffected by drama. In truth, you are already equipped to navigate rough seas. And if you ask, I will guide you to a safe harbor. Reflect on this today.

MEDITATION ONE HUNDRED THREE

The best way to honor the past is to live in the present. Therefore, the best way to honor a loved one who has died is to be at peace with the present moment; to be happy in the here and now. And to find peace and happiness, you must forgive the past and let it go. Hear the truth: Because life is for the living, allow the dead to bury the dead. Reflect on what this means to you.

MEDITATION ONE HUNDRED FOUR

My kingdom has colors and beauty you haven't yet seen. My kingdom has music and praise you haven't yet heard. In truth, my kingdom has wonders and joys beyond what you can imagine. So I tell you again: Believe in me, and you will see the glory of heaven! Remember this today.

MEDITATION ONE HUNDRED FIVE

Deep, emotional expressions – both loving *and* fearful ones – affect organic life at the molecular level and beyond. Therefore, be slow to anger and quick to praise. Be slow to scold and quick to forgive. Work on this today.

MEDITATION ONE HUNDRED SIX

Money cannot free you; work cannot redeem you; and alliances cannot heal you. Only my truth will liberate you. Only my love will save you. And only a relationship with me will bring you lasting peace. Reflect on this today.

MEDITATION ONE HUNDRED SEVEN

As you face changes – changes in health, relationships, finances, or careers – turn to me. I am the certainty that your heart is looking for. My love for you is the same today as it was before the stars were born. Turn to me and receive the timeless comfort that your soul is yearning for.

MEDITATION ONE HUNDRED EIGHT

Are you looking for happiness? Are you searching for peace? There is a time and a season for everything under heaven. Yet, I tell you truly: As your faith grows, happiness can be found in the most perilous times. And as your love grows, peace can be found in the most hostile seasons. Remember this today.

MEDITATION ONE HUNDRED NINE

Listen to the One who sees, but is not seen. Do not deny what is already happening, and do not resist what you cannot change. Instead, see beyond it; bless it; and let it go. Work on this today and be at peace with the world.

MEDITATION ONE HUNDRED TEN

It is hard to feel my presence when your mind is flooded with thoughts. And it is hard to experience my peace when your day is filled with activities. Today, make sure you have some unscheduled time. Then, find a quiet place and allow your mind to be still. Do this today and be renewed.

MEDITATION ONE HUNDRED ELEVEN

As you think about the past, you reinvent history. And as you reinvent history, you create a false reality. Why be loyal to what is no more and never was? Why be enslaved by misguided illusions? I tell you: Let go of imagined enemies and contrived grievances. Think no more about the past!

MEDITATION ONE HUNDRED TWELVE

You hear of men harming their brothers. You hear of women hurting their children. In despair, you ask: "What is happening to the world?" Yet, I tell you: What someone may do with an intention to harm, I will use to promote the greater good. And what someone may do with an intention to hurt, I will use to serve the greater whole. Reflect on what this means to you.

MEDITATION ONE HUNDRED THIRTEEN

In all things, I come to those who love and serve me. Therefore, devote this day to servitude. Find new ways to help the disheartened. Do this in remembrance of me.

MEDITATION ONE HUNDRED FOURTEEN

As you pause in silence, you shall hear my voice of faith. And as you wait in stillness, your heart shall fill with hope. This is a day of faith, and now is a time of hope. Reflect on what this means to you.

MEDITATION ONE HUNDRED FIFTEEN

There are many who are tragically confused. And there are some who think that I have forsaken them. So hear the truth: I want to help you, not punish you. I want to heal you, not condemn you. And I want to save you, not abandon you. Remember this as the day unfolds.

MEDITATION ONE HUNDRED SIXTEEN

You can solve a problem on your own. But will your solution be the best one? Will your answer lead to a desirable outcome? So I ask: Why not reach out to me? Come to the One who will give you inspired clarity. Turn to the One who will guide you to an optimal result. Remember this today.

MEDITATION ONE HUNDRED SEVENTEEN

There are those who believe that truth and reality have no Maker. So I ask: Is inspiration just imagined? Is hope simply a mirage? Is faith just a dream? And is love merely an accident? Make this a day of reflection. What is true, and what is not? What is real, and what is illusion?

MEDITATION ONE HUNDRED EIGHTEEN

There are some who are lost, and others who are broken. So I ask: Are you willing to serve the lost? For as you serve them, you are serving me. And are you willing to help the broken? For as you help them, you are helping me. Remember this today.

MEDITATION ONE HUNDRED NINETEEN

Praise me, and I will bless you and keep you. Trust me, and my face will shine upon you. Love me, and I will fill your heart with peace. Reflect on this as the day unfolds.

MEDITATION ONE HUNDRED TWENTY

Balance promotes happiness, and rest promotes healing. Therefore, maintain a steady balance between the secular and the sacred. And be sure to set aside time for rest and leisure. Remember this today.

MEDITATION ONE HUNDRED TWENTY-ONE

If you are fearful of death, are you ready to live? If you are fearful of life, are you able to love? How is fear allayed? How is doubt overcome? And how is faith restored? Reflect on these questions as your day unfolds.

MEDITATION ONE HUNDRED TWENTY-TWO

You connect with me during periods of deep sleep, where thoughts and dreams are not. We commune in silence and stillness. Are you aware of these holy times we share together? Be assured: They are powerful and restorative. In truth, you cannot live without them. Reflect on what this means to you.

MEDITATION ONE HUNDRED TWENTY-THREE

There are some who have broken bodies. And others have weakened minds. Perhaps you pity such people. Yet, do not be misled; for their souls are shining far brighter than you know. In truth, if I were to unveil their collective light, the sun would envy such brilliance. Remember this today.

MEDITATION ONE HUNDRED TWENTY-FOUR

Like a flower to its stem, faith and trust are connected. Like a mother to her child, faith and trust are joined. Believe in me, and I will show you miracles. Trust in me, and I will work miracles through you. Reflect on this as your day unfolds.

MEDITATION ONE HUNDRED TWENTY-FIVE

There are some who brag about their wealth. And others boast of their achievements. They pray on street corners to be watched and admired. Yet, I tell you: Only the humble can earn greatness. Remember this today.

MEDITATION ONE HUNDRED TWENTY-SIX

Do you want to take charge of your life? Do you want to control your own destiny? Then, why not take charge of your negative thoughts? Why not take control of your misguided perceptions? Today, see every obstacle as an opportunity. Today, perceive each trial as a blessing.

MEDITATION ONE HUNDRED TWENTY-SEVEN

A sick child can help you remember what is truly important in your life. A disabled child can help remind you of your own gifts and blessings. Today, reflect on what this means to you.

MEDITATION ONE HUNDRED TWENTY-EIGHT

I tell you the truth: Those who believe in me will live, even though they die. And whoever lives and believes in me will never die. Remember this today, for it is hope which feeds your soul.

MEDITATION ONE HUNDRED TWENTY-NINE

I know your every thought and word and deed. Yet, I tell you: Rest easy, for my gifts are not tied to what you think or say or do. My mercy is your birthright, and my peace is your inheritance. Reflect on this today.

MEDITATION ONE HUNDRED THIRTY

I prayed for those who followed me, and I prayed for those who despised me. So I tell you the truth: Pray for the oppressed *and* the oppressors. Lift up the conquered *and* the conquerors. Make this a day of prayer, and remember to pray as I have taught you.

MEDITATION ONE HUNDRED THIRTY-ONE

Oppression cannot result in long-term gain, for I will not allow it. And exploitation cannot result in long-term benefit, for the scales of justice are destined to be balanced. So believe me when I tell you: Today's vanquished will be tomorrow's victors. Accept this truth. Then, look upon the world and judge it not.

MEDITATION ONE HUNDRED THIRTY-TWO

Those who are entering and leaving the world need only to be safe and loved. How then, could all of the in-between wants and desires be something more than passing illusions? Trust me when I say: You have already received everything you truly need. Reflect on this today.

MEDITATION ONE HUNDRED THIRTY-THREE

The Holy Spirit is my voice, the Counselor of your heart. When you are afraid, accept my comfort. When you are confused, heed my advice. And when you are lost, welcome my guidance. Work on these things today.

MEDITATION ONE HUNDRED THIRTY-FOUR

I ask you to forgive. Yet, you needn't be a close friend of someone who has tried to hurt you. In truth, forgiveness – like a prayer – can be offered and received from a great distance. Still, I tell you: To love your enemies is to have no fear as you dine with them. Reflect on what this means.

MEDITATION ONE HUNDRED THIRTY-FIVE

Perhaps a majestic mountain will help you remember me. Or maybe a glorious sunrise will remind you of me. Yet, you can turn to me at any time; you needn't wait for a special moment. In truth, you can reach out to me in the most humble environment. Do this one simple thing today.

MEDITATION ONE HUNDRED THIRTY-SIX

Though there is sickness, I am not its cause. Though there is pain and suffering, I am not their source. Yet, I remind you: Sickness opens doors of kindness and compassion; pain opens windows of trust and faith; and suffering opens hearts to my love and grace. Remember this today.

MEDITATION ONE HUNDRED THIRTY-SEVEN

In its purest form, love has no needs or desires. In its truest form, love is selfless and fearless. And in a state of perfection, love has no conditions, exceptions, or agendas. Devote this day to love. And remember, there is no limit to the love you can give!

MEDITATION ONE HUNDRED THIRTY-EIGHT

While growing up, you are aware of getting stronger. And while growing old, you are aware of getting weaker. Yet, as your body goes from weak to strong and from strong to weak, the awareness will stay the same. And I tell you: That which is changeless is eternal. Today, reflect on what this means to you.

MEDITATION ONE HUNDRED THIRTY-NINE

Shortly before death, there is a realization that your life will continue. And at that moment, worry and anxiety are replaced by relief and freedom. Next, you will understand that everything is exactly as it should be. And at that moment, relief and freedom are replaced by peace and joy. Such is my gift of grace!

MEDITATION ONE HUNDRED FORTY

Learning and growing include painful moments. Yet, if not for the sting of pain, how could there be healing? If not for the grimace of suffering, how could there be comfort? And if not for the burn of anguish, how could there be mercy? Today, reflect on what this means to you.

MEDITATION ONE HUNDRED FORTY-ONE

Solitude is a holy space. In truth, I often touch the hearts of those who walk a path less travelled. So trust me when I say: In solitude, you are sanctified. Today, reflect on what this means.

MEDITATION ONE HUNDRED FORTY-TWO

First, you confront a problem. Next, you search for a solution. And though your ego is quick to respond, its answers cannot be trusted. There is a better way; for when the Holy Spirit solves a problem, no one loses. Today, listen to the voice of wisdom. Today, ask the Holy Spirit to solve your problems.

MEDITATION ONE HUNDRED FORTY-THREE

There are many who look upon others with disdain. Their egos see only the unworthy. Their hardened hearts see only the undeserving. Yet, I tell you: Not a single child of mine is unworthy, and not a single child of mine is undeserving. My love is a birthright, and my grace is a gift. Remember this today.

MEDITATION ONE HUNDRED FORTY-FOUR

The world's distractions hinder our relationship. And in truth, the pursuit of wealth and status is particularly alluring. That is why the rich and powerful struggle to find my peace. Today, be mindful of these pitfalls. As your day unfolds, remember to place me above all earthly treasures.

MEDITATION ONE HUNDRED FORTY-FIVE

Some wish to be healed, but they are not yet willing to love. Others wish to be healed, but they are not yet ready to forgive. So I tell you: Healing is a spiritual endeavor, a personal journey needing both love *and* forgiveness. Today, reflect on what this means to you.

MEDITATION ONE HUNDRED FORTY-SIX

Through your gifts and talents, my voice is heard. And through your faithful service, my will is done. Today, make the most of your unique abilities. Today, serve others as you would have others serve you. Do this in remembrance of me.

MEDITATION ONE HUNDRED FORTY-SEVEN

In all of its elegance and beauty, the world was born of my love. And in all of its glory and splendor, life was born of the same love. Today, celebrate life. And as the day unfolds, praise my love. For I tell you truly: Love is all there is!

MEDITATION ONE HUNDRED FORTY-EIGHT

My mercy is expressed through your love of others. And my grace is expressed through your love of self. Does your heart not tell you this? Therefore, look inward today. And in all things, follow your heart. Work on this as the day unfolds.

MEDITATION ONE HUNDRED FORTY-NINE

I am the Source of comfort. So why look elsewhere? I am the Source of well-being. So why turn to another? Come to me for reassurance. Turn to me for safety. Do this today, and wander no more.

MEDITATION ONE HUNDRED FIFTY

There are some who search for creative improvements, for a better tool or an easier way. Others look for creative challenges, for new mediums of artistic expression. So listen to the truth: Your creative abilities are unfathomable. Indeed, your lack of faith is all that stands between you and the miraculous. Reflect on this today.

MEDITATION ONE HUNDRED FIFTY-ONE

Is peace waiting just around the corner? Is joy resting just beyond your reach? Then turn to me and search no longer. I tell you truly: Your trust in me will give you peace. And your faith in me will bring you joy. Accept nothing less today.

MEDITATION ONE HUNDRED FIFTY-TWO

Are your problems too big for me? Are your worries too small? Maybe you can never find the right moment to ask for my help. So hear the truth: This is a new and different day! Today, you will bring every single problem and worry to me. And today, each moment will be a perfect time to quietly seek my help.

MEDITATION ONE HUNDRED FIFTY-THREE

You attach a high value to your intellect. Yet, your thoughts cause us to drift apart. Negative, cynical, and doubting thoughts create distance between us. So today, make better choices. Let go of negativity, and dismiss all doubt. Today, nurture optimism by focusing on positive thoughts. Work on this as your day unfolds.

MEDITATION ONE HUNDRED FIFTY-FOUR

There are many who fail to practice what they preach. And many others promote untenable beliefs while walking a self-righteous path. So I ask: Do you love your religion more than you love me? And are your creeds more important than your relationship with me? Today, reflect on what this means to you.

MEDITATION ONE HUNDRED FIFTY-FIVE

Have you forgotten who you really are? Believe me: You are light and love, whole and complete. Do you remember your true self? Trust me: You are kind and helpful, glorious and eternal; for you are just as I created you. Remember this today.

MEDITATION ONE HUNDRED FIFTY-SIX

I am all-powerful; yet, you needn't cower. I am ever-present; yet, you needn't look over your shoulder. And though my ways are much higher than yours, you needn't be ashamed. Today, look to the sky and offer sweet praise. Do this, and walk with confidence.

MEDITATION ONE HUNDRED FIFTY-SEVEN

Sacraments promote healing and comfort. They replenish the heart. They nourish the soul. Therefore, drink from my cup. Drink until your heart's content. Do this in remembrance of me. Do this, and rejoice; for what once was lost has now been found.

MEDITATION ONE HUNDRED FIFTY-EIGHT

Remember me with each beat of your heart. Think of me with your every breath. For I was your first home and your first love, and nothing in the world can separate us: not time, not space, not sickness, not even death. Today, reflect on what this means to you.

MEDITATION ONE HUNDRED FIFTY-NINE

There are some puzzles that cannot be solved, and there are certain mysteries that cannot be unraveled. Yet, I tell you: Heaven celebrates every life lesson that is taught by a sick child. Reflect on this today.

MEDITATION ONE HUNDRED SIXTY

While on earth, I chose to teach and to serve. And you can choose a similar ministry, if you wish. Today, teach lessons of love and forgiveness. Today, serve others with kindness and compassion. Do this in remembrance of me.

MEDITATION ONE HUNDRED SIXTY-ONE

If you want to honor me, then accept the perfection of my creations. Be at peace with the world I have made. Believe me when I say: Earth is not a place of exile, and life is not a form of punishment. Today, praise the world's beauty! Behold my glory and embrace my joy!

MEDITATION ONE HUNDRED SIXTY-TWO

There are many ways to express love and countless opportunities to be helpful. And in truth, there are times when you can help others by *not* doing something. Today, express your love by *not* controlling or manipulating the people around you. Remember this as the day unfolds.

MEDITATION ONE HUNDRED SIXTY-THREE

To pray without ceasing is to keep an uninterrupted connection with me, and to maintain a spiritual focus on all that you think, say, and do. To pray without ceasing is to keep me in the forefront of your mind. Work on this today.

MEDITATION ONE HUNDRED SIXTY-FOUR

Nothing happens that is not part of the greater whole and its purpose. By keeping calm during troubled times, you show your trust in me. By offering praise during unexpected hardships, you demonstrate your abiding faith. And through your faith and trust, something good shall come from each and every trial. Today, reflect on what this means to you.

MEDITATION ONE HUNDRED SIXTY-FIVE

What evil has done with intent to harm the world, I will use to accomplish good. Because of this, miracles often emerge from the depths of despair. And believe me when I tell you: Not a single child of mine is undeserving of a miracle. Remember this today.

MEDITATION ONE HUNDRED SIXTY-SIX

As you join with me, nothing is routine or boring. As you connect with me, nothing is without meaning or purpose. Today, ask me to walk at your side. Do this, and every step will be holy, every moment will be sacred.

MEDITATION ONE HUNDRED SIXTY-SEVEN

Is eternity enough time to find mercy? Is eternity enough time to seek justice? I tell you truly: There is a higher plan you know nothing of. And in accordance, I call my children home at just the right time; not a moment too soon or too late. Today, reflect on what this means to you.

MEDITATION ONE HUNDRED SIXTY-EIGHT

When the time is right, my angels will guide your precious soul to heaven. In truth, this is a gift of reassurance; for even that which is invulnerable yearns for safety and comfort. Remember this always.

MEDITATION ONE HUNDRED SIXTY-NINE

There are some who run from me. Yet, my only desire is for them to find peace. There are others who hide from me. Yet, my only wish is for them to find happiness. Do my desires frighten you? Do my wishes threaten you? Reflect on these questions as your day unfolds.

MEDITATION ONE HUNDRED SEVENTY

Problems not only begin in your mind, they end there as well. So I ask: Why offer a rude comment that is likely to hurt someone's feelings? Why offer a spiteful remark that is likely to sabotage a relationship? Today, choose your words carefully. Do this one simple thing as the day unfolds.

MEDITATION ONE HUNDRED SEVENTY-ONE

Today is a brand new day! Receive it as the gift it truly is. Today is a brand new beginning! Accept it as the blessing it really is. As the day unfolds, search for opportunities to love and to serve. Find ways to inspire and uplift those who come your way.

MEDITATION ONE HUNDRED SEVENTY-TWO

Today, be confident as you turn to me. Receive my counsel with a grateful heart. Then, go forth with my blessing. Do this, and be not afraid.

MEDITATION ONE HUNDRED SEVENTY-THREE

My love cannot be earned, for what is freely given requires no labor. My grace cannot be purchased, for what is freely given requires no money. Yet, I tell you: Redemption has come at a cost, and salvation has come with a sacrifice. Today, reflect on this means to you.

MEDITATION ONE HUNDRED SEVENTY-FOUR

When your mind is racing, you do not hear me. And when your day is busy, you do not have time for me. So I ask: Are you able to calm your mind? Are you willing to clear your schedule? Spend time with me today, for I have so much to teach you.

MEDITATION ONE HUNDRED SEVENTY-FIVE

How long do earthly fortunes last? How long can trophies sustain you? Follow me, and I will guide you to heavenly treasures. Trust me, and I will lead you to eternal riches. Love me, and I will take you to a place where no thief comes near and no moth destroys. Reflect on what this means to you.

MEDITATION ONE HUNDRED SEVENTY-SIX

Come to me and no burden will crush you. Talk to me and no problem will overwhelm you. Today, I am here to help and to guide you. Today, you are not alone.

MEDITATION ONE HUNDRED SEVENTY-SEVEN

There are times when you lack confidence, and there are moments when you are fearful. So hear the truth: I have ordained your immortality. Nothing can take that from you, and no one can ever harm you. Today, reflect on what this means.

MEDITATION ONE HUNDRED SEVENTY-EIGHT

Where there is beauty, you see my creations; and where there is mercy, you look upon my grace. Where there is kindness, you see my angels; and where there is love, you look upon my face. Remember this today.

MEDITATION ONE HUNDRED SEVENTY-NINE

You have searched far and wide for me. You have looked high and low for me. Yet, those who are wise have learned that I am closer than breathing; nearer than hands and feet. Today, reflect on what this means to you.

MEDITATION ONE HUNDRED EIGHTY

There are many who shed tears. And many others wallow in despair. Yet, what have they lost? Is there not another who provides comfort and safety? Is there not another who offers love? Reflect on this as your day unfolds.

MEDITATION ONE HUNDRED EIGHTY-ONE

Many believe they have lost their innocence. They hang their heads in shame, thinking they are unworthy of love. They carry the yoke of guilt, thinking they are undeserving of grace. Yet, I say: Rejoice, for your sins are forgiven! Be joyful and dance in the streets! Remember this today.

MEDITATION ONE HUNDRED EIGHTY-TWO

To practice law or medicine, you must have a license. To counsel or to teach, you must have a certificate. These documents come from secular authorities. And while there is nothing wrong with standardized competency or ceremonial commissioning, I tell you the truth: Only the Holy Spirit can anoint and ordain. Reflect on this today.

MEDITATION ONE HUNDRED EIGHTY-THREE

In heaven, my light is all that's needed to guide you. In heaven, my face is all that's needed to inspire you. And in heaven, my love is all that's needed to sustain you. Reflect on this today.

MEDITATION ONE HUNDRED EIGHTY-FOUR

Why condemn life's hardships? Is each trial not an opportunity to reach out to me? Is every challenge not a chance to whisper my name? Speak to me today. Then, listen intently. For I have so much to share with you.

MEDITATION ONE HUNDRED EIGHTY-FIVE

The sky is a rich blend of colors, shapes, and textures. It expresses beauty, majesty, and infinity. During the day, the sky has one kind of glory; the night sky's glory is of a different kind; and each sunrise and sunset has its own perfect splendor. And there is a paradox as well; for the sky is timeless, yet ever-changing. Over the next twenty-four hours, set aside time to gaze at the sky. Do this, if you are able.

MEDITATION ONE HUNDRED EIGHTY-SIX

Eternal life is my promise to you. Accept this truth and rest easy. Immortality is my covenant with you. Embrace this reality and be at peace with the world. Reflect on this today.

MEDITATION ONE HUNDRED EIGHTY-SEVEN

Today, you wear my armor. Today, you carry my shield. As the day unfolds, remember that evil cannot harm you and malice will not touch you. As the day unfolds, remember that you are safe.

MEDITATION ONE HUNDRED EIGHTY-EIGHT

Sometimes, you get confused and lose your way. Other times, you become distracted and forget where you are going. So I say this once more: Heaven is your final destination, and let nothing stand in your way. Reflect on what this means to you.

MEDITATION ONE HUNDRED EIGHTY-NINE

Quite often, a keen sense of humor is a sign of wisdom. And a sense of humor can indicate a balanced worldview as well. So listen to the truth: Life needn't ever be grim. This is a new and different day! Today, greet the world with good cheer!

MEDITATION ONE HUNDRED NINETY

Allow me to form a new star before I right the wrongs in your life. Allow me to shape a new mountain before I cast out your demons. And believe me when I say: Patience is holy. Today, be willing to wait.

MEDITATION ONE HUNDRED NINETY-ONE

Those who believe in chaos also believe in random events. And those who believe in random events also believe in chance encounters. Yet, trust me when I say: Life has countless activities, but very few random events. And life has countless interactions, but very few chance encounters. Reflect on this today.

MEDITATION ONE HUNDRED NINETY-TWO

Do you thirst for peace? Then drink from my cup of redemption and be born again. Do you thirst for joy? Then drink from my cup of salvation and be forever transformed. I tell you truly: Make these choices and worry no more. Reflect on what this means to you.

MEDITATION ONE HUNDRED NINETY-THREE

Trust me completely. Do this, and no one can disturb your inner peace. Trust me completely. Do this, and nothing can disrupt your heart's serenity. Today, surrender your pride and place your trust in me. Make this choice, and bathe in heaven's peace.

MEDITATION ONE HUNDRED NINETY-FOUR

Today, when you are burdened, lean on me. When you are saddened, talk to me. And when you are weary, rest in me. Do these simple things, and make this a day of healing.

MEDITATION ONE HUNDRED NINETY-FIVE

The supernatural cannot yet be proven empirically. For now, miracles seem to contradict natural laws. Still, is your life not a miracle? And are there not moments of your life which defy logic and reason? Reflect on these questions today.

MEDITATION ONE HUNDRED NINETY-SIX

Consciousness is a phenomenon which is not understood. And love is a mystery which cannot be unraveled. Yet, both are undeniably real. Are there other enigmas which scientific formulas cannot define? Are there other aspects of life which mathematical equations do not explain? Explore these questions today.

MEDITATION ONE HUNDRED NINETY-SEVEN

Just as a divided house cannot stand, a divided mind cannot be whole. On one hand, the ego announces your greatness. On the other hand, the ego proclaims your unworthiness. So hear the truth: The ego is a liar and deceiver. Tame this beast and regain your clarity! Work on it today.

MEDITATION ONE HUNDRED NINETY-EIGHT

Your day will be filled with conscious and unconscious judgments. And though they are based on past experiences, judgments can misguide you nonetheless. In truth, your memories are clouded because your ego has rewritten history. Its revisionist nature means that many of your judgments are founded on lies. And that makes you an unqualified judge. Reflect on this today.

MEDITATION ONE HUNDRED NINETY-NINE

You see just a sliver of what is happening in the world. Actually, you see just a fraction of what is happening right in front of your eyes. This limited perspective causes confusion, and your confusion makes it even more important to trust me. Remember this today.

MEDITATION TWO HUNDRED

Truth is the heart's domain. And because of this, your mind neither recognizes nor accepts your true identity. Your mind thinks that you are nothing but flesh and bones. Your mind thinks that when your body dies, your life will end. So I tell you: Accept no reality in which death plays a role. Today, reflect on what this means.

MEDITATION TWO HUNDRED ONE

Spontaneity and randomness are neither identical nor interchangeable; for life is spontaneous, but not random. And believe me when I say: Life is complexly interconnected. What appears to be chaos is, in truth, the work of a higher plan. Reflect on this today.

MEDITATION TWO HUNDRED TWO

The past is just a memory; the future is but a dream. Only this moment is real. Accept this, and you are ready for happiness. Embrace this, and you are ready for peace. Today, choose to live in the present. Do this, and have no regrets.

MEDITATION TWO HUNDRED THREE

The world is a projection of your thoughts. So trust me when I say: As your thoughts become more and more caring, the world becomes more and more friendly. And as your thoughts become more and more loving, the world becomes a kinder, gentler place. Remember this today.

MEDITATION TWO HUNDRED FOUR

As you offer love, you do my work. As you offer forgiveness, you do my will. And as you pray, you receive my gift of peace. Remember this today.

MEDITATION TWO HUNDRED FIVE

Why blame a friend for self-inflicted torment? Why blame an enemy for self-created pain? Accept responsibility for what you see, what you think, and what you believe. Only then will your mind be transformed. And only then will truth be your reality. Reflect on this today.

MEDITATION TWO HUNDRED SIX

Much like medicine heals a wound, discipline heals your mind. For I tell you the truth: Your mind cannot rest until it stops blaming others for your woes. And your mind cannot heal until it stops condemning your heart. Reflect on this as the day unfolds.

MEDITATION TWO HUNDRED SEVEN

Within the backdrop of awareness, there is a memory of being safe. And within the blankness of sleep, there is a memory of being loved. That is why silence is sacred and stillness is holy. Today, reflect on what this means to you.

MEDITATION TWO HUNDRED EIGHT

Are your triumphs genuine or counterfeit? Are your trials authentic or imaginary? Believe me when I say: The mind creates an abyss which only the heart can bridge. Today, let your heart determine what is true and what is not. Today, follow your heart to reality.

MEDITATION TWO HUNDRED NINE

As you move from one room to the next, you will love me more and more. As you move from one room to the next, you will trust me more and more. In truth, you will never stop growing in love and faith. So I tell you: Shed your complacency! Do this now, and waste no more time!

MEDITATION TWO HUNDRED TEN

There are many who ask: "Why must I suffer? Why must I die?" So hear the truth: Only the unborn cannot suffer; only the unborn escape death. Remember this today.

MEDITATION TWO HUNDRED ELEVEN

At this very moment, my mercy is comforting you. At this very moment, my love is uplifting you. And through this day and the night which follows, my will light shine upon you. So go forth with joy in your heart!

MEDITATION TWO HUNDRED TWELVE

Is life not evidence of my love? Is innocence not evidence of my grace? Hear the truth: By my love, you shall always be safe. And by my grace, you shall never be alone or comfortless. Remember this today.

MEDITATION TWO HUNDRED THIRTEEN

Arrogance argues that some must have less before others can have more. Yet, be assured: You can gain *all* without loss; you can have *everything* at no one's expense. For my blood has made further sacrifice unnecessary. Today, reflect on what this means to you.

MEDITATION TWO HUNDRED FOURTEEN

When obedient to the heart, your mind is a helpful friend. Yet, when given too much authority, your mind can be a menacing tyrant. Today, make sure that your mind is a faithful servant of your heart. Today, act as though the only thing possible is what I would have you do.

MEDITATION TWO HUNDRED FIFTEEN

Those who are wise look at the world and see unity. They look at the world and see but one religion, one church, and one healer. The religion is love; the church is kindness; and the healer is forgiveness. Reflect on what this means to you.

MEDITATION TWO HUNDRED SIXTEEN

There are some who are hungry. And others have no protection from the heat or the cold, the rain or the snow. Yet, I tell you: While it is possible to lack food and shelter, not a single child of mine can ever be homeless. Reflect on this today.

MEDITATION TWO HUNDRED SEVENTEEN

There are many who yearn for healthy bodies and sound minds. And there is nothing wrong with such hopes. Yet, I tell you: In heaven, broken bodies and splintered minds are but a distant memory. And as such, they are quickly forgotten. Remember this today.

MEDITATION TWO HUNDRED EIGHTEEN

As you retreat from pain and suffering, you needn't be less nurturing. And as you detach from wants and desires, you needn't be less passionate. For I tell you truly: Fewer needs and less anguish will bring a renewed zest for living and loving. Today, reflect on what this means.

MEDITATION TWO HUNDRED NINETEEN

An illness might cause you to be more sedentary and quiet. And when sick, perhaps you may choose to isolate yourself. Yet, I ask: Do great wonders not arise during periods of silence? Do revelations not occur during times of solitude? Reflect on what this means to you.

MEDITATION TWO HUNDRED TWENTY

Evil and darkness are not always the same. Life actually thrives in darkness: A seed grows beneath the soil; a baby develops in the womb. And you needn't be afraid of the dark, for my resurrection occurred within a pitch-black tomb. Reflect on this today.

MEDITATION TWO HUNDRED TWENTY-ONE

My love for you is more than you can know or comprehend. My plan for you is beyond what you can believe or imagine. So I ask: Is your heart now open to my love? And is your mind now open to my plan? Have faith in me today, and the lamb and the lion shall dwell in peace.

MEDITATION TWO HUNDRED TWENTY-TWO

Call out to me, and I will hear you; for already I stand at your side. Is it strength you want? Is it courage you seek? Call out to me, for already I know what you need. Do this today, and have the strength and the courage you hope for.

MEDITATION TWO HUNDRED TWENTY-THREE

Why carry such a heavy load? Have you forgotten that I am nearby? Have you forgotten that I am eager to help? Ask me to lift the yoke from your shoulders. Do this today, and know what it feels like to be worry free.

MEDITATION TWO HUNDRED TWENTY-FOUR

Even now, there is a place for you in heaven. Even now, there is a room where you shall be safe. For I have made a special place for you to rest and to heal. I have prepared a special room where you shall remember your wholeness and perfection. Reflect on what this means to you.

MEDITATION TWO HUNDRED TWENTY-FIVE

In crowded cities, there are many who feel isolated and threatened. And on busy sidewalks, there are many who feel alone and unsafe. Yet, comfort and protection are closer than they think; for my angels are always within reach. Reflect on this today.

MEDITATION TWO HUNDRED TWENTY-SIX

Your mind is troubled and confused. It thinks I want to punish you. Yet, this is a delusion – an unconscionable lie! I tell you truly: Open your heart to my love, for that is all I want. That is all I have ever wanted. Remember this always.

MEDITATION TWO HUNDRED TWENTY-SEVEN

Today, your unshakable love will make every relationship a holy relationship. And today, your unwavering kindness will make every encounter a holy encounter. Settle for nothing less!

MEDITATION TWO HUNDRED TWENTY-EIGHT

There is but One who is qualified to judge. There is but One who offers the wisest counsel. And I tell you: Release your guilt and claim heaven as your rightful home. Release your shame and accept immortality as your rightful inheritance. Work on this today.

MEDITATION TWO HUNDRED TWENTY-NINE

Do you pay attention to the lost as they offer guidance? Do you listen to the confused as they give advice? I tell you the truth: I do not pay attention to those who claim to be undeserving of my mercy. Nor do I listen to those who say they are unworthy of my grace. Reflect on this today.

MEDITATION TWO HUNDRED THIRTY

Be wary of cloaks made from lamb's wool, as wolves will sometimes don them. And be wary of serpents which cross your path, as some will surely tempt you. Draw near to me today. Stay close to me and be safe from deceivers in search of an acolyte.

MEDITATION TWO HUNDRED THIRTY-ONE

There are many who run from conflict, and many others choose to hide from their enemies. Yet, I say: Opportunities to grow in faith come as you confront the storms of life, including the trials that you share with others. Such times offer a chance to forgive. They offer a pathway for sinners to become saints. Reflect on this today.

MEDITATION TWO HUNDRED THIRTY-TWO

Special celebrations are deserving of thoughtful gifts. Yet, trust me when I say: Kindness is an appropriate gift for all occasions. Today, offer unconditional kindness to everyone you meet. Work on this as your day unfolds.

MEDITATION TWO HUNDRED THIRTY-THREE

Regardless of what you think, I have nothing to do with your pain and suffering. And despite what you believe, life's trials are not a form of punishment. Still, if you insist on identifying the cause of your anguish – the source of your suffering – then you need only look into a mirror. Remember this today.

MEDITATION TWO HUNDRED THIRTY-FOUR

I am the Redeemer who holds your right hand and whispers, "You are safe." I am the Comforter who walks at your side and whispers, "You are loved." Therefore, trust in me and worry no more. Do this, and have heaven on earth.

MEDITATION TWO HUNDRED THIRTY-FIVE

Your future is much more promising than you think. And I tell you the truth: My plan for you is far more glorious than you know. Therefore, keep a cheerful heart today. Wear a bright smile and live as though you haven't a care in the world.

MEDITATION TWO HUNDRED THIRTY-SIX

It is easy to stray from righteousness, for its path is straight and narrow. In the blink of an eye, you may become lost or confused. So I tell you: Seek my face always, and look to me for guidance. Work on this today, and go forth with confidence.

MEDITATION TWO HUNDRED THIRTY-SEVEN

There are many who disregard my willingness to help them. Some wish for total independence. Others dream of absolute self-reliance. And still others are certain they can do just fine without me. So I ask, what are your excuses? Reflect on this today.

MEDITATION TWO HUNDRED THIRTY-EIGHT

Give thanks to me and praise my name! Bow down to me and sing joyful songs! Behold my glory and rejoice! Today, accept nothing less!

MEDITATION TWO HUNDRED THIRTY-NINE

Those who follow me shall never be in darkness. And those who walk with me shall never be alone. So I ask: Will you not follow me today? Will you not walk with me now?

MEDITATION TWO HUNDRED FORTY

If you are fearful, come to me. Come to me for safety. If you are worried, come to me. Come to me for peace. And if you are weary, come to me. Come to me and rest. Remember this as your day unfolds.

MEDITATION TWO HUNDRED FORTY-ONE

Sensations can be comforting: a pastoral landscape, a soothing sound, or a gentle touch. That is why so many people are disturbed by deprivation; by complete silence, absolute darkness, or total isolation. Yet I ask: Can you not converse in silence? Can you not contemplate in darkness? And can you not commune in solitude? Reflect on this today.

MEDITATION TWO HUNDRED FORTY-TWO

Just as there is human love and divine love, there is human law and divine law. There are many who obey the laws of man but ignore mine. So hear the truth: Only *my* commandments lead to untold treasures and everlasting joy. Remember this today.

MEDITATION TWO HUNDRED FORTY-THREE

Turn to me; turn to me now; and your worries will disappear like night at the break of dawn. Talk to me; talk to me now; and your fears will dissolve like mist in the morning sun.

MEDITATION TWO HUNDRED FORTY-FOUR

I ask for your undivided attention. So in this regard, I am jealous indeed. Direct your focus entirely on me. Do this today and tomorrow. Do this through the weeks and months ahead. Make this a lifelong pursuit. And in return, you shall have wealth beyond measure. Are you more accepting of my jealousy now?

MEDITATION TWO HUNDRED FORTY-FIVE

Share your innermost thoughts and feelings with me. Tell me about your deepest worries and your darkest fears. Do this today. For when monsters are cast from the shadows, they are weak and vulnerable. And when demons stand in the light of truth, they are sheepish and impotent.

MEDITATION TWO HUNDRED FORTY-SIX

You may confront the world by yourself if you wish. You may stand alone while facing your fears. Yet, there is an easier way. Take my right hand. Do this, and follow a gentler path. Do this today, and arrive at a better place.

MEDITATION TWO HUNDRED FORTY-SEVEN

Love me, and your cup will overflow. Trust me, and your wealth will be too vast to measure. And by sharing your riches with others, you shall gain heavenly treasures that can never be plundered. Today, reflect on what this means to you.

MEDITATION TWO HUNDRED FORTY-EIGHT

Before you were conceived, I protected you. Before you were born, I counseled you. And as you leave this world, I will comfort you. In truth, I shall never stop loving you. Remember this today.

MEDITATION TWO HUNDRED FORTY-NINE

There are many who believe they can neither see, nor hear, nor feel me. So I ask: Am I not seen in the colors of a rainbow? Am I not heard in a songbird's melody? And am I not felt in a loved one's embrace? Reflect on this today.

MEDITATION TWO HUNDRED FIFTY

You have but one life, yet it lasts forever. So I ask: Is this not a reason to celebrate? Is this not a time of triumph? Rejoice today! Wait not a moment longer!

MEDITATION TWO HUNDRED FIFTY-ONE

I am the light which conquers darkness. I am the hope which follows a storm. So hear the truth: There shall never be a place where darkness reigns. And there shall never be a time when hope is vanquished. Reflect on what this means to you.

MEDITATION TWO HUNDRED FIFTY-TWO

What is timelessness? What is divinity? How can they be described? Think of it this way: I was; I am; and I shall always be. Or if you prefer, I have always loved; I love now; and I shall always love. Remember this as the day unfolds.

MEDITATION TWO HUNDRED FIFTY-THREE

As you praise me, you are awakened to my presence. As you give thanks to me, you are reminded of my glory. So praise me today, and know that I am with you. Thank me today, and remember that I love you.

MEDITATION TWO HUNDRED FIFTY-FOUR

You needn't be perfect for me to be pleased. And you needn't be faultless for me to love you. So I ask: Why do you feel guilty? Why are you ashamed? In truth, guilt and shame are your greatest barriers to peace and happiness. Today, reflect on what this means to you.

MEDITATION TWO HUNDRED FIFTY-FIVE

Open your heart to my strength. Do this right now, and break free from destructive desires. Open your heart to my courage. Do this today, and be safe from damning temptations.

MEDITATION TWO HUNDRED FIFTY-SIX

When you ask me for help, your problems are less daunting. And as you grow to trust me more and more, you shall never feel overwhelmed. Is there something which troubles your heart? Are you ready to ask for my help? Are you willing to trust me wholly? Reflect on these questions as your day unfolds.

MEDITATION TWO HUNDRED FIFTY-SEVEN

A single flame may light a thousand candles, and it can do this without sacrifice. Love is much the same. The love in your heart may comfort a thousand souls, and it can do this without loss. No matter how many people you inspire, your love shall not be diminished. No matter how many people you uplift, your light shall never dim. Remember this today.

MEDITATION TWO HUNDRED FIFTY-EIGHT

There are many who ask: "Why is this happening?" Others will ask: "Where is God now?" Yet, such questions do not trouble me; for my ways are higher than yours. And I tell you truly: Draw closer to me during moments of doubt. Work on this today.

MEDITATION TWO HUNDRED FIFTY-NINE

There are many who claim to not know me. Yet, believe me when I say: You know me well, for I am your heart's desire. You know me well, for I am the way and the truth and the life. Today, reflect on what this means to you.

MEDITATION TWO HUNDRED SIXTY

Resistance is the source of your stress. Yet, resistance is a choice that you make. Choosing to resist is much like choosing to forget. Therefore, accept whatever is happening. You gain nothing by denying the obvious and by fighting what cannot be changed. Remember this today.

MEDITATION TWO HUNDRED SIXTY-ONE

Today, focus on me. Concentrate on our relationship. And when you notice that your mind has wandered, gently steer it back to me. Practice and determination will yield a favorable outcome. This is your pathway to peace, for an undisciplined mind is the devil's playground.

MEDITATION TWO HUNDRED SIXTY-TWO

Stubbornness is not an attribute, and a closed mind is not a virtue. So today, let go of what you think you want. And after doing this, I will give you what you need.

MEDITATION TWO HUNDRED SIXTY-THREE

I am your Savior, your ever-present help in times of trouble. Be not afraid, though oceans rise and mountains quake. Be not worried, though kingdoms battle and nations fall. I am your comfort and strength, your ever-present help in times of trouble. Reflect on this today.

MEDITATION TWO HUNDRED SIXTY-FOUR

The Holy Spirit is the voice within your heart. Listen closely, for I often whisper. And trust me when I say: As you follow your heart, you promote my will. Today, promote a legacy of kindness and helpfulness. Work on this as your day unfolds.

MEDITATION TWO HUNDRED SIXTY-FIVE

Disease plays a role in natural death. First, the tree is born. Next it grows up, and it grows strong. Then it grows old, it grows weak, and it grows sick. Finally, the tree dies. Its epitaph: I was sinless. Reflect on what this means to you.

MEDITATION TWO HUNDRED SIXTY-SIX

There are some who feel threatened by my love. Others are fearful of my presence, and still others are afraid of my name. In desperation, they flee to the shadows. In despair, they abuse my name. Yet, those who run from me shall be lost; and those who curse me shall suffer. Reflect on what this mean to you.

MEDITATION TWO HUNDRED SIXTY-SEVEN

Wisdom prepares you to see the world as neutral and benign. You alone can accept my truth and reality. You alone can free your mind of fear and worry. Today, there is nothing in the world that threatens your well-being. Today, you are safe in my infinite arms.

MEDITATION TWO HUNDRED SIXTY-EIGHT

Instead of giving up on me, simply ask, "God, where are you?" Instead of taking my name in vain, simply say, "God, help me." Remember this today.

MEDITATION TWO HUNDRED SIXTY-NINE

A relentless pursuit of wealth will only lead to frustration. And a ruthless quest for power can only lead to disappointment. So I ask: Are these wise decisions? Today, look closely at the choices you make. And by doing this, you may learn a great deal about yourself.

MEDITATION TWO HUNDRED SEVENTY

At certain times, everyone is a teacher. There are some who teach through harmful intentions. They teach how *not* to live. So I remind you: Teach only love, for that is what you are. Remember this today.

MEDITATION TWO HUNDRED SEVENTY-ONE

Nothing in the world can separate you from my love – not distance, not time, not pain, not sadness, not even sin. Does this surprise you? Today, reflect on the nature of my love.

MEDITATION TWO HUNDRED SEVENTY-TWO

At first, it might feel awkward to offer endless praise to me. Your mind may balk at the very thought of it. Yet, your heart will urge you to push forward. And in time, it will seem natural. In time, your unending praise will feel normal and routine. Work on this today.

MEDITATION TWO HUNDRED SEVENTY-THREE

Perhaps today, I am but a poor reflection – as in a mirror. Yet one day, you will know me more fully. One day, divine perfection will be wholly revealed. Reflect on what this means to you.

MEDITATION TWO HUNDRED SEVENTY-FOUR

I have asked you to make disciples of all nations. Yet, I do not expect you to save the world. So rest easy, my child. Simply live your faith, for this will be enough. Work on it today.

MEDITATION TWO HUNDRED SEVENTY-FIVE

You needn't travel far in your search for me. I am closer than you may think. To find me, look inward. Search the infinite stillness of your heart. Look for me in the quiet solitude of your soul. Make this journey today.

MEDITATION TWO HUNDRED SEVENTY-SIX

There are many who do not believe in heavenly angels. Yet in truth, there are more angels than you can possibly count. And trust me when I say: They gather around you more often than you know. Remember this today.

MEDITATION TWO HUNDRED SEVENTY-SEVEN

Although the laws of man can be helpful, they are often misguided. And while the laws of religion are well-intended, they are sometimes misused. Distance yourself from religious legalism, for it has little to do with me. Reflect on what this means.

MEDITATION TWO HUNDRED SEVENTY-EIGHT

That which saddens the caterpillar brings joy to the butterfly. So I ask: Will you be satisfied with a heavenly body made of flesh and bone? Reflect on this today.

MEDITATION TWO HUNDRED SEVENTY-NINE

When I came to the world, humanity was hopelessly lost. And still, there is confusion about my time on earth. So hear the truth: My ministry was not of the human condition, but of its potential. My ministry was not of a troubled world, but of what it might become. Reflect on what this means to you.

MEDITATION TWO HUNDRED EIGHTY

Why languish in the gutter of self-pity? Believe me when I say: You cannot possibly be a victim, for I have never created one. Take my hand today. Do this, and I will lead you to a breathtaking summit. Let me guide you to a place where there is no despair.

MEDITATION TWO HUNDRED EIGHTY-ONE

Are you feeling depleted? Are you thinking that compassion has limits? Do you hear a voice that suggests you have nothing left to give? Come with me on a respite. Let me guide you to a destination of renewal. As you talk to me, your fatigue will wane. As you walk with me, your stress will dissolve. Do this today, and be not disheartened.

MEDITATION TWO HUNDRED EIGHTY-TWO

There are many who are painfully confused. And many others accept suffering as their destiny. So trust me when I say: The time for righteous pain is over. The time for redemptive suffering has passed. Reflect on what this means to you.

MEDITATION TWO HUNDRED EIGHTY-THREE

I dwell in the stillness of your soul; and in the silence of your heart, you will feel my presence. Therefore, find a holy sanctuary. Retreat to a sacred space. Then, pray in silence and meditate in stillness. Do this simple thing today.

MEDITATION TWO HUNDRED EIGHTY-FOUR

I understand that fear and worry are products of your mind. So you needn't be ashamed of your thoughts, and you needn't apologize for your feelings. Yet, listen to the truth: If you ask that *my* will be done, your fears shall disappear. And if you ask that *my* will be done, your worries shall vanish. Work on this today.

MEDITATION TWO HUNDRED EIGHTY-FIVE

There are many who believe they walk alone. Soon, they grow weary. And feeling overwhelmed, they compound their problems by making destructive choices. Some will turn to self-abuse. Others will adopt hedonism. So believe me when I say: You can serve but one master. Reflect on what this means to you.

MEDITATION TWO HUNDRED EIGHTY-SIX

Hearing your prayers of thanksgiving, I send even more blessings your way. Hearing your songs of praise, I give you even more reasons to be joyful. Remember this today.

MEDITATION TWO HUNDRED EIGHTY-SEVEN

Most everyone has heard of hell. And in truth, many dwell there. Yet, there shall never be a place where you cannot call out to me. And there shall never be a time when I cannot come to you. Today, reflect on what this means.

MEDITATION TWO HUNDRED EIGHTY-EIGHT

There are some who travel the world to witness my beauty. Yet, those in search of holiness needn't walk very far. Look closely at your surroundings. Search for signs of my love. Hunt for evidence of my glory. And as you follow this path, perhaps holiness will be found where you least expect it. Work on this today.

MEDITATION TWO HUNDRED EIGHTY-NINE

Today, look at the world through the innocent eyes of a child. And as you look at others, you will see my face. Today, look upon creation through a lens of awe and wonder. And as you do this, you will live in paradise.

MEDITATION TWO HUNDRED NINETY

As you move from room to room, the joys of higher realms remain a mystery. Yet, as you grow in faith, you learn to accept what *is*. You learn to be at peace with life's circumstances. Then, frustration and disappointment can no longer haunt you. Today, reflect on what this means.

MEDITATION TWO HUNDRED NINETY-ONE

Even as your life appears to be spiraling out of control; even then, you have choices. Do you not control your perception of a hardship? Do you not choose a solution to your problem? And do you not choose how to cope with your pain? Reflect on this today.

MEDITATION TWO HUNDRED NINETY-TWO

Holy unions are formed when – with my blessing – two are joined as one. Marriage is but one kind of holy union. Others include the joining of love and forgiveness, the coupling of kindness and compassion, and the bonding of respect and unity. In truth, holy unions are stepping stones to heaven. Remember this today.

MEDITATION TWO HUNDRED NINETY-THREE

Much has been said about lost innocence. And much has been taught about living in a fallen world. So hear the truth: In order to find innocence, you must first be willing to love. And in order to live in a sinless world, you must first be willing to forgive. Work on these things today.

MEDITATION TWO HUNDRED NINETY-FOUR

Do not be paralyzed by doubting thoughts. And do not be delayed by sanctimonious words. Glorify me through selfless service. Honor me by helping others. Work on this today, and I will ask for nothing else.

MEDITATION TWO HUNDRED NINETY-FIVE

Do not form alliances with worldly deities, for such pairings distract you from exploring your inner self. They distract you from searching your heart, the home of my light and truth. Now you know why heaven's path is straight and narrow. Reflect on this today.

MEDITATION TWO HUNDRED NINETY-SIX

Quiet faith is your strength; silent hope is your guide. Commune with me in nakedness and be not vulnerable. Join with me in solitude and be not alone. Remember this today.

MEDITATION TWO HUNDRED NINETY-SEVEN

There are times when those who love me are ridiculed. There are places where those who love me are persecuted. Are you shouldering the yoke of righteousness? Are you bearing the cross of humiliation? I tell you once more: Rejoice and be glad, for heaven awaits you! Reflect on this today.

MEDITATION TWO HUNDRED NINETY-EIGHT

You were not made in an image of frailty. Nor did I create you to be alive for a moment and to be dead forever. So hear the truth: Though you have but one life, it is a life without end. Celebrate your immortality, for no one can take it from you. Go forth this day with joy in your heart!

MEDITATION TWO HUNDRED NINETY-NINE

There are some who spend money, but have no food. Others spend time, but are not fulfilled. So I ask: Why pay for things that cannot nourish? Why focus on things that cannot satisfy? Today, reflect on what this means to you.

MEDITATION THREE HUNDRED

Some are fearful of silence, and others are wary of solitude. Yet, when you run from silence, you run from me. And when you flee from solitude, you flee from me. Listen to the truth: From the depths of silence and solitude, I speak to you. Remember this today.

MEDITATION THREE HUNDRED ONE

Pain is a part of learning and growing. Yet, suffering occurs only when a label is attached. If you label something – if you choose to call it "bad" – then suffering will surely follow. So hear the truth: Labeling is a choice. Therefore, suffering is a choice as well. Today, be strong and resist the temptation to label. Work on this, and put an end to your suffering!

MEDITATION THREE HUNDRED TWO

You needn't worry about clothing or shelter, for I comfort all who reach out to me. You needn't worry about food or water, for I nourish all who trust in me. And you needn't worry about the kingdom of heaven, for I welcome all who open their hearts to me. Remember this today.

MEDITATION THREE HUNDRED THREE

You live in a transparent world. And as you walk, my light shines upon you. I truth, I am always at your side. So I ask: Why are there places where you cannot find me? And why are there times when you do not see me? Reflect on this today.

MEDITATION THREE HUNDRED FOUR

For now, there are gaps in your understanding of my ways. For now, there are divine mysteries you cannot solve. Yet one day, an explosion of light shall reveal my plan and explain my ways. Some will call it a revelation. Others will know it as a second coming. But all will see it as a new world. Reflect on what this means.

MEDITATION THREE HUNDRED FIVE

There are many who believe that only the weak surrender. Yet, I tell you: Those who bow to my mercy are the strongest of the strong. And those who kneel to my grace are the bravest of the brave. Reflect on what this means to you.

MEDITATION THREE HUNDRED SIX

As you follow your heart, you learn to look inward. And by looking inward, you grow in faith. Ultimately, it is faith which empowers you to accept that your life is, in truth, an inner journey. Reflect on this today.

MEDITATION THREE HUNDRED SEVEN

There are many who follow their minds and trust their bodies. They will ask: How is it possible to be born again? So hear the truth: Only those who follow their hearts shall find a better world. And only those who trust in me shall discover peace on earth. Reflect on what this means to you.

MEDITATION THREE HUNDRED EIGHT

Most unions are the joining of two. Yet sometimes, holy unions are formed by the joining of three: Hope, faith, and love; Solitude, silence, and prayer; Father, Son, and Holy Spirit. Can you identify others? Reflect on this as your day unfolds.

MEDITATION THREE HUNDRED NINE

You must learn to ask me for certain things. If you want mercy, then ask and it shall be given. If you want grace, then ask and you shall have it. But I tell you the truth: You needn't ask for my love, for it is already yours. Remember this today.

MEDITATION THREE HUNDRED TEN

When pinned to a cloud, hope will surely drift away. When placed upon the sand, a dream is sure to crumble. Yet I tell you: What is built upon the rock of faith shall last forever more. Today, reflect on what this means.

MEDITATION THREE HUNDRED ELEVEN

Each drop of seawater has the same salty taste. So there is no such thing as a good drop or a bad one. Life is much the same. Be it a triumph or a trial, each situation holds the promise of growth. Each experience has the potential to bring you closer to me. Remember this today.

MEDITATION THREE HUNDRED TWELVE

I ask you to give thanks before meals. Not only does your blessing honor me, it pays tribute to the love which produces, prepares, and serves the food. And with certain meals, your blessing pays homage to an ultimate sacrifice. Remember this today.

MEDITATION THREE HUNDRED THIRTEEN

There are many who yearn to be free, and many more who wish to be happy. So hear the truth: Freedom begins when life's journey becomes an inner one. And happiness begins when peace and uncertainty dwell in harmony. Work on this today.

MEDITATION THREE HUNDRED FOURTEEN

Perhaps you've read the Bible, but have you turned to me for mercy? Perhaps you've gone to church, but have you come to me for grace? And maybe you've listened to sermons, but have you prayed to feel my peace? Reflect on what this means to you.

MEDITATION THREE HUNDRED FIFTEEN

Remember that each new day offers perfect moments for gift giving. I tell you the truth: Angels sing with your every gift of love. And heaven rejoices with your every gift of forgiveness. Be sure to give generously today.

MEDITATION THREE HUNDRED SIXTEEN

Disingenuous contrition is an arrogant attempt to portray oneself as a martyr. And condescending forgiveness is a childish effort to make oneself "better" than the person who tried to harm you. In truth, such deceptions have nothing to do with real forgiveness. Today, remember that the road to hell is paved with self-righteous indignation.

MEDITATION THREE HUNDRED SEVENTEEN

There are places where violence is glorified. There are times when immorality is presented as entertainment. And because of this, there are many who think deviant behavior is normal. Some are tempted to mimic the depravity they watch. Others lose touch with the sanctity of life. So I ask: Are violence and perversion harmless? Are their promoters blameless? Are their defenders faultless? Reflect on this today.

MEDITATION THREE HUNDRED EIGHTEEN

The more you love me, the more you will become like me. And the more you become like me, the more you will feel heaven's peace. Work on this today.

MEDITATION THREE HUNDRED NINETEEN

There are some who ask: Why should I meditate? Why must I pray? So hear the truth: Meditation awakens you to my love. Prayer awakens you to my will. Remember this as your day unfolds.

MEDITATION THREE HUNDRED TWENTY

To the humble, I offer peace. To the thankful, I give blessings. And to the faithful, I reveal my love in the promise of each new day. Reflect on what this means to you.

MEDITATION THREE HUNDRED TWENTY-ONE

There are many who choose to wear a disguise. Next, they wonder why no one can recognize them. So trust me when I say: As you work to discover your true identity, you work on your salvation. Today, reflect on what this means.

MEDITATION THREE HUNDRED TWENTY-TWO

You are free to live the way you wish. You are free to walk the path of your choice, and you are free to walk alone. Yet ask, and I will guide you. And then, together, we shall create your destiny. Remember this today.

MEDITATION THREE HUNDRED TWENTY-THREE

Those who are wise have learned that laughter promotes healing. Like a soothing elixir, laughter eases stress. Like a loyal friend, laughter helps you cope with anxiety. So remember to look for the right moments to laugh. Work on this today.

MEDITATION THREE HUNDRED TWENTY-FOUR

When serving others, reach out to them with kindness and compassion. Instead of criticism, offer them comfort. Instead of disapproval, give them affirmation. Offer them assurance, not doubt. Give them hope, not despair. Do this in remembrance of me.

MEDITATION THREE HUNDRED TWENTY-FIVE

Love is patient, love is kind. It is not easily angered, and it keeps no record of wrongs. Love rejoices with the truth. It always protects, always trusts, always hopes, and always perseveres. And I remind you: Seeds of love yearn for the fertile soil of freedom. Reflect on this today.

MEDITATION THREE HUNDRED TWENTY-SIX

Contemplation is the echo of my voice, the one that whispers: There is no distance between you and me, and time hasn't the power to separate us. Today, reflect on what this means to you.

MEDITATION THREE HUNDRED TWENTY-SEVEN

Unblemished by corruption, your Sacred Heart is the home of purity and sanctity. Upon its altars, I have placed my love. And within its chambers, I have written my name. Remember this today.

MEDITATION THREE HUNDRED TWENTY-EIGHT

Prayer is a language which transcends the jealousies of religion. It is a passage that circumvents all barriers, a bridge that connects all gaps. Prayer is a direct voice from your heart to mine. Reflect on this today.

MEDITATION THREE HUNDRED TWENTY-NINE

Why are you infatuated with your thoughts? Are the mist and the fog deserving of your loyalty? Are the fleeting and fragile worthy of your trust? Today, count on the One who is timeless and changeless. Trust in the One who is immortal and almighty.

MEDITATION THREE HUNDRED THIRTY

I hear your every prayer, and each of them is treasured. Yet, when you offer a prayer of praise and thanksgiving, all of heaven rejoices! Reflect on this as your day unfolds.

MEDITATION THREE HUNDRED THIRTY-ONE

Have you forgotten the feeling of joyfulness? Are you still searching for the relationship that will make life perfect? I tell you truly: Place your relationship with me above all others. Work on this today. And as your devotion grows, I will gently restore your memory of perfection and joy.

MEDITATION THREE HUNDRED THIRTY-TWO

Those who cling to past grievances are held captive by their thoughts of revenge and feelings of bitterness. So I say this once more: Only forgiveness has the power to restore freedom. In truth, forgiveness is a gift which is given to oneself. Today is a perfect day for you to give and receive this gift. Now is a perfect time for you to regain your long lost freedom.

MEDITATION THREE HUNDRED THIRTY-THREE

Are you counting on future happiness? Those who are wise have learned that life is what happens as you plan for the future. So hear the truth: Like a lifeline that dangles just beyond your reach, tomorrow's happiness is today's torment. Reflect on what this means to you.

MEDITATION THREE HUNDRED THIRTY-FOUR

Adequate rest and sleep are vital, not optional. Those who are overly fatigued participate in life but miss its meaning. Today, set aside time to rest. And remember to pray before going to bed, for prayer sets the stage for a good night's sleep. Do these simple things today.

MEDITATION THREE HUNDRED THIRTY-FIVE

There are many who live in the world, yet fail to see my light. Many others look upon creation, yet fail to see my love. Still, this does not trouble me; for paradigms are ever-shifting. And as the wise have learned: You do not see the world as it is, you see the world as you are. Reflect on this as your day unfolds.

MEDITATION THREE HUNDRED THIRTY-SIX

As you place the past in my capable hands, you eliminate every reason to be ashamed. As you place the future in my capable hands, you eliminate every reason to be worried. And as you place this moment in my capable hands, you eliminate every reason to be afraid. Work on this today.

MEDITATION THREE HUNDRED THIRTY-SEVEN

There are many who gaze at the moon and the stars and believe them to be everlasting. Yet, much of the world is not as it appears to be. So I tell you: Trust not in what you see, for what you see will surely betray you. Instead, place your trust in the invisible and the timeless. Reflect on this today.

MEDITATION THREE HUNDRED THIRTY-EIGHT

Come to me. Come to where brokenness can no longer haunt you. Turn to me. Turn to the Source of wholeness and wellness. Do this today, for I tell you the truth: An unhealed healer helps no one.

MEDITATION THREE HUNDRED THIRTY-NINE

There are many who dwell on the past. Yet, I tell you: The past is no more. Therefore, it can neither harm nor help you. Let go of bitterness and reclaim your peace. Let go of revenge and regain your happiness. Work on this today.

MEDITATION THREE HUNDRED FORTY

Do you value our relationship? Would you like for us to grow even closer? Then I tell you once again: Do not be fooled into thinking that good deeds are more important than prayer. Remember this today.

MEDITATION THREE HUNDRED FORTY-ONE

Your thoughts are important, but what you think isn't who you really are. Your words are important, but what you say isn't who you really are. And your deeds are important, but what you do isn't who you really are. Today, reflect on what this means to you.

MEDITATION THREE HUNDRED FORTY-TWO

There are many who hunt for earthly treasures. And many others search for worldly pleasures. Next, they wonder why life is filled with frustration and disappointment. These misguided souls have not yet learned the ego's motto: Seek but do not find. Reflect on what this means to you.

MEDITATION THREE HUNDRED FORTY-THREE

Yes, there will be periods of sadness and regret. Of course, there will be moments of anger. And I know that, at times, your anger will be directed at me. So hear the truth: There is nothing you can think or say or do that I cannot forgive. Remember this as your day unfolds.

MEDITATION THREE HUNDRED FORTY-FOUR

Each and every day offers a wide range of choices. Do you say one thing, or say something else? Do you do one thing, or do something different? So today, each time you face a decision, ask this simple question: Which choice expresses love? Devote this day to making better choices.

MEDITATION THREE HUNDRED FORTY-FIVE

Your *story* follows a linear path of days, months, and years. Yet, your *life* unfolds in the timeless present. Having no ties with the past or the future, the present moment is nonlinear. And owing no debt to time, the present moment is the essence of reality. So listen to the truth: Though your story is important, it is your life which changes the world. Reflect on what this means to you.

MEDITATION THREE HUNDRED FORTY-SIX

Do you still have hope for a better world? Do you still have faith in humanity? This is a day of trust. Today, look upon the world and behold my perfect plan. Look upon the world and see that everything and everyone belong. Trust me today, and be not worried.

MEDITATION THREE HUNDRED FORTY-SEVEN

Human beings cannot win the war on disease any more than governments can win the war on poverty – not in this world, not at this time. Yet, there is a paradox; for people can focus on healing. People can pray. They can receive medical treatments. They can make healthier choices. And their broken bodies may, for a while, be well again. Today, reflect on what this means.

MEDITATION THREE HUNDRED FORTY-EIGHT

Perhaps certain people bother you. Maybe there are some you dislike. And perhaps there are a few you despise. Yet, believe me when I say: As you see the holiness of your enemy, you see the holiness of yourself. Work on this today.

MEDITATION THREE HUNDRED FORTY-NINE

An epiphany is a radical transformation, a profound metamorphosis. Epiphanies have enabled the blind to see. They have allowed the lost to find their way. In short, an epiphany empowers the mind to accept what the heart has always known: With love, all things are possible. Reflect on this today.

MEDITATION THREE HUNDRED FIFTY

Why are you forlorn? Have your sins not been forgiven? Trust me when I say: Nothing you have said or done has eluded my grace. Your slate is wiped clean. Therefore, today's tears shall be tears of joy!

MEDITATION THREE HUNDRED FIFTY-ONE

There are many who start on the straight and narrow path, but somehow lose their way. And many others have perfect eyesight, yet they cannot see. So I tell you: Open your eyes to the light of my truth. Now is the time for a new beginning. Today is the day to shed all memories of blindness.

MEDITATION THREE HUNDRED FIFTY-TWO

There are some who think that happiness will come on the day they buy a new car or land a better job. Others believe that happiness will come when they take an exotic vacation or find a new relationship. So hear the truth: Your ego wants you to miss today's joy while waiting for tomorrow's excitement. Reflect on what this means.

MEDITATION THREE HUNDRED FIFTY-THREE

Has immortality not quenched your thirst for riches? Has eternal life not quelled your yearning for justice? And has salvation not already solved your biggest problems? Reflect on what these questions mean to you.

MEDITATION THREE HUNDRED FIFTY-FOUR

There are some who know my ways better than others. And always, there are some who are eager to emerge from the shadows of illusion. Using the tools of logic and clarity, the Holy Spirit reveals my truth and light. The Holy Spirit calms the mind and awakens the heart. And illumination will dawn when the seeker is ready. Reflect on this today.

MEDITATION THREE HUNDRED FIFTY-FIVE

Your every thought is accounted for. In truth, the bookshelves of the universe hold the records of each word and deed. For how else could the scales of justice be balanced? Part of you is afraid these archives will be used to condemn you. Yet, I say: This very evidence will prove your innocence. Reflect on what this means to you.

MEDITATION THREE HUNDRED FIFTY-SIX

Much like life, human love is always changing, adapting, and evolving. An infatuation may escalate to a romance. A romantic love might change to a nurturing love. Yesterday's dear friend may become tomorrow's life partner. And a life partner's love could evolve to a caregiver's love. Still, no matter how it is expressed or how it may change, it is love in all its glory! Remember this today.

MEDITATION THREE HUNDRED FIFTY-SEVEN

The world is transformed as each newborn arrives. Infants become children who become men and women. Some will be famous, others will be infamous. And still others will live and die unnoticed. Yet, I tell you: Each and every person plays a crucial role in my perfect plan. In truth, there is no other who can do what I ask of you. Reflect on this today.

MEDITATION THREE HUNDRED FIFTY-EIGHT

A holy relationship is an expression of my love. Therefore, it is a relationship which has my blessing. It is a joining founded on respect, a pairing graced by freedom, a union in which exploitation has no home. Remember this today.

MEDITATION THREE HUNDRED FIFTY-NINE

You cannot change what others may think or say So I tell you: Forgive what you can neither control nor understand. Do this, and reclaim your peace of mind. Do this today, and enjoy newfound happiness.

MEDITATION THREE HUNDRED SIXTY

There are many who sleepwalk through life. In truth, they have created a parallel reality. They have chosen to live in a make-believe world. So trust me when I say: First, you must awaken. Then, you can start making your dreams come true. Reflect on this today.

MEDITATION THREE HUNDRED SIXTY-ONE

By changing the way you view the world, you can change the way you view worldly circumstances. You can see situations, even life's darkest clouds, as fleeting and nonthreatening. Work on this today.

MEDITATION THREE HUNDRED SIXTY-TWO

Energy and spirit are two threads intertwined in the cloth of divinity. Though born of the same love, energy and spirit are neither identical nor interchangeable. I tell you the truth: Energy propels life. Energy fuels life. But spirit *is* life. Reflect on this today.

MEDITATION THREE HUNDRED SIXTY-THREE

When you see someone as weak or lacking, you impose these limits on yourself. When you perceive someone as broken or inferior, you adopt these traits as your own. So hear the truth: My eyes see only strength and wholeness, glory and perfection. Reflect on what this means to you.

MEDITATION THREE HUNDRED SIXTY-FOUR

You have attached values to everything. Yet, they are *your* values, not mine. Your values are tied to the past, and the past is but a confusing dream. Now is the perfect time to rethink what you value. Today is the perfect day to realign your values with mine.

MEDITATION THREE HUNDRED SIXTY-FIVE

Let not your heart be troubled, for no one walks alone when crossing the bridge to eternity. And I tell you the truth: This world's beauty falls far short of what awaits you as the pathway vanishes and time ends with it. Remember this always.

POSTLUDE

We live in a world of form *and* content. Indeed, both are necessary. Form and content are partners: connected, yet distinctly individual. Religion is form, while faith is content. The body is form, while the soul is content. A good deed is form, while kindness is content. A relationship is form, while love is content. Sin is form; guilt is content. Believing is form; knowing is content. Assaults and attacks are form; fear and rage are content. Heaven and hell are form; joy and torment are content.

Though the mind is fixated on form, the heart is drawn to content. Spiritual seekers should look beyond form; for we cannot learn and grow simply by staring at a book, by admiring its cover and flipping through the pages. We have to read it. We have to understand its message and apply its wisdom. Deeper levels of awareness and higher realms of consciousness are reached as we explore life's content. And ultimately, that is why you must follow your heart.

God has given you life everlasting. His plan is for you to have heaven on earth. Your Loving Father has graced you with the Light of Christ, and your sins have been forgiven. Are there grander gifts than these? Could you wish for blessings more glorious? And should not your prayers, then, ask for what you already have?

Closing Thoughts and Acknowledgments

The needs of the sick are constantly changing. At first, perhaps a family member can provide capable assistance to a loved one. But professional help might be needed as disease progression leads to greater dependency. When a loved one declines, family members face tough questions. Where can I find the best care? Who can I trust? Is it possible to be a daughter, a wife, a mother, *and* a good caregiver at the same time?

There's a learning curve to providing effective care. Like many things, practice leads to improvement. Most professional caregivers have had years of training. They've fulfilled licensing requirements and have attended countless continuing education classes. Still, patience and a kind heart are among the most important qualifications. Because the bedside is a sacred place, care giving is actually a ministry, an opportunity to serve and comfort those who are hurting. And because pain – be it physical, emotional, or spiritual – is very real, it carries a sense of urgency. This reality can add a significant burden to family members and professional caregivers alike.

My ministry as a hospice chaplain is the most challenging work I've ever done. Yet it's also, by far, the most rewarding. Let me be candid: Hospice is a blessing. And my passion for it keeps growing as I see patients and families receiving wonderful benefits from the services that only hospice provides. With this in mind, I want to share some things I've learned while working as a staff chaplain for Hospice of Dayton. And I'll try to dispel a few of the myths associated with hospice care as well.

I feel especially blessed to work for a nonprofit hospice because, contrary to what you may think, all hospices are *not* the same. People with life-threatening illnesses can turn to Hospice of Dayton for palliative care, even when they're receiving curative treatments. Simply defined, palliative care is comfort care and pain management. And if curative options are exhausted or no longer desired, then dignified end-of-life care is available as well. A medical assessment confirming eligibility is all that's required.

Hospice care is a celebration of life. Therefore, our mission is to provide care which promotes the best possible quality of life. This includes maintaining that high standard of care and support to the time of natural death or to medical ineligibility, which normally results from symptom stabilization. Hospice of Dayton achieves its goals through holistic care focused on the body, mind, and spirit. Professional caregivers provide pain management, medical care, personal care, psycho-social support, and spiritual support. Our experienced staff also offers respiratory therapy, occupational therapy, massage therapy, music therapy, and art therapy. In addition, two Hospice Houses serve our patients with acute medical needs. And most notably, our community support and nonprofit status ensure that every eligible patient receives our benefits, regardless of their ability to pay.

For more than 35 years, Hospice of Dayton has served in nearly every care environment, including private residences, nursing homes, and assisted living and independent living facilities. As a team member, I've seen new patients receive immediate help from our expert pain management. I've watched our patients of faith experience a renewed inner peace after receiving a prayer. I've heard the reassuring words offered by our nurses and aides. I've watched our staff physicians making their daily rounds, taking all the time needed to answer questions, and giving heartfelt hugs. I've witnessed the relief provided by therapeutic massage, and I've seen the joy inspired by a music therapist. I've seen children smile as they express their feelings through art therapy. And yes, I've felt the loving presence of heavenly angels as they gather at a patient's bedside. I assure you, it *does* happen.

During this time of change for America's healthcare providers, hospice services continue to be an attractive option. In fact, the need for palliative and end-of-life care is greater than ever before. And families who take the time to research and compare their local hospices stand to gain huge dividends.

Myth: There is only one hospice.

Truth: Most of the time, patients and families have several hospices in their community. That's why it's important to carefully compare the services and qualifications of each one.

Myth: A doctor chooses which hospice to use.

Truth: Although a doctor's referral is normally required for eligibility, it's the responsibility of the patient or family to decide which hospice to use.

Myth: Hospice care is for someone who has "given up" and wants to die.

Truth: Hospice is for the living! In fact, families often say, "I only wish we had come to you sooner."

Myth: There's no difference between for-profit and not-for-profit hospices.

Truth: Nonprofit hospices are closely connected with local neighborhoods and are supported, in part, by the communities they serve. And while for-profit hospices are accountable to shareholders and investors, nonprofit hospices typically use revenues to expand patient services.

Myth: All hospices require the same professional licensing for their staff.

Truth: Some hospices have adopted licensing policies which far exceed the minimum government requirements.

Myth: Every hospice offers the same standard of patient care.

Truth: Yes, every hospice organization must maintain an established minimum standard of patient care. However, some hospice organizations provide a much higher standard of care and earn special recognition from the Joint Commission for exceptional performance.

Myth: Hospice care doesn't allow chemotherapy or radiation treatments.

Truth: Some hospices review these clinical options on a case-by-case basis. Approval may be granted if such treatments help manage pain and improve the patient's quality of life.

Myth: Hospice care is only for the wealthy.

Truth: Usually, hospice costs are covered by either private insurance, Medicare, or Medicaid. And some hospices provide benefits regardless of a patient's ability to pay.

★★★

Quite often, professional caregivers don't have the chance to learn much about the lives of their patients. And at first, this was the case with George, a new patient at our Hospice House. I met him for the first time when he was eighty-five years old, minimally responsive and unable to speak. Seated next to his bed, I introduced myself and reassured George that he was in a safe place. I explained that he had an entire team of people looking after his needs and making sure that he would be comfortable. I offered him a gentle touch, a silent prayer, and a ministry of presence. I reminded him that he was loved. Then, I left George and called his daughter, Judy, who lived out of state. She provided the details of her father's faith history and asked me to visit him as often as possible. Judy said that she would be travelling to Dayton later in the week, and that she would stay at her father's bedside until God called him to heaven.

As promised, Judy arrived at our Hospice House and kept a devoted vigil. During my subsequent visits, I learned more and more about George. Judy said that he was a loving husband and father. He was an excellent provider and a loyal worker who retired from a local paper mill after forty years of service. He volunteered at a shelter which served the homeless. And yes, he loved the Lord. But there was more. During one of our conversations, Judy shared an extraordinary story about her father – a story I will never forget.

George was driving his car one winter's day with Judy, who was ten at the time, sitting in the passenger's seat. Suddenly, George steered the car to the curb, stopped, and dashed out. Judy watched as her father exchanged words with a man on the sidewalk. Next, George took off his coat and helped the man put it on. The two men shook hands, and

George returned to the car. Judy asked, "Dad, who was that man?" And her father replied, "I don't know, but he looked very cold. And he was happy to wear my coat."

Judy looked at me and said, "That was just how Dad lived. He did things like that all the time. And being so young, I just thought that every Dad did the same things; that every Dad lived like he did. Now, of course, I know that he's special."

And so it is with caregivers as we, for a brief moment, enter the rooms and the lives of our patients. Let us remember that they are real people with real stories, even when they can no longer tell them. Let us realize that they are real people who we actually don't know at all. For in truth, no one is defined by a pulse rate, a temperature, or a disease. And let us remain hopeful that, after serving a patient, we will not be leaving the room of a stranger.

★★★

I was on my way to visit Michael, a hospice patient. Earlier that day, my team meeting had been rescheduled and some other unexpected things had popped up. The day seemed to be spiraling out of control, and I was frustrated and feeling sorry for myself. Still, I pushed these thoughts aside as I entered Michael's room. Confined to a wheelchair, Michael's debilitating disease has ravaged his body, but has left his mind alert and healthy. And in Michael's case, it's also very difficult to speak. Near the end of my visit, Michael wanted a prayer. And following the prayer – as I was getting ready to leave – a determined look appeared on Michael's face. Then, with great effort, he said, "God bless you."

Walking from Michael's room, I felt utterly humbled. Here is a man who seemingly has so little, yet he continues to give to others. Here is a man who faces incredible hardship, yet he uplifts the people around him. So Michael, thank you for your ministry. Thank you for showing me what is really important. Thank you, Michael, for reminding me of my blessings. And thank you for being a light in the world. In truth, I have many patient visits like this one. It's a different name, of course, and a different terminal disease; yet with the same result: I receive more than I give. Sometimes, we help the dying; other times, they help us. And we never know when or where or from whom our next gift will come.

★★★

When you were growing up, your mother would leave you alone for periods of time. Or if you needed help, there were times when she would let someone else provide it. Yet, that didn't mean your mother had stopped loving you. Remember this if you ever become exhausted while providing care for a loved one. Remember this if you ever become overwhelmed when keeping a bedside vigil.

★★★

This past Christmas season, my wife, Lynn, and I drove to Cincinnati's Music Hall for a performance of Handel's *Messiah*. I typically experience mixed feelings around Christmas. On one hand, there's the bustle and stress of the secular traditions, like shopping. But on the other hand, there's the joy of the spiritual traditions and the celebration of a holy birth.

While driving to the concert, part of me wished to attend the performance, but another part of me wanted to be relaxing at home. Several years had passed since I last listened to the *Messiah*. It's a masterwork which uses Scripture and music to depict the Advent, the Passion, and the Resurrection of Christ. A music critic for the *Chicago Tribune* wrote: "Other oratorios may be compared one with another, but *Messiah* stands alone. It is a majestic monument to the memory of the composer; an imperishable record of the noblest sentiments of human nature and the highest aspirations of man."

Just minutes into the performance, I was overcome with awe and wonder. I was reminded that music touches our hearts in a way which words alone cannot. And my welling tears were testaments to what happens as we connect with the sacred and the real. Of course, the sacred and the real are ever-present. Yet when we're depleted, this truth eludes us.

The soloists were superb, as were the guest conductor and members of the Cincinnati Symphony Orchestra. And upholding their sterling reputation, the May Festival Chorus sang with precision and exuberance. As the orchestra and chorus performed the final, glorious Amen, I knew that I was just where I needed to be. Joyful smiles beamed from the musicians on stage and from the audience too. The music had been exhilarating and healing. I gained a renewed inner peace and was reminded that all is well with the world. Everywhere I looked, there were people who, it seemed, had just witnessed a miracle.

★★★

For three and a half years, I've been writing material to include in *Fearless Living and Loving*. And for the past year and a half, I've done most of my weekend writing in the Nashville community of Brown County, Indiana. Lynn and I have always enjoyed vacationing in Brown County and, from time to time, we would rent one of the rustic cabins available for visitors. There's an abundance of natural beauty in the area: rolling hills, woods, streams, and a wide range of plants, birds, and animals. Nashville is a small, quaint town with lots of interesting shops and great places to eat. And since the early 1900s, it's been a haven for artisans of all kinds: musicians and instrument makers, potters, writers, painters, weavers, basket and broom makers, wood carvers, sculptors, art glass and furniture makers, and so on.

The shopkeepers and locals are warm, friendly people. It's like travelling back to an era when life was slower paced and less complicated. Still, something else attracted us to Brown County, a spiritual beckoning of sorts. We realized this would be a perfect place to spend our retirement years. So with the future in mind, we bought ten acres of wooded land. It has a delightful pond and a suitable building site. For now, we've added a tiny, one-room cabin and this secluded place has become my personal retreat – a sanctuary of peace.

Native Americans were first to discover the holy places tucked away in our vast country. Today, they're called vortexes. Veins of quartz and other crystalline minerals have been credited for the special serenity found in these locations. Maybe the mineral deposits create electro-magnetic anomalies which calm us. But regardless of how or why, the peaceful energy is undeniable and people are clearly drawn to these unique areas. It seems that Brown County is just such a place. Yes, there's plenty of visual beauty and lots of things to do, but there's an intangible attraction as well – that feeling of tranquility.

Perhaps this explains why so many artists have made their way to the Nashville area. Every work of art is the product of a creator, meaning that artistic expression is a spiritual experience. So it's perfectly natural for artists to gather in an environment which enhances their creativity. Most of the time, we make important life choices – such as, where we live and work – for rational, identifiable reasons. But could there be subtle influences as well? Perhaps human decisions are impacted by mystical forces which cannot be seen or touched. And if I were a betting man . . . .

★★★

In 2011, I was privileged to attend the last public speaking appearance of physician and humanitarian David Hawkins. Several thousand admirers travelled to Sedona, Arizona including a surprising number of people from Europe and Asia. On that day, the diminutive master teacher displayed immense intellectual prowess and spiritual depth – all of it graced by wit and humility. I will always remember the peace and love I felt that day. He died one year later.

★★★

I never met Helen Schucman, Bill Thetford, or Ken Wapnick. However, I feel that I got to know Ken indirectly though his published material and recorded lectures on *A Course in Miracles*. Though all have died, their legacies are alive and strong, a reminder that lessons of love and forgiveness are timeless. *Course* lessons also point out that the Holy Spirit works in and through believers *and* nonbelievers. And in both populations, the Holy Spirit's influence may go entirely undetected. A number of my reflections and meditations are founded on *Course* concepts which are now public domain.

★★★

I received Sarah Young's stunning book of devotions as a gift. Titled *Jesus Calling: Enjoying Peace in His Presence*, it's the only devotional book I'm aware of that is written in the first-person, as if Jesus is speaking directly to the reader. Published in 2004, Young's powerful book convinced me to use a first-person format as well. And frankly, it's doubtful I would have had the creative genius or the courage to do so without the venerable Ms. Young lighting the way.

★★★

Glenda Green's spirit-themed writing and painting have inspired countless people of faith. Most of us can only dream about having such talent. Her artistic ministry continues.

★★★

The work of Episcopal priest Barbara Brown Taylor served as the inspiration for Meditation Two Hundred Twenty. She points out that we can connect with God in any situation, including a state of absolute darkness. In truth, we can embrace the absence of light as a perfect environment for spiritual growth. And for those who have a fear of blindness, this perspective is deeply reassuring.

★★★

The late Leo Bascaglia was a dynamic speaker, writer, and professor. His book *Living, Loving, Learning* includes a message on forgiveness which influenced Reflection 53. I also want to credit Eckhart Tolle, whose spiritual writing inspired parts of Reflection 76 and Meditation Three Hundred Forty-One.

★★★

In 2009, I spent an afternoon with Howard Storm, another gifted artist. At the time, he was the senior pastor of a United Church of Christ in rural Ohio. Although I had previously read his book, he offered fresh insights on his personal epiphany. I observed that Howard exudes serenity and calmness. But then, who wouldn't be filled with peace after being cradled by the infinite arms of the Lord? Howard expressed concern over the drop in church attendance, especially among older teens and young adults. He was skeptical when I offered that many people, even as they withdraw from religion, are becoming more spiritual. Howard is retired now, but still painting.

★★★

A quote by the Dalai Lama inspired Meditation Two Hundred Fifteen. Moreover, I've learned a great deal from the books penned by Thomas Merton, Cardinal Joseph Bernardin, the Dalai Lama, and Sri Nisargadatta Maharaj; and I've long been an admirer of Billy Graham, preacher and crusader extraordinaire. That's why I presented brief overviews on their lives and teachings. It's intriguing how the common thread of love is woven through the tapestry known as world religions. As for Merton, I believe that he stands at the pinnacle of modern-day theologians. While still a young man, Merton wrote: "Why should anyone be shattered by the thought of hell? It is not compulsory for anyone to go there. Those who do, do so by their own choice, and against the will of God; and they can only experience hell by defying and resisting all the work of Providence and grace. It is their own will that takes them there, not God's." And on prayer, Merton explained: "If God's answer to your prayer is 'No' then you can be certain that his plan includes something much better."

★★★

A bona fide miracle worker, Elisabeth Kubler-Ross was an early pioneer of hospice care and a tireless advocate for those with terminal illness. She literally wrote the book on matters of death and dying. Moreover, her models for grief counseling and for providing compassionate and dignified end-of-life care are still used today. By all accounts, Elisabeth was a woman of deep faith; and her spiritual roots were fully integrated with her work as a physician. She wrote, "Everything in this life has purpose. There are no mistakes or coincidences. All events are blessings given to us to learn from."

★★★

Kudos to David Kessler, a protégé of Kubler-Ross. Kessler has written helpful guidelines for counselors whose clients are facing terminal illness. His insights have influenced the material I've presented in *Fearless Living and Loving*.

★★★

Thanks to Richard Arthur and David Macey for their meticulous editing. Special thanks to Julie Keene, a kind servant and a passionate teacher.

★★★

When I was growing up, my mother and father took me to worship services every Sunday. In a quaint, country church in Western Pennsylvania, I was introduced to Christianity. And for this, I shall be forever grateful to my loving parents.

★★★

My wife, Lynn, is a supportive partner and a trusted confidant. And with beauty inward and out, she's my soul mate as well.

★★★

And finally, Jesus is my Healer, my Teacher, my Comforter, and my Redeemer. Jesus is the shepherd whose voice I know. Glory to God in the highest!

June, 2014

ABOUT THE AUTHOR

John is a staff chaplain at Hospice of Dayton. He has earned an undergraduate degree in music from the University of Cincinnati, Cincinnati, Ohio; a graduate degree in education from Miami University, Oxford, Ohio; and a graduate degree in theology from Liberty Baptist Theological Seminary, Lynchburg, Virginia. John and his wife, Lynn, live in Cincinnati with their Australian Shepherd, Cody.

John is available for speaking engagements, spiritual counseling, bereavement support, caregiver workshops, and spiritual wellness presentations. Visit John's website at www.johnalove.com or contact him by e-mail at chaplainjohnalove@gmail.com

CPSIA information can be obtained at www.ICGtesting.com
Printed in the USA
BVOW07s1734010215

385783BV00001B/32/P